A Whig Embattled

JOHN TYLER

A portrait by George P. A. Healy hanging at Sherwood Forest, the Tyler home in Charles City County, Virginia.

A Whig Embattled

The Presidency under John Tyler

by

Robert J. Morgan

with a new preface by the author

ARCHON BOOKS
1974

Library of Congress Cataloging in Publication Data

Morgan, Robert J.
    A Whig embattled; the Presidency under John Tyler.
    Reprint of the edition published by University of
Nebraska Press, Lincoln; with new pref. by the author.
    Bibliography: p.
    1. United States—Politics and government—1841-1845.
2. Tyler, John, Pres. U.S., 1790-1862.   I. Title.
[E396.M6 1974]   973.5'8'0924   74-2004
ISBN 0-208-01428-4

Printed in the United States of America

TO

M. L. M. and G. L. M.

ACKNOWLEDGMENTS

THE very helpful assistance which I have received from numerous individuals deserves at least the recognition of the printed word. I owe to my friend and former teacher at the University of Virginia, Professor James Hart, a major debt of gratitude, for without his encouragement this study would have remained no more than a manuscript. Professors Norman Hill and Lane Lancaster of the University of Nebraska gave me the benefit of their comments on portions of the final manuscript. Mrs. James Southall Wilson of Charlottesville, Virginia, kindly aided me in the search for the frontispiece. Mrs. J. Alfred Tyler of Sherwood Forest, Holdcroft, Virginia, generously permitted the use of a copy of the portrait of President Tyler now hanging in her home. Mr. James R. Short of the Virginia State Library, Richmond, also spared no effort to find a suitable picture of John Tyler. My wife, Naomie Pegues Morgan, not only witnessed the birth pangs of this study with the encouragement of patience, but also read the manuscript repeatedly and gave valuable advice. Miss Emily Schossberger and her staff at the University of Nebraska Press, especially Mr. Stanley Moon, guided me with patience and good humor through the final stages of preparing and publishing the study.

ROBERT J. MORGAN

The author expresses his thanks for permission, generously granted by the publishers, to quote passages from the following books: to the American Historical Association, publishers of the *American Historical Review*, for "The Diary of Thomas Ewing" (Vol. XVIII, No. 1); to Rinehart & Company, Inc., publishers of *Presidential Leadership* by E. Pendleton Herring; to Harper & Brothers, publishers of *The President of the United States* by Woodrow Wilson; and to the Public Administration Service, publishers of *The President and the Presidency* by Louis Brownlow.

TABLE OF CONTENTS

PREFACE TO THE 1974 EDITION

The decade between 1963 and 1973 undoubtedly has been one of the most turbulent in the history of the American Presidency. Spanning the incumbencies of three men, it opened with the assassination of John F. Kennedy. Crisis spread quickly with racial strife and deepened ominously, when Lyndon Johnson plunged the nation ever deeper into an undeclared war to attain uncertain objectives. His decision strained civil comity to the point where he felt constrained to deny himself a President's traditional candidacy for a second term. This distressing decade has closed with the disgrace of the Vice-President and public distrust of the incumbent President which is probably unparalleled except during the administration of Andrew Johnson. Election to one of the most coveted offices in the world has cost one President his life and damaged the reputations of the other two, one of them irreparably. Allusion to the first Johnson reminds us that other Presidents have suffered similar fates. The congressional Whigs of the early 1840's fought for nearly four years to prevent John Tyler from casting the Presidency into the Jacksonian mold. Few Presidents have suffered more than he from the lash of criticism intended to drive him from office by all means short of impeachment.

This study of Tyler's Presidency was published twenty years ago under the heroic spell of Franklin Roosevelt's twelve years in office. Then it seemed to be the only institution capable of making the Constitution capable of serving modern needs.

Consequently, studies of the Presidency emphasized description, analysis and prescription of institutional roles, often to exclusion of the social context. Subsequently, attention was shifted to other matters such as decision-making and the means of aggregating sufficient power to make the President effective in mediating the infinite variety of conflicts to be resolved in a pluralist society. These scholarly concerns reflect political reality. All the deepest tensions of American society have become focused most visibly upon the Presidency for solution. Power to match these demands has been sought by incumbents and eulogized by supporters of presidential government. But the terrible stresses of the past decade have prompted a new look. Now critics express a widening concern over an office which seems to have attained imperial dimensions beyond effective control of the electorate, Congress and the Courts. With terrifying military power to be unleashed at his exclusive command, his acts often clouded in a secrecy rationalized in the national interest, and a sweeping delegation of legislative authority, the modern President appears to be a Colossus astride the world. Anxieties arising from our fear that, like Dr. Frankenstein, we have created a monster capable of destroying representative democracy have stimulated a re-examination of the institutional role of the President in the political system. In part, this reassessment requires reconsideration of the heritage bequethed by the men who founded our institutions and contributed significantly to their development. In this context, Tyler's theory and practice are worthy of notice.

At the risk of making these remarks merely topical, I would like to suggest that Tyler's experience bears some resemblance to that of recent Presidents', especially Mr. Nixon's. Both he and Tyler tried to lead at a time when party alignments were undergoing changes which were not fully comprehended nor controllable. Consequently, they both faced congressional majorities hostile out of both sheer partisanship and differences over major issues. In a political system divided by both party and governmental institutions, each man attempted to serve simultaneously as party leader and "constitutional" chief executive standing above mere partisanship. Tyler scarcely had a party to stand above after the congressional Whigs expelled him from their ranks. Mr. Nixon, while appearing to take the statesman's high road to office without a party which needed him more than he needed it, nevertheless permitted some of his aides to pervert the electoral process to the point where he has suffered an embarrassing *denouement*, to say the least.

There is also a striking resemblance in their reputations for conducting successful foreign policies. Tyler's handling of boundary disputes and his annexation of Texas in all but formal fact were major events in nineteenth century American diplomacy. Nixon's conduct of relations with China and the Soviet Union have been viewed as important accomplishments. In their vetoes of legislation, their refusal to yield information to Congress, their difficulties in securing confirmation of some nominees to the Supreme Court they have shared in the trials of Presidents determined to maintain the independent authority of the office. Nevertheless, there are some important differences arising from the evolution of the office itself.

By far the most important of these changes is the exponential increase in the scale on which national power is used to affect the lives of Americans directly and people throughout the world, notably by our use of immeasurable military might. A reader familiar with the contemporary Presidency will be struck by the limited number of participants in the political struggles of Tyler's era. I refer not so much to the relatively smaller and more homogenous electorate as to the number and variety of associations, especially private, with which the President must have direct relations in the daily conduct of his office. A President no longer deals merely with Congress, a few foreign nations and, more remotely, the Courts. In domestic affairs he faces a vast federal bureaucracy only formally subject to his control. He must deal with the leaders of a bewildering range of groups particularizing their visions of the common good. Private power is now widely believed to be stronger than public authority. President Kennedy was reduced to "jaw-boning" with the heads of the giant steel corporations to reduce their prices in order to stem inflation. It is inconceivable to picture Tyler and his contemporaries in this situation.

As federalism has evolved, the range of contacts between a President, state governors and mayors of big cities has increased to a degree which I believe would have been literally unimaginable to Tyler. His only serious communication with a governor concerned Dorr's Rebellion in Rhode Island and that was by letters and the reports of intermediaries. In domestic affairs he could confine his attention almost exclusively to Congress and thereby function within a political arena confined to the formal, governmental institutions in Washington.

The fact that the President now operates in a far broader political environment has produced another difference which deserves attention, although its consequences are too elusive to fix with certainty. In Tyler's day most communications between President and Congress were deferential in tone to a degree strange to us now. To be sure, there was acrimony aplenty, when Tyler denounced the House of Representatives in his Protest Message. A majority had excoriated his policies and impugned his motives without having the courage to vote a bill of impeachment. Deference was paid by the President to Congress in the normal course of events, however. It can be interpreted as a manifestation of Whig ideology and dismissed today as no more than a matter of style. On the other hand, it may reflect a reversal in the value placed upon deliberation and action. The older view, derived from Aristotle, was that collective deliberation produces prudent judgments more often than the decisions of a single man. The contemporary view is that the popular longing for a secular messiah justifies action by a pale imitation of a philosopher-king. One man's lust for fame can determine the destiny of a democracy.

There is evidence of this difference in the President's view of his role in an incident which I overlooked in the original edition of this book. In April, 1846, after Tyler vacated his office to Polk, critics in the House secured passage of a resolution directing the President to provide information which might prove that Daniel Webster had used public funds for personal expenses while serving as Tyler's Secretary of State. Polk refused this request, not on the ground of executive privilege now invoked almost daily, but because the statute authorizing the use of a secret, diplomatic fund directed the President merely to certify expenditures from it instead of accounting for them in the usual public fashion. Polk construed his duty to extend retroactively to Tyler's administration in order to protect current diplomatic negotiations. Dissatisfied, the House then created a select committee to probe this matter. It requested and secured from Tyler permission to visit him and take his deposition. He declined to invoke a privilege of silence because a subordinate's conduct in office involved possible criminal behavior. His information satisfied the committee which then sealed his deposition by order of the House. Tyler appears to have acted on the principle enunciated by Polk in response to the House's demand for information. The "safety of the republic should be the supreme law . . ." When that is at issue, the House can "penetrate into the most secret recesses of the executive departments."[1]

A third important difference between past and present consists of the consequences of the President's exposure to the public through television. Tyler could reach the public only through the press. In turn, the public could know him, if at all, only by the same means. The bulk of the American people lived and died without ever seeing what a President looked like. A hostile press could—and did—damage him, but it could never drive a President out of office. The advent of radio seemed to give a masterful President an irresistible advantage over all rivals in molding public opinion to support him. Television seemed only to add further to his commanding presence. Today there is reason to believe that it may be a double-edged sword. The capacity to inform has turned into an instrument of exposure in the hands of able journalists. Congress has only begun to tap the potential of this instrument which is not dramatically effective in conveying deliberation. Now virtually every detail of a President's life is exposed to daily viewing. Dignity, miracles and mystery are all stripped from authority, leaving it clearly revealed too often as the sordid means of gaining wealth, power and status for the ag-

[1] *Journal of the House of Representatives*, 29th Cong., 1st Sess., p. 693.

gressive few. Even when exposure reveals only that every President is doomed to disappoint many Americans because he cannot serve every particular interest, the cumulative effect is to personalize the office in a dramatic fashion which the printed word alone cannot match. Certainly, this has been a factor in the paradoxical development of the office to the point at which it seems simultaneously to be both too powerful and too weak to serve American democracy well.

These brief reflections lead me to one final point. In writing this book, I tried to follow in a modest way the exemplary model of the late Edward S. Corwin. I declined to follow him in one important respect, however. I rejected his conclusion that the power of our modern Presidents has become dangerously personalized. Now Corwin's fears do not seem to be entirely misplaced. As we pile ever increasing responsibilities and discretionary authority on the President, the distinction between leading the nation and governing it disappears. It has been confused in this age of personal diplomacy and continuous, domestic crisis-management. The obliteration of this distinction has seduced Presidents into "governing" through the crude manipulation of the public. It requires the perfection of mythological heroes to redeem an imperfect society and defend it against powerful enemies. When expectation does not coincide with reality, the temptation to merge the real man with his official image apparently becomes irresistable. Because the man in office is neither omnipotent nor omniscient, the chances that his integrity will survive this transformation are not high. Corwin was right. Presidential power has become dangerously personalized for reasons not clear a generation ago.

Many of us have contributed to this situation, although unintentionally. We have eulogized the Presidency as the ultimate and perfected manifestation of the nation's will and the hope for its secular salvation. In evaluating the contributions to this office of a man such as Tyler one can easily exaggerate the importance of the abstraction called the Presidency and ignore other more concrete elements in the existential world of politics. Consequently, it is useful to ponder Thucydides' judgment that Athenian democracy might have avoided self-destruction had it chosen as its leader Nicias, the man of integrity, over Alcibiades, master of the arts of political manipulation and servant of anyone who would pay his price. The question for those of us living in a society dominated by images is whether, in a world haunted by Alcibiades' ghost, the means can be found to elect men of integrity and depersonalize the power of future Presidents. This book is a reminder that the search is unending.

In the interval since 1954, one major biography of Tyler has been published. Biographies of his contemporaries and historical studies of the period have appeared, also. Useful general studies of the Presidency have been written, also. The most useful of these books to a reader desiring to know about Tyler's life is the biography by Robert Seager II, *And Tyler Too* (New York: McGraw Hill, 1963). It is an extended social history of the Tyler and Gardiner families linked by Tyler's second marriage. It covers nearly one hundred years; only three chapters deal with the period of his Presidency. Of these, chapter nine is a useful supplement to my study of Tyler's efforts to build a political party on the issue of annexing Texas. Other studies which might be noted are Claude H. Hall, *Abel Parker Upsher* (Madison: The State Historical Society of Wisconsin, 1964) chapters six and eight. Frederick Merk, *Fruits of Propaganda in the Tyler Administration* (Cambridge: Harvard University Press, 1971) supplements my chapter five. It is an account of Tyler's use of special agents and Webster's use of secret funds to muster journalistic support for the administration's foreign policies. Tyler's part in the investigation of Webster's alleged misuse of these funds is described.

None of these studies contradicts mine in its essentials and, therefore, I have chosen to leave my text unchanged. Were I writing the book now, I might reach some different conclusions; even one's own judgments are not incontrovertible. Still, I believe that an author ought to change his mind in his new books, not his old ones.

R. J. M.

Charlottesville, Va.
January 1974

INTRODUCTION

IT HAS often been said that the American Presidency is not alone what the Constitution says it is but also what the occupants of the White House have made it. Law and custom have made the office the remarkable institution that it is today, although the latter force has had the major share in the development. There is general agreement among observers of the Presidency that the power and influence of the office have ebbed and flowed with the personalities of Presidents and with the circumstances in which they found themselves; but, nevertheless, no one of them has closed his administration without making some contribution which has influenced his successors. In a few instances there has been a forceful display of leadership; in some other cases the contribution has been modest. In sum, however, a vast store of precedent has been accumulated to buttress the view commonly accepted today that the Presidency is the mainspring of leadership within our constitutional framework. Given our system of divided powers, however, this position is one which has only slowly been attained and it is one which can be lost, at least temporarily, by a President who does not understand the institutional gulf which ordinarily separates the executive and legislative branches. The framers separated the governing powers and established a balance of authority that almost certainly precludes a harmonious relationship between the President and Congress. In fact, more often than not, the reign of sweet harmony has been of brief duration.

When the power to govern is so divided, it encourages conflicts, tests for power, and inevitably raises the question: where does the preponderence of influence or control lie—with the President or with Congress?

In the study of our constitutional history my curiosity was piqued a few years ago by the furious battles over both the policies of government and the place of the Presidency in the administration of John Tyler. Tyler's administration was, as most schoolboys know, unique, if only because it served to test the constitutional provision for succession in the case of the President's death. In our written history Tyler was long pictured as one of the poorest of our Presidents. In the light of the circumstances in which he became President and also because many of the principal issues discussed in his administration had continued from the Jackson era, Tyler's Presidency seemed due for some special study.

There is no lack of historical scholarship covering this period, although no study focused solely on the Presidency appears to have been attempted. Lyon G. Tyler, son of the President, published a three-volume labor of vindication called *The Letters and Times of the Tylers*, which has been useful because it contains many letters written by Tyler and his contemporaries. Useful, too, was Hugh Fraser's *Democracy in the Making*. In his study, *John Tyler: Champion of the Old South*, Oliver Perry Chitwood undoubtedly did much to set Tyler in a favorable historical perspective. Several other works touch at least indirectly on Tyler's life. But none, so far, has been concerned primarily with his theory and practice in the Presidency.

A word or two of biographical information about Tyler may help the reader who does not have a full account of his life at hand. He was born in Charles City County, Virginia, on March 29, 1790—the first "natural born" President of the United States. His family was sufficiently distinguished that his father became Governor of Virginia while John was a student at the College of William and Mary. After terminating his studies there, Tyler was admitted to the bar and two years later, at the age of twenty-one, entered the Virginia legislature. From that point forward, until his death, he intermittently held various public offices. He served successively in the House of Representatives of Congress from 1817 to 1821. After a brief retirement caused by impaired health, he returned to the Virginia legislature and followed one term there first as rector and then as chancellor of the College of William and Mary. In 1825 he was chosen Governor of Virginia, a post to which he was once re-elected. He was then chosen by the legislature to be United States Senator late in 1826 and remained in that office until he resigned his seat in February, 1836, rather than obey the instructions of the Virginia legislature to vote for the expunging resolution to remove the censure of Jackson from the official records of the Senate. In that same year he was a Southern Whig candidate for Vice-President and received forty-seven electoral votes out of a split field. Returning to the Virginia legislature as a member in 1838, he was again nominated for the Vice-Presidency in 1839, this time by the national Whig convention. After his Presidency, Tyler retired to private life until the calamitous events of 1860 and his personal convictions compelled him to declare his allegiance to Virginia, once the efforts at peace failed in early 1861. He died in Richmond in January, 1862.

I have used freely the materials of history, but I have not attempted to unfold the drama of Tyler's Presidency in a chronological narrative. To do so would be to fail in giving proper emphasis to the various facets of the presidential office. Although students of the Presidency do not all agree on an exact cataloguing of the various roles played by the President, there seems to be a consensus with regard to some. At different times—and sometimes simultaneously—he is cast as Chief of State, "the oldest institution of the race, the elective kingship";[1] Chief Executive in theoretical command of the bureaucracy; Chief of Legislation, Chief of Foreign Relations, and Chief of Party. Around at least some of these aspects of the Presidency I have arranged the materials of this study.

[1] Henry Jones Ford, *The Rise and Growth of American Politics*, p. 293.

Chapter I

A PRESIDENT BY CHOICE

HISTORY has an odd way of softening most of the animosities created by our vigorous and independent Presidents while they were in office. In fact, in judging the great, the ordinary and the unsuccessful, we have generally shown a decided preference for the imaginative, bold and vigorous ones. All of them, however—the great, the near great and the ordinary—have shared a common experience at the hands of their contemporaries. "Every President of the United States, with but one exception, when he has been in office has been denounced as a despot, a tyrant, a dictator, as one who was using the power of the government to further his own personal ends and to achieve his own personal ambitions. The only President who was not so denounced was William Henry Harrison: he lived only one month after he was inaugurated."[1] Whatever denunciation Harrison was spared was heaped in double measure on his successor, John Tyler, the first Vice-President to become the President of the United States. Tyler had been in office a scant five months before he found his political reputation consumed in a blaze of partisanship, his association with his party dissolved and his name an object of derisive carricature throughout the land. Curiously enough, Tyler became the fallen angel of Whiggery largely because he chose to follow his independent judgment on important issues and to use some of the powers of his office with considerable vigor—sometimes with boldness.

[1]Louis Brownlow, *The President and the Presidency*, pp. 17-18.

1

The system of government created at Philadelphia in the summer of 1787 was one deliberately calculated to produce friction among the various parts, especially between the President and Congress. As Madison, the constitutional philosopher who was a colorless President, put the matter in Number Fifty-one of the *Federalist*: ". . . the great security against a gradual concentration of the several powers in the same department consists in giving to those who administer each department the necessary constitutional means and personal motives to resist encroachments of the others. The provision for defence must in this, as in all other cases, be made commensurate to the danger of attack. Ambition must be made to counteract ambition. The interest of the man must be connected with the constitutional rights of the place."[2] The framers chose to balance the doctrine of legislative supremacy as the shield of popular government with their own inclinations to support a vigorous executive. The precise nature of the relationship between the executive and Congress, however, was left to be shaped by time and experience, although among the delegates at the constitutional convention the advocates of a strong executive were able to articulate their position without serious challenge. As Gouverneur Morris said in his great speech on the executive on July 19, 1787: "It is necessary then that the Executive Magistrate should be the guardian of the people, even of the lower classes, against legislative tyranny, against the great and the wealthy who in the course of things will necessarily compose the legislative body."[3] It was not, however, until the Jacksonian Revolution that the Presidency became the constitutional focal point for that democratic uprising which has been associated with Andrew Jackson's name. During the first forty years under the Constitution the system of checks eulogized by Madison did not produce the turbulent struggle between President and Congress which was an outstanding feature of both the Jackson and the Tyler administrations. On the contrary, during that time the executive-

[2] *The Federalist*, p. 337. All references are to the Modern Library edition.
[3] Max Farrand, *Records of the Federal Convention*, II, 52.

legislative relationship developed little open and serious conflict.

Under Washington the Federalists put into practice the theory of vigorous executive leadership of Congress which Hamilton had advocated in the debate over ratification.[4] With his customary energy and persistence Hamilton practiced his theory as Washington's virtual prime minister. When Hamilton passed from the scene, executive leadership of Congress faded, so that when Jefferson assumed the Presidency with the triumph of his agrarian republicanism, a new relationship between President and Congress had to be established. It was fundamental to the republican faith that the legislature was the direct agent of the people and the mainspring of the constitutional system.

During the generation from Jefferson's second administration to the accession of Jackson Congress reigned supreme within the governmental system. Jefferson had proved to be clever and able in guiding Congress by party manipulation and direct personal contact with his lieutenants strategically placed in both houses. No such skilled player followed him, however, and his successors in the "Era of Good Feeling" were even reduced to the impotence of being selected by the congressional caucus merely to be ratified by the electoral college. Thus did the framers' plan to make the President independent of the legislature fail—at least temporarily— within the first generation of government under the new Constitution.

The eclipse of the Presidency in the shadow of a powerful Congress came to such a violent end under Jackson that it shook the foundations of the Constitution and dismayed the advocates of congressional hegemony. To begin with, Jackson was not the choice of Congress, as his predecessors had been from Madison to the second Adams. Moreover, Jackson, with a friendly majority in Congress, especially in the House, was able in his first administration to secure an organization favorable to his objectives, although he suffered reverses in the Senate before he left office. When his control of Congress

[4] *The Federalist,* No. 70.

was thwarted by the Whig opposition which rose to challenge him, he resorted to a vigorous and previously unknown use of the veto power. In addition, in his bitter struggles with the Senate over the rechartering of the Bank of the United States Jackson firmly asserted the doctrine that all the department heads were responsible to him alone and were loyally subject to his direction and control. His construction of the President's appointing power was novel and shocking even to some of his early supporters, like Tyler. As the spokesman for the newly enfranchised small farmers and laborers, and the chief of a triumphant Democratic party, Jackson became the first President to fulfill Morris's conception of a vigorous chief executive standing forth as "the guardian of the people." In the Senate, meanwhile, the new opposition led by Clay and Webster, who had made their careers in Congress, whipped themselves into a fury of incredulity over the President's bold claim of freedom from congressional guardianship. Henry Clay declaimed on the floor of the Senate: "We are in the midst of a revolution . . . the concentration of all powers in the hands of one man."[5] The climax of Jackson's bitter struggle with the Senate Whigs came with the passage of a resolution censuring the President for his "usurpations" of power, only to have Jackson direct a campaign which culminated in the adoption of a counter-resolution to expunge the censure from the *Journal of the Senate.* It is one of the ironies of history that John Tyler, Senator from Virginia, refused to obey the instructions of the Virginia General Assembly to vote for the expunging resolution. Instead, he resigned his seat and retired from public life rather than admit the unconstitutional triumph of a President over the Senate of the United States, thereby stamping himself a true Whig.[6]

The anti-Jackson opposition in Congress and in the country assumed the sobriquet *Whig* in symbolic defiance of what

[5]*Congressional Debates,* Vol. X, Part 1, p. 60. One of the best discussions of the early development of the Presidency is to be found in Wilfred E. Binkley, *President and Congress,* especially chapters ii-iv.

[6]Lyon G. Tyler, *The Letters and Times of the Tylers,* I, 536.

they called the monarchial despotism of Jackson. Historic-
ally, of course, in the eighteenth-century struggles between
the King and Parliament the term connoted superiority of
the legislature over the executive as the organ of popular
government.[7] In opposing executive dominance over Congress Whigs prided themselves in preaching the dogma that
they were true disciples of Jeffersonian Republicanism. Incongruous as it may seem, no Whigs were more emphatic
than the old National Republicans in their espousal of congressional supremacy. It was incomprehensible to them that
Jackson, the President, should defeat the very legislative
program which Hamilton had made the springboard for
vigorous executive leadership under Washington. The deep
divisions between the Whigs and the Jacksonian Democrats
over the Presidency did not occur in a vacuum, of course.
The great domestic issues of the day: the questions of protective tariff, internal improvements, the banking and mone-
tary system, and the disposal of the public lands furnished
the grist for the great constitutional debates over the shift
of power from Congress to the Presidency. But on these
issues the Whigs were themselves a house divided by apparently unbreachable ramparts. They needed only to elect
their first President in order to prove the frailty of their
party tie.

In the election campaign of 1840, the Whigs avoided discussion of the domestic issues of the day but devoted their
energies to damning twelve years of "executive usurpation"
under Jackson and Van Buren. Overshadowing any serious
discussion, however, were the nonsense and humbuggery of
the campaign of the log cabin and hard cider. "Tippecanoe
and Tyler, too!" shouted conservative Whig gentlemen from
the factories of New England to the sugar plantations of
Louisiana. William Henry Harrison, aged and frail, was
swept into office with the Virginian States' Rights Whig,
Tyler, who was safely embalmed in the Vice-Presidency
where his peculiar anti-nationalist ideas could not be expected to cause trouble. In his Inaugural Address a dutiful

[7]See E. M. Carroll, *Origins of the Whig Party*, pp. 123-124.

Harrison echoed the victory of a cardinal Whig principle: ". . . it is preposterous to suppose that a thought could be entertained for a moment that the President, placed at the capital, in the center of the country could better understand the wants and wishes of the people than their own immediate representatives who spend a part of every year among them . . . bound to them by the triple tie of interest, duty and affection."[8] Shivering in the damp cold of a northeaster on inauguration day, the victorious Whigs must have felt like the poet Thomas Stanley, who said:

> Yet no new sufferings can prepare
> A higher praise to crown thee.

Before dawn on April 4, 1841, William Henry Harrison, first Whig and ninth President of the United States, was dead.[9]

Harrison's death created something of a constitutional crisis in its time even though the issue it raised inflames few tempers today.[10] Little time was to pass, also, before it became clear that Tyler's accession to the office was to create the sort of political crisis which appears inevitable in our system as long as the candidate for Vice-President represents the faction of his party which failed to nominate its man for the Presidency. For much of the time prior to 1841 the Vice-Presidency had been a comfortable sinecure with which to honor some of the country's more able politicians. Such was the case with Tyler. His nomination was a gesture of compromise from the National Republican Whigs to the Southern States' Rights members of the party. John Adams, Jefferson and Van Buren alone among the early Vice-Presidents were elected to the Presidency; so obscure did the office become after the ratification of the twelfth amendment that under the Virginia dynasty the Secretary of State was

---

[8]J. D. Richardson, *The Messages and Papers of the Presidents*, V, 1865. All references are to Vol. V.

[9]Of Harrison's election John Quincy Adams said: "Harrison comes in on a hurricane; God grant he may not go out upon a wreck!" *Memoirs of John Quincy Adams* (Charles Francis Adams, ed.), X, 366. Cf. Nathan Sargent, *Public Men and Events*, II, 114, 117.

[10]Even as late as 1927, however, it was claimed that Coolidge was merely "acting President" in succeeding Harding. Edward S. Corwin, *The President, Office and Powers*, p. 66.

in virtual succession to the Presidency. The elder Adams is said to have chafed in the office, Jefferson supposedly considered it an innocuous post, and Calhoun is described as scheming his intrigues while presiding over the Senate with dignity and poise.[11] Even the venerated framers were at a loss to discuss the office with their usual omniscience. As Williamson observed on September 7, 1787, "such an officer as Vice-President was not wanted. He was introduced merely for the sake of a valuable mode of election, which required two to be chosen at the same time."[12]

John Tyler was in Williamsburg when Fletcher Webster delivered the news of Harrison's death in a message signed by the members of the cabinet and addressed to "John Tyler, Vice-President of the United States."[13] Nathan Sargent, one of the Whig chroniclers of the period, claimed that the cabinet discussed the proper address to Tyler and concluded that "Mr. Tyler must, while performing the functions of President, bear the title of Vice-President, acting President."[14] Such a view was in keeping with the extreme Whig theory of a limited chief executive—one who was not even to be independent of the judgment of his cabinet. Tyler hastened at once to Washington where, on April 6, 1841, he took the oath swearing that he would faithfully execute the office of President. After the ceremony Judge Cranch issued a sworn statement which has always raised some questions about Tyler's motives and intentions. Cranch said that Tyler had appeared before him "and although he deems himself qualified to perform the duties and exercise the powers and office of the President . . . without other oath than that which he has taken as Vice-President, yet as doubts may arise, and for greater caution, [he] took and subscribed the . . . oath before me."[15]

Tyler's decision to take the oath, apparently arrived at after some hesitation and doubt on his own part, established

[11]Corwin, *op. cit.*, 73, 408. Cf. Margaret Coit, *John C. Calhoun*, p. 160.
[12]Farrand, *op. cit.*, II, 537.
[13]Richardson, *op. cit.*, pp. 1877-1878.
[14]Sargent, *op. cit.*, p. 122.
[15]Richardson, *op. cit.*, pp. 1886-1887.

a constitutional usage of the first importance. As he said in an inaugural address issued to the country three days later,

> This . . . occurrence has subjected the wisdom and sufficiency of our institutions to a new test. For the first time in our history the person elected to the Vice-Presidency of the United States . . . has had devolved upon him the Presidential office.[16]

More than mere niceties of language were involved in this matter. The question was: does the Vice-President merely act as President upon the death of the latter, or does the Vice-President vacate the office to which he was elected and become the President? Had Tyler decided that he was merely the Vice-President *acting as* President, undoubtedly the oath he had already taken as Vice-President to "support the Constitution of the United States" was sufficient.[17] On the other hand, once he decided to *become* President, it would appear from a plain reading of the Constitution that he was legally enjoined to subscribe to the oath provided especially for the President. For Article Two, Section One, provides that: *"Before he enter on the Execution* of his Office, he shall take the following Oath or Affirmation . . ."[18] The act of taking the oath marks the President's first official duty in office.[19] The doubts that might arise, then, as Cranch said, would have been well founded if Tyler laid claim to the presidential office without ever taking the presidential oath. The "greater caution" appears to have been the mark both of prudence and of necessity.

The constitutional significance of Tyler's decision to take the presidential oath seems to lie not so much in the legal realm as it does in the political aspects of the office. It would be difficult to see how there could be any important legal difference between the powers of a Vice-President who had become President and one merely exercising the powers and duties of the office, if such a distinction be possible. Tyler's

[16]*Ibid.*, p. 1889.
[17]1 *Statutes at Large* 23 (Law of June 1, 1789).
[18]*Constitution of the United States,* Art. II, Sec. 1 (italics added).
[19]See Corwin, *op. cit.*, p. 72.

whole course of conduct in the first few days after he arrived
in the capital demonstrated plainly that he acted with conscious deliberation to establish himself as a President in his
own right and not as a mere caretaker for the departed
Harrison. There is ample evidence to support the conclusion
that he was aware of his unique position in history and that
he anticipated a determined effort from within his own party
to minimize the moral and political influence which, together
with the legal powers of the office, make the American Presidency a remarkable institution for leadership. Tyler knew
that if he viewed his own administration as a mere regency,
he could not follow the independent course of action which
he had determined upon. On April 9, he wrote to William
C. Rives, Senator from Virginia:

> Apart from my apprehension of my want of the necessary
> qualifications for the discharge of the important functions
> of chief magistrate, even under the most favorable circum-
> stances, I am under Providence made the instrument of a
> new test which is for the first time to be applied to our
> institutions. The experiment is to be made at the moment
> when the country is agitated by conflicting views of public
> policy, and when the spirit of faction is most likely to
> exist. Under these circumstances the devolvement upon
> me of this high office is peculiarly embarrassing.[20]

On the same day Tyler issued an "Inaugural Address" in
which he outlined his intended policies and expressed his
misgivings for the future:

> The spirit of faction, which is directly opposed to the spirit
> of lofty patriotism, may find in this occasion for assaults
> upon my Administration; and in succeeding, under cir-
> cumstances so sudden and unexpected and to responsibili-
> ties so greatly augmented, to the administration of public
> affairs, I shall place in the intelligence and patriotism of
> the people my only sure reliance.[21]

Apparently, Tyler's friend Littleton Tazewell had warned
him of the probability of a severe trial in office, for in October, 1841, after the accuracy of Tazewell's prediction was

[20]Tyler, *op. cit.*, II, 20.
[21]Richardson, *op. cit.*, p. 1890.

confirmed, Tyler wrote his confidant, saying, "I well remember your prediction of Gen. Harrison's death, and with what emphasis you enquired of me whether I had thought of my own situation upon the happening of that contingency. You declared in advance much of the difficulty by which I have already been surrounded."[22] In writing to the Norfolk Democratic Association in 1844 Tyler elaborated this prophecy:

> ... he [Tazewell] drew a fearful picture to myself of what would be my situation on the occurrence of such contigencies. He spoke of violent assaults to be made upon me unless I yielded my conscience, judgment—everything, into the hands of the political managers ... and even anticipated my resignation as a measure to be forced upon me.[23]

These statements, together with Tyler's actions in issuing an Inaugural Address and moving into the White House, lend considerable weight to the conclusion that he had consciously decided that the Vice-President must become the President both in law and in fact. The wisdom of his decision became ever clearer as the portentous struggle over the President's relations with Congress and his cabinet developed in the early months of his administration.

Tyler's decision to assume both the dignities and the powers of the presidential office apparently stirred a considerable amount of discussion in the press, in fact, so much so that the editor of *Niles Register* spoke up in protest:

> May not the good people of this *republic* be spared from an idle controversy in regard to the *appellation* by which the person now at the head of its executive department shall be designated? The *Richmond Enquirer* took occasion conspicuously to style Mr. Tyler as the 'acting president.' The *National Intelligencer* insists that the vice president ... succeeds to the appellation of, as well as the power and duties of 'president of the United States.' The *New York Post* takes part with the *Enquirer*.[24]

The *Pennsylvanian* sided with the view that Tyler would act as President, hastening to assure its readers that no special

[22]Tyler to Tazewell (Oct. 11, 1841), Tyler, *op. cit.*, II, 127.
[23]*Ibid.*, p. 96.
[24]*Niles National Register*, LX, 113.

presidential election would take place, since this would occur only if both the President and the Vice-President vacated their offices. It added the view that Tyler should take the presidential oath since this constituted the inauguration of the President. He could then ". . . communicate to his fellow citizens, by an address, the principles upon which he intends to administer the government."[25] The Whig organ, the *National Intelligencer*, in urging the view that Tyler was the President, and neither the acting President nor President *ad interim*, said that:

> by the terms of the Constitution, the *office* of President *devolves* upon the vice-president. . . . The Constitution uses very different terms when it comes to provide for the removal, death, etc., both of president and vice president. For such a case Congress is empowered to provide 'by declaring what *officer* shall then *act* as president . . . until the disability be removed, or a *president* shall be elected.' The *office* of President devolves not upon him. . . .[26]

Ex-President John Quincy Adams did not permit party loyalty to obscure his judgment of the matter. He noted in his diary on April 4, 1841, anticipating the later discussion of the problem, that ". . . this event . . . makes the Vice-President . . . John Tyler . . . Acting President of the Union for four years less one month."[27] He added gratuitously his unflattering personal judgment of Tyler as a man and as a statesman, a judgment which colored all his relations with the President for the remainder of their lives:

> Tyler is a political sectarian, of the slave-driving, Virginian, Jeffersonian school, principled against all improvement, with all the interests and passions and vices of slavery rooted in his moral and political constitution—with talents not above mediocrity, and a spirit incapable of expansion to the dimensions of the station upon which he has been cast by the hand of Providence. . . . This day was in every sense gloomy. . . .[28]

[25]*Ibid.*, p. 88.
[26]*Ibid.*, p. 98.
[27]Adams, *op. cit.*, X, 456.
[28]*Ibid.*, pp. 456-457.

On April 16, after public discussion of the problem had commenced, he added:

> I paid a visit this morning to Mr. Tyler, who styles himself President . . . and not Vice-President acting as President, which would be the correct style. But it is a construction in direct violation of both the grammar and context of the Constitution . . . a strict constructionist would warrant more than a doubt whether the Vice-President has the right to occupy the President's house, or to claim his salary, without an Act of Congress. He moved into the house two days ago.[29]

Before Tyler's succession to the Presidency became a closed public matter through congressional confirmation, there occurred two other events which strengthened the new President's viewpoint respecting the succession. As Adams indicated in his *Memoirs*, the President moved into the White House on April 14, 1841. The White House, of course, is the residence of the President, although it could, as well, be the residence of an acting President. Nevertheless, a scrupulously correct strict constructionist might, as Adams suggested, be chary of taking such a step as Tyler did. In fact, a conscious unwillingness to take this step might well have symbolized the position of a Vice-President who took the view that he had not become the President.

On April 24, 1841, the President met the diplomatic corps in the White House, where Bodisco, the Russian minister, made a brief speech in which he said: "Mr. President . . . the constitution has invested you with the chief magistracy of the Union. . . ."[30] The President's reply accepted this view and further expressed a hope for continued peaceful relations between this nation and the others of the world. Although it could be argued that the members of the diplomatic corps would have been unwise had they addressed the head of this nation in any other fashion under the circumstances, it still remains a fact that this act marked a further acceptance of the newly established usage.

[29]*Ibid.*, pp. 463-464.
[30]*Niles Register*, LX, 130.

Congressional confirmation of the fact that John Tyler had succeeded to the name as well as to the powers and duties of the presidential office came in the opening days of the special session called by Harrison to meet on May 31, 1841. In the House of Representatives Henry A. Wise of Virginia, one of Tyler's supporters, who was often troublesome, moved the adoption of the customary resolution informing "the President of the United States" that Congress was ready to receive communications from him.[31] Immediately McKeon of New York moved an amendment to insert the words "Vice-President, now exercising the duties of" before the word "President."[32] Whether McKeon's appellation would have accorded Tyler a level of dignity one step above or one below Adams' title of acting President seems to matter only from the standpoint of the President's role as the chief of his party and as the "embodiment of the people's elective will."[33] McKeon had the grace to claim that it was not out of political malice that he had moved his amendment, but rather out of a genuine concern that the Constitution be properly interpreted and that the question be settled for all future time. Quoting the relevant provisions of the Constitution, he claimed they indicated clearly enough that only the powers and duties of the Presidency, but not the office, devolved upon a Vice-President in case of *any* of the contingencies provided for.[34] He asserted that the debates in the constitutional convention gave weight to his view and yet he

[31]*Journal of the House of Representatives*, 27th Cong., 1st Sess., p. 19.

[32]*Congressional Globe*, 27th Cong., 1st Sess., p. 5.

[33]This suggestive phrase is used by George F. Milton, *The Use of Presidential Power*, p. 3.

[34]*Const. of U.S.*, Art. I, Sec. 3, Cl. 5: "The Senate shall chuse their other officers, and also a President pro tempore, in the absence of the Vice President, or *when he shall exercise the Office* of President of the United States." The italics are mine and the words emphasized seem clearly to nullify McKeon's argument. Art. I, Sec. 1, Cl. 6: "In case of the Removal of the President from Office, or of his Death, Resignation, or inability to discharge the Powers and Duties of the said office, the same shall devolve on the Vice-President, and the Congress may by law provide for the *case of* Removal, Death, Resignation or Inability, *both* of the President and Vice-President, declaring what Officer shall *then act* as President" (italics added).

voiced his intention to vote the President's salary to Tyler.
Invoking a superfluous divine sanction, Wise concluded the
extremely short debate by saying that Tyler "would claim
the position that he was, by the Constitution, by election
and by the act of God, President of the United States."[35]
The House adopted Wise's motion without either amendment or a record vote.

The issue was debated somewhat more fully in the Senate.
On June 1, Allen of Ohio moved to amend the House resolution of the previous day by striking out the words "President of the United States" and inserting in their place the
phrase "the Vice-President, on whom by the death of the
late President, the powers and duties of the office of President have devolved."[36] Allen, too, foreswore any spirit of
political malice toward Tyler in proposing this amendment.
He noted the ambiguity of the Constitution which failed to
distinguish the succession in the case of a President's death
from a situation involving a temporary presidential inability
to perform duties. In the latter instance, Allen observed, the
President would recover his official powers as soon as he
recovered from his disability. In the case before the Senate,
however, he felt that the real problem stemmed from the
fact that "if the presidential [office] was indeed now held by
the Vice President, that fact recognized the existence of a
case where the highest office in the Republic may be held
otherwise than by an election of the people."[37] Tappan of
Ohio supported this view and added his argument that Tyler,
like the second in command of a military organization, had
assumed the office of President only temporarily and "is now
no more than the Vice-President . . . entitled to the salary"
of the President.[38] Tyler might, he added, be addressed in
personal conversation as President, but never in official communications from one department of the government to an-

[35]*Cong. Globe*, 27th Cong., 1st Sess., p. 5.

[36]*Journal of the Senate of the United States*, 27th Cong., 1st Sess., p. 3.

[37]*Cong. Globe*, 27th Cong., 1st Sess., p. 4. Allen apparently discounted the *election*
of the Vice-President in this case.

[38]*Ibid.*, pp. 4-5.

other. The logic of paying the Vice-President the President's salary but not according to him the dignities of the office (granting that he fully possesses the powers of it) is not clear. There is here a suggestion that a distinction exists between an office and the powers and duties associated with it, but such is not the case in our jurisprudence.[39]

Senator R. J. Walker of Mississippi arose and remarked that he had not before this day been aware of any movement in the Senate to bring up the question. He had, however, some observations to make before recording his vote. He argued, first of all, that proper grammatical construction of the succession clause would permit only one conclusion. The antecedent of "the same" was "the said office."[40] More than the powers and duties of the Presidency—in fact, the office itself—devolved upon the Vice-President in case of the death of the President. Walker, like others, distinguished this situation from one in which both the President and Vice-President were removed from the scene. In the latter case only was there an acting President, according to the very words of the Constitution, Walker noted. To clinch his point Walker asked rhetorically, "Is Mr. Tyler still the Vice President discharging additional duties? If so, why is he not here performing the duties of Vice President?" He was not so acting, Walker concluded, because he had vacated the office. Presiding over the Senate at that moment was a President *pro tempore* who was chosen, as the Constitution provided, "when he *shall exercise the office* of President. . . ."[41] The grammatical difficulty with Walker's position was that the antecedent of "he" is "Vice-President."

Calhoun entered the debate only long enough to observe dryly that the question of presidential inability to act posed by Allen was not in fact before the Senate. The sole issue involved was the succession in the event of the President's death. The Senate immediately availed itself of this highly

---

[39]The term *office* embraces concepts of tenure, compensation, duration of activities and duties. *United States* vs. *Hartwell*, 6 Wallace 385.

[40]See footnote 34 *supra*.

[41]*Cong. Globe*, 27th Cong., 1st Sess., p. 5. Cf. footnote 34 *supra*.

practical observation by voting 38 to 8 against Allen's amendment.[42] The vote clearly was not along party lines, since the
Whig majority at the time was seven members. Even the
Clay Whigs did not at this time challenge Tyler's claim to
the full and unstigmatized title of President.

While it is true that any present discussion of this particular succession problem seems to have been mooted by
usage, the issue was clearly alive in April, 1841. Tyler was
faced with a constitutional crisis of sorts which he had to
resolve within the letter and spirit of the Constitution according to the lights of his own conscience. While he has
been adversely criticized for his "caution" or "doubts" in
making his decision, the fact of the matter is that he showed
good judgment and courage in reaching his decision. He
determined for the future the rule that an "accidental" President shall possess every scintilla of power, right and influence enjoyed by one elected to the office.[43] The truth of the
matter appears to be that the Constitution contained so
many provisions which were either ambiguous or conflicting
that the matter had to be decided within the spirit but outside the literal letter of the instrument. The succession clause
which ought to be regarded as paramount in case of doubt
or conflict appears to say, as Senator Walker concluded, that
the "office" shall devolve upon the former Vice-President.
Unfortunately, however, the succession clause is intertwined
with the inability clause. The provision for selecting a president *pro tempore* of the Senate is operative "when he [the
Vice-President?] shall exercise the office of President." The
twelfth amendment, ignored in the congressional debate,
further confuses the issue, at least according to Horwill, by

---

[42]*Senate Journal*, 27th Cong., 1st Sess., p. 3.

[43]Herbert W. Horwill in his *Usages of the American Constitution*, p. 59, considers
Tyler's decision and the usage which it established to be one of the most important elements of our unwritten constitution. Ruth C. Silva in *Presidential Succession*, p. 51, concludes that Tyler's decision to claim that he was President set
an unfortunate precedent in violation of the framers' intent. It is her view that
as a result of the succession precedent, but not of constitutional provision, a
person who has not been elected to the office serves for as much as nearly four
years. Tyler's accession is discussed in detail, pp. 14-51 *passim*.

providing that when the House shall have failed to make a choice of President by the start of his term "the Vice-President shall *act as President, as in the case of the death* or other constitutional disability of the President." It is argued that had the framers of this amendment wished the Vice-President to be the President in case of the latter's death, they could have done so simply by saying that he shall *become*, and not merely "act as," the President. The argument is, however, not persuasive for the simple reason that this provision, like the one in the succession clause providing for the death of both the President and the Vice-President, is to apply only during an interval in which a President is yet to be selected, either by the House in the one case or by a possible special election in the other.[44] The Constitution, as Tyler surely must have realized, spoke no clear and unequivocal command. The institutional test caused by Harrison's death was, as Tyler said in his Inaugural Address, a new one well calculated to assay the good judgment of any man.

The succession issue appears to have been closed with the vote in Congress so that even John Quincy Adams referred to Tyler as "the President" in his *Memoirs* for June 25, 1841.[45] So deep, however, were the wounds later inflicted by Tyler on his political adversaries and so venomous was their response that in 1848 he had occasion to write to Buchanan, saying: "The enclosed package is returned in such manner to meet your own eye. I cannot recognize myself in the address of *ex-vice-president;* for the *third* time it is repeated in annual communications from your department, and obviously arises from a studied purpose . . . in what spirit I will not undertake to say, from some subaltern in your department."[46] For the moment, however, sweet harmony appeared to reign within the ranks of the Whig party. On April 8,

[44]For further discussion of the latter point (special election) see Corwin, *op. cit.*, pp. 70-71. Cf. Everett S. Brown and Ruth Silva, "Presidential Succession and Inability," *Journal of Politics*, Vol. XI, No. 1 (Feb., 1949), pp. 236-256.

[45]Adams, *op. cit.*, X, 486.

[46]Oct. 16, 1848. Tyler, *op. cit.*, II, 13. Apparently Tyler did not think that Buchanan knew of this incident; he wrote his son later saying that Buchanan had apologized.

1841, the Washington Whigs met and adopted a series of resolutions praising Tyler. The last of these implied clearly the price at which future peace would be bought. "In his prompt and cordial invitation to President Harrison's wise and patriotic cabinet to continue their services . . . and with adherence to the administrative policy to which his predecessor stood pledged . . . John Tyler . . . will be the president of the people."[47]

Before another day was out, however, the nationalist Whigs had reason to know, if they but had eyes to see, that the cost of their support was higher than Tyler would pay. For on April 9th Tyler told the nation, "The usual opportunity which is afforded to a Chief Magistrate of presenting to his countrymen an exposition of the policy which will guide his Administration, in the form of an inaugural address, not having . . . been afforded me, a brief exposition of the principles which will govern me in the general course of my administration . . . would seem to be due to myself as to you."[48] This step alone should have been a clear warning to the Whigs that Tyler did not intend to be a compliant servant of the party masters. Had Tyler intended merely to stand in the shadow of Harrison, it would have been inappropriate for him to address the nation with a statement of his own principles. Consciously and boldly, however, Tyler unfurled his sail before political winds that were soon to blow with hurricane force.

Many aspects of Tyler's Inaugural Address stood in naked contrast to Harrison's flatulent address, often said to have been prepared with the approval of Clay and Webster. Harrison admitted that disputes had occasionally arisen over the amount of power constitutionally granted to Congress, but he consoled his listeners with the assurance that "*most of the instances of alleged departure from the letter or spirit of the Constitution have ultimately received the sanction of a majority of the people.*"[49] With this obvious reference to

[47]*Niles Register*, LX, 115.
[48]Richardson, *op. cit.*, p. 1889.
[49]*Ibid.*, p. 1860.

the constitutionality of the Bank of the United States he
further averred that the real source of danger to the nation's
liberties was the growth of executive power. He added his
view that the veto power, a seeming incongruity in our system, ought to be used only with the greatest forbearance.
Modestly Harrison mortgaged his future by stating that he
would set a proper example in declining a second term.

John Tyler had no taste for such principles. After declaring a spirit of friendliness toward all nations (but one based
on the strengthening of our military and naval forces), he
comforted the Whigs by decrying the "union of the purse
and sword" in the hands of the President, pledged to make
no purely spoils removals or appointments, and took the
vow of poverty when public spending was concerned. Moving closer to the heart of Whig dogma, however, he declared
that "if any war has existed between the Government and
the currency, it shall cease. Measures of a financial character now having the sanction of legal enactment shall be
faithfully enforced until repealed by the legislative authority." With this reference to the fiscal policies of Jackson and
Van Buren he further stated that he considered them to
be unwise. He then made a somewhat enigmatic statement
which cheered the Clay Whigs until it was later elaborated
with his vetoes, and drove the advocates of rechartering the
Bank of the United States into a frenzy of frustration:

I shall promptly give my sanction to any constitutional
measure which, originating in Congress, shall have for its
object the restoration of a sound circulating medium. . . .
In deciding upon the adaption of any such measure to the
end proposed, as well as its conformity to the Constitution, I shall resort to the fathers of the great republican
school for advice and instruction, to be drawn from their
sage views of our system of government. . . .[50]

Yet, incredible as it may seem, given the views of such
republican fathers as Jefferson and Madison toward the
Bank, the old National Republicans saw in this passage
assurance that Tyler would not oppose their drive to re-

[50]*Ibid.*, p. 1892.

charter the Bank. In contrast to Harrison's nationalist care-
lessness with constitutional principle Tyler added his long-
standing view that:

> Those who are charged with its [the national government's]
> administration should carefully abstain from all attempts
> to enlarge the range of powers thus granted to the several
> departments of the government other than by an appeal
> to the people for additional grants, lest by so doing they
> disturb the balance which the patriots and statesmen who
> framed the Constitution designed to establish between the
> Federal Government and the states composing the Union.
> . . . An opposite course could not fail to generate factions
> intent upon the gratification of the selfish ends, to give
> birth to local and sectional jealousies, and to ultimate
> either in breaking asunder the bonds of union or in build-
> ing up a central system which would inevitably end in a
> bloody scepter and an iron crown.[51]

In this brief address Tyler stated views which were un-
comfortably independent of those expressed by Harrison and
preached by the Nationalist leaders of the Whig party.
Harrison advocated loose construction of the powers of Congress in obvious support of a revived Bank, but Tyler warned
against disturbing the federal balance of powers without
resort to the amending process. Harrison condemned the

[51]*Ibid.* Tyler's views concerning the Bank of the United States were expressed with
such consistent uniformity in opposition to this favorite agency of nationalist
politicians that one is at a loss to understand either the Whigs of 1841 or histo-
rians who have since then spoken of Tyler's "treachery" or inconsistency on the
bank question. In 1832 he supported Jackson's veto of Clay's bill to extend the
charter of the existing bank, and in 1834, while disapproving Jackson's removal
of the deposits as a violation of statutory law, Tyler repeated his damnation of
the bank. Writing to Littleton W. Tazewell, then Governor of Virginia, Tyler
called the bank "the original sin against the Constitution, which in the progress
of our history has called into existence a numerous progeny of usurpations." He
viewed the bank as being inimical to Southern interests: "The Southern states
are in constant apprehension lest the government should be converted into a
mere majority machine. To appeal to the source of all power here, the States,
for a grant upon a subject such as this, would be in every view highly important.
It would arrest the action of the mere majority principle—would be the fore-
runner of other submissions to the same legitimate source, and go far toward
arresting the government in its downward tendency. The States would come
again to be elevated in our system, and nationalism, if I may coin a word, lose
many of its votaries." Tyler, *op. cit.*, I, 499.

Jacksonian use of the veto power, but Tyler warned that he would give his approval only to the financial measures acceptable to true Jeffersonian Republicans (and, by inference, his veto to those which were not). Any opposite course, he admonished his party and the country, would only result in factional and sectional conflicts. Harrison decried the expansion of independent executive power, but Tyler did little more than to disapprove the union of purse and sword and unchecked spoilsmanship. Harrison announced his unavailability for renomination to the Presidency, but Tyler remained silent on this issue. Harrison declaimed with the eloquence of a true Jeffersonian Republican against presidential domination of Congress, the real representatives of the people, but on this issue Tyler said nothing. The polite approval with which Tyler's message was received by the Whigs belied the anxious conferences of their leaders as they gathered in Washington for the special session of Congress called by Harrison to meet on May 31.

Chapter II

THE CHIEF OF VETO

In 1840 the Whig leadership had staked the success of its legislative program on the control of Congress by Henry Clay and the party caucus and a manipulation of the Presidency through the selection of a politically inexperienced Harrison, who had called the veto power an incongruity in our constitutional system. The power and influence of Congress were to be expanded at the expense of executive direction. Moreover, the Whigs of nationalist persuasion were determined to enact their program of bank, high tariff and internal improvements regardless of southern sensibilities. With the accession of Tyler, the whole scheme, legislative and constitutional, hinged on an uncertain balance. Would Tyler, the strict constructionist from Virginia, dare use the veto to thwart eight years of Whig hopes?

Although the framers of the Constitution embodied Hamilton's twin principles of unity and responsibility in the Presidency as the nation's chief executive and as its sole organ of foreign relations, they did not clearly define the President's legislative role. The President is able to perform his function as the chief law enforcement officer free of congressional control in so far as the Senate does not oppose his appointments to office, and the two houses do not seek either to control his power of removal or to limit his freedom of action by drawing in on the purse strings. The President also enjoys perhaps an even greater freedom in directing the course of the nation's foreign policy, except in so far as the

Senate thwarts him by refusing his appointments or the
treaties which he may negotiate. However, the President's
initiative in the legislative process, if he has any at all, is
at best held precariously. It has been observed that what
the framers had in mind was the "balanced constitution of
Locke, Montesquieu and Blackstone which carried with it
the idea of a *divided initiative in the matter of legislation and
a broad range of autonomous executive power or prerogative*"
with respect to those functions which we designate as being
peculiarly executive in nature.[1]

Aside from the devices of party which a President may
utilize with varying degrees of skill, the legal tools which
give to him a share in the legislative process are few in
number. It will be recalled that he may call special sessions
of Congress, recommend measures for congressional consideration, and withhold his assent to bills. Even these instruments cannot be used very successfully without the link
of party between the President and Congress. Furthermore,
although all three of these devices may be used positively
by the President to secure desired results, the fact remains
that the veto power is essentially negative in nature. The
simple fact is that a President may propose a legislative
program and employ, to maximum advantage, his personal
influence as well as the patronage with the leaders in Congress, or he may believe that his constitutional duty is done
when he has tied together the problems of the day in a State
of the Union Message and dropped them all in the legislative
lap. He may look upon the veto as a stick with which to
threaten or chastise a Congress which passes legislation
which he considers unwise, or he may regard it as a sor-
cerer's broom capable only of causing trouble. Modern Presidents are apt to be guided by the first of these views, although this was not always the case. Among the early Presidents only Jackson and Tyler demonstrated the potentialities of the veto at a time when its use still raised furious
opposition in Congress.

1
Corw in, *op. cit.*, pp. 15-16.

While the latent opportunity for the President to seize the legislative initiative exists, not every President has been both willing and able to take advantage of it. Faced with a situation in which the initiative is seized by congressional leaders, the President can do little to gain that initiative for himself. He may by the courageous use of the veto power prevent the passage of bad legislation, but that does not guarantee always that Congress will be compelled then to enact good legislation. In isolated instances this may be the case, but it does not enact a program. The record of the legislative relationship of Presidents to Congress has amply demonstrated what may be accepted as a political maxim: that divided initiative tends to produce divided responsibility, which more often than not has produced collision and stalemate. That is both the virtue and the shortcoming of our system of checks and balances.

Viewed in broad perspective, the problem of the legislative relation of the President to Congress involves the two steps of proposing and approving legislation. The questions left unanswered by the framers, to be worked out in practice, were essentially these: Do these two steps belong substantially to the legislature despite the constitutional requirement that the President approve or disapprove all bills and resolutions presented to him? Does the Constitution vest one step in the executive and the other in the legislature? Does the executive propose and the legislature approve? Or is the process reversed by the potentialities of the veto power? Yet further, does the President merely inform, while the legislature proposes and approves? Is there, on the other hand, some constantly fluctuating balance among these various alternatives? The answer during much of the twentieth century has been that the executive must propose legislation both in detail and in broad outline, while the legislature performs the deliberative function in granting or withholding its approval. As Woodrow Wilson observed, the nineteenth century was marked by legislative ascendancy over the executive, who was still identified to a marked degree with absolute rule.

It is in this latter context that the struggles between President Tyler and Congress over these questions make sense to us today. The Jackson and Tyler Presidencies mark a point of crisis involving the executive-legislative relationship. Jackson could interrupt the period of legislative supremacy because he, and not Congress, was the symbol of the newly enfranchised masses. Tyler played no such symbolic role, and yet his States' Rights convictions forced him to use the veto vigorously and thereby to thwart the determined bid of the Whigs in Congress again to impose upon the President both Senator Henry Clay's program and the doctrine of legislative guardianship over the executive.[2]

There is no little irony in the fact that John Tyler, the first President put in office by the Whigs, used the veto power more than any of his predecessors except Andrew Jackson.[3] In the Tyler Administration a struggle over the legislative process took place between one of the greatest of all congressional party leaders and one of the most obdurate of all Presidents.[4] This struggle took a form which was dictated at least as much by circumstances as it was by personalities. Clay was an original National Republican who became a Whig when Andrew Jackson identified the Presidency with the interests of the farmer and small manufacturer. Clay represented the capitalist's interests in the Senate and controlled the House in large measure through loyal lieutenants. While Tyler was perfectly willing to bear the name Whig in the campaign of 1840, he found no inconsistency in considering himself at the same time a true disciple of Jeffersonian Republicanism. He was outspoken in his opposition to national republicanism in any form, including Clay's cleverly named "American System." Like other Whigs, he grew alarmed at Jackson's use of the appointing and removal powers, although far more threatening was the

[2]See Binkley: *op. cit.*, chapter iv.

[3]*Historical Statistics of the United States, 1789-1945*, p. 291. Jackson used the veto twelve times, Tyler ten. Of the earlier Presidents only Madison with seven vetoes was close to Jackson and Tyler.

[4]A. N. Holcombe, *Our More Perfect Union*, pp. 96, 252-253

Force Bill. Southern States' Rights politicians saw it as a terrifying union of executive influence with expanded national power. It is not to be wondered at that Harrison, in a speech made during the "issueless" campaign of 1840, promised that a Jeffersonian broom would be used to cleanse the Augean stables of Van Burenism.[5] All that was necessary to complete the triumph of Whiggery and Clay's "American System" was the meeting of a Congress organized by Whigs under the nominal leadership of a Whig President who understood his proper place in the constitutional scheme.

The most notable fact which contributed to the failure of John Tyler to become chief legislator during his administration is that he almost never told Congress precisely what detailed legislation *he* thought should be enacted. Moreover, Tyler was guilty of this omission on occasions when positive action would quite probably have saved him grave political embarrassment. Tyler sought carefully to avoid raising the cry that his actions constituted dictation to Congress. In short, with very few exceptions, Tyler considered it to be the President's function to inform, but not to lead, Congress. In his Annual Messages to Congress Tyler rarely made a detailed recommendation, but he did touch upon the major problems of the day. Frequently, as in his message to the special session of the 27th Congress and in his first Annual Message, he indicated to Congress that, should that body desire it, he would submit the detailed plans drawn up by the heads of the departments. He was willing to say that something should be done by Congress, but he was unwilling to say *how* it should be done. Thus, there was virtually no executive bill-drafting in the Tyler Administration. Moreover, Tyler's direct supporters in Congress were so few in number, even from the very start of the 27th Congress, that he did not even enjoy the advantage of having his stalwarts in key committee posts where they might have drafted bills for him. Probably nothing more than a cunning and sadistic wit prompted the one exception to this general rule. In the

[5]Binkley, *op. cit.*, p. 88.

second session of the 27th Congress Caleb Cushing was re-
lieved of his assignment as chairman of the House Committee on Foreign Affairs and made chairman of a select
committee on the currency. In this new post he had the
frustrating duty of considering the President's ill-fated exchequer plan—to the high glee of the Clay Whigs who had
no intention of passing legislation embodying the President's
recommendations.[6]

In his first message to the special session of the 27th Congress, Tyler refrained from urging the very measures which
he knew were closest to the hearts of the Whigs descended
from the National Republican school. He considered it undesirable either to urge the creation of a bank in any way
resembling the first and second banks of the United States
or to seek an increase in the protective tariff. Since the program of internal improvements and the distribution of the
proceeds from the sales of the public lands depended upon
continuation of a high tariff, Tyler had no enthusiasm for
these measures. On the other hand, Clay, with substantial
working majorities in both houses of Congress at his command, saw the opportunity for the triumph of his "American
System"—high protective tariff, the rechartering of a national bank, internal improvements, and the distribution to
the states of the proceeds from the sales of the public lands
at prices which encouraged land speculation.

As early as April 25, 1841, Tyler knew that he should
have either to fight or to agree to Clay's financial program,
which offended his constitutional scruples. On that date he
wrote to Judge Tucker that "my fear is now that nothing
short of a National Bank, similar in all its features to that
which has recently passed out of existence, will meet the
views of the prominent men of the Whig party."[7] Five days
later Tyler wrote to Clay a frank letter in which he made
his position on measures clear to the real leader of the Whig
party:

[6]Claude M. Fuess, *The Life of Caleb Cushing*, I, 333.
[7]Tyler, *op. cit.*, II, 32.

Considering the brief time allowed me and the extreme pressure on my time, it will not be expected that I shall come before Congress with matured plans of public policy connected with deeply interesting and intricate subjects . . . As to a Bank, I design to be perfectly frank with you —I would not have it urged too prematurely. The public mind is in a state of great disquietude in regard to it . . . I have no intention to submit anything to Congress on this subject to be acted on, but shall leave it to its own action, and in the end shall resolve my doubt by the character of the measure proposed, should any be entertained by me.[8]

By this letter each side knew rather clearly where the other stood, although the Whigs later made a great point of expressing public surprise over the President's veto of the two bank bills in the following summer.[9] It should have been crystal-clear to Tyler, that if Clay did lead the Whigs to accept a legislative program embodying all their pet measures, he would either have to bow to their wishes or use the veto power to thwart them. Despite his knowledge of the situation Tyler chose not to assume the legislative initiative. It appears that he did not intend to follow any other course of action.

In the opening paragraphs of his message to the special session of the 27th Congress, which met May 31, Tyler combined a strong hint to the effect that he had not looked with favor on this session when it was originally called, with lip service to Whig views of the exalted position of Congress, "the immediate representatives of the States and the people."[10] He would rely, he said, on the combined wisdom of the two houses of Congress "to take their counsel and advice" so as to extricate the country from its financial embarrassments.[11] He also called for the distribution of proceeds from the sales of the public lands, provided that this did not result in higher tariff duties. He observed that the Com-

[8]*Ibid.*, III, 92-93.

[9]George R. Poage, *Henry Clay and the Whig Party*, pp. 68-72, 99, 106.

[10]Richardson, *op. cit.*, p. 1893. It is generally conceded that the session was called by Harrison at the behest of Whig leaders, especially Clay; Poage, *op. cit.*, p. 32.

[11]Richardson, *loc. cit.*

promise Tariff of 1833 had one year to run, and that it
should not be disturbed, since it would bring most bene-
ficial results. The sub-treasury system, he said, "does not
seem to stand in high favor with the people, but has recently
been condemned in a manner too plainly indicated to admit
of a doubt."[12] Decrying alike the monster of the old-fashioned national bank and the pet banks, Tyler said pointedly:
"Thus in the short period of eight years the popular voice
may be regarded as having successively condemned each of
the three schemes of finance to which I have adverted."[13]
He then cast the initiative to the winds by deferring to congressional judgment in the formulation of proper legislation.
He had no accurate means, he said, of gauging the wishes
of the public except by appealing to "their more immediate
representatives." Harrison's election had been decided on
"principles well known and openly declared," although the
net result was confined to condemnation of the sub-treasury
system enacted in Van Buren's administration. Confessing
helplessness, he threw himself into the waiting arms of Henry
Clay and the Whig majority in Congress whose members
had "come more directly from the body of our common
constituents." He would remain aloof, waiting: "I shall be
ready to concur with you in the adoption of such system as
you may propose, reserving to myself the ultimate power of
rejection . . . a power . . . which I will not believe any act of
yours will call into requisition."[14] Despite the exaggerated
deference to Whig sensibilities regarding the President's role
in the legislative process, the reference to the veto was an
ominous warning of stormy reefs yet to be crossed.

In a sense the message typified the sort of "Newtonian
balance" which Tyler conceived to be the proper legislative-
executive relationship.[15] What the President said was that
he would not presume to know better than Congress, the
more *immediate* representatives of the people, what scheme

[12]Richardson, *op. cit.*, pp. 1896, 1898.
[13]*Ibid.*, p. 1898.
[14]*Ibid.*, p. 1899.
[15]Cf. Woodrow Wilson, *The President of the United States*, p. 6.

of finance ought to be formulated. He indicated what he thought the people had plainly showed they *did not* want— pet banks, national bank, or sub-treasury—but it was unbecoming of him to say what the people *did* want. In short, he conceived it to be his function to inform, but not to lead, Congress, while reserving to himself the power to judge both the constitutionality and the propriety of such measures as Congress might propose to enact. Congress could go its way, and the President would permit the powers of his office to languish.

The result of this baiting of Congress could be only disastrous. As Woodrow Wilson observed some years later, "leadership and control must be lodged somewhere. . . . There can be no successful government without leadership or without the intimate, almost instinctive, coordination of the organs of life and action."[16] The fact of the matter is that in the first and perhaps most significant test of presidential attitude and leadership Tyler was totally unprepared to act positively, although his inaction may well have been aimed at a calculated political effect. He refused to step into the vacuum that was bound to be created if his own suggestion for repealing the sub-treasury were acted upon favorably by Congress. Yet he knew that the key measure of the financial program which the Whig leaders in Congress hoped to enact into law was the rechartering of a national bank of the sort vetoed by Jackson.

After the legislative storms of the summer of 1841, Tyler shifted his position slowly but noticeably by taking a somewhat more positive stand in making proposals dealing with financial problems. He told Congress in his first Annual Message that "the Secretary of the Treasury will be ready to submit to you, *should you require it,* a plan of finance

---

[16]*Ibid.*, pp. 2, 6. In fairness to Tyler, however, it should be noted that the bank bill framed by Secretary of the Treasury Thomas Ewing in response to a Senate resolution on June 7, 1841, was generally known as an administration measure which was the product of the President's consultations with the cabinet—one designed to secure his approval. He indicated in the message to the special session that he would propose a measure if Congress called for it. The Ewing bill was essentially Judge White's bill from 1832. See Poage, *op. cit.,* p. 45.

which, while it throws around the public treasury reasonable guards for its protection and rests on powers acknowledged in practice to exist from the origin of the government
. . . it proposes . . . to separate the purse from the sword . . .
[and] denies any other control to the President over the
agents who may be selected to carry it into execution but
what may be indispensably necessary to secure the fidelity
of such agents. . . ."[17] The plan to which the President referred was one to which he had personally given careful
thought in the interval since the two bank bill vetoes of the
previous summer. In fact, he felt that the country expected
him to formulate some bank plan in view of the vetoes, but
he entered upon the task with tepid enthusiasm.[18] In the
same message he dealt with the tariff question by saying
only that:

> Should it be necessary, in any view that Congress may
> take of the subject, to revise the existing tariff of duties,
> I beg leave to say that in the performance of that most
> delicate operation moderate counsels would seem to be the
> wisest. The Government under which it is our happiness
> to live owes its existence to the spirit of compromise.[19]

The chief quality of this message seemed to be its moderate
tone. The President left with Congress the initiative in framing laws unless Congress saw fit to call upon *him* for his plans.

By March, 1842, however, Tyler had become so alarmed
at the distressed state of the public treasury that he sent to
Congress two special messages dealing with the problem. On
March 8, he forwarded to the House a report of the Secretary of the Treasury indicating that a deficit of about three
million dollars was anticipated at the time. In this message

---

[17]Richardson, *op. cit.*, pp. 1937-1938. Tyler's insistence on minimizing the President's control over his proposed agency was consistent with his earlier views on
the Bank and with his criticisms of Jackson's removal of the deposits of federal
funds from the Bank of the United States in 1834. At that time Tyler said:
"Concede to the President the power to dispose of the public money as he pleases,
and it is vain to talk of checker and balances. The presidential office swallows up
all power, and the president becomes every inch a king." Tyler, *op. cit.*, I, 491.

[18]Tyler, *op. cit.*, II, 129. Cf. Tyler to Tazewell (Oct. 11, 1841), John Tyler Papers,
Vol. II, No. 6409, Library of Congress.

[19]Richardson, *op. cit.*, p. 1934.

he said that he was submitting the suggestions made by the Secretary and inviting the prompt action of Congress on the matter.[20] When no quick action was forthcoming from Congress, on March 23 he again sent a message—this time to both houses—in which he detailed plans to meet the financial crisis. The difference in tone between this message and his earlier messages is notable:

> Notwithstanding the urgency with which I have on more than one occasion felt it my duty to press upon Congress the necessity of providing the Government with the means of discharging its debts and maintaining inviolate the public faith, the increasing embarrassments of the Treasury, impose upon me the indispensable obligation of again inviting your most serious attention to the condition of the finances . . . Under the circumstances I am deeply impressed with the necessity of meeting the crisis with a vigor and decision which it imperatively demands at the hands of all intrusted with the conduct of public affairs. . . . Relying, as I am bound to do, on the representatives of the people . . . I shall not shrink from the responsibility imposed upon me by the Constitution of pointing out such measures as will in my opinion insure adequate relief.[21]

Tyler then outlined in the message the steps he considered necessary. These included an extension of the time in which the five million dollar loan authorized in the previous session could be taken, a moderate increase in the tariff, and a cessation of the distribution of the proceeds of the sales of the public lands.

His recommendations of a higher tariff and cessation of distribution constituted departures from his previous views, but Tyler justified this change by pointing to the distressing condition of the country, which, he added hopefully, "is such as may well arrest the conflict of parties."[22] This message had a tone which was sufficiently imperative to attract the attention of Congress and the country alike. It marked the

[20]*Ibid.*, p. 1955.
[21]*Ibid.*, pp. 1959, 1961.
[22]*Ibid.*, p. 1959.

first and only occasion on which Tyler tried to seize the legislative initiative by sending Congress a program of action to meet a critical situation. His relations with the parties were such, however, that his plea for a suspension of partisanship fell on deaf ears.[23]

In dealing with legislative matters Tyler was extremely sensitive to the charge that he was dictating to Congress. This is clearly revealed in the deferential tone in which he couched nearly all his messages to Congress and in his personal dealings with the members of the houses. On June 30, 1841, he sent a message to the House communicating a memorial favoring a bankruptcy law. He told the House, "whether Congress shall deem it proper to enter upon the consideration of this subject at its present extraordinary session it will doubtless wisely determine. I have fulfilled my duty to the memorialists in submitting their petition to your consideration."[24] After his veto of the first bank bill, during a cabinet meeting, the President said that "he did not think it became him to draw out a plan of a bank . . ."[25] In the negotiations on the second bank bill Tyler asked Representative Stuart of Virginia "not to expose him to the charge of dictating to Congress."[26] In his Annual Message of December 7, 1841, the President recommended that Congress provide by law for transferring to federal courts cases arising in state courts and involving questions touching upon the faithful discharge of the international obligations of the United States.[27] Again on March 8 the President repeated this recommendation in a special message.[28] Unknown to the President, however, Webster wrote to Senator Berrien, chairman of the Senate Committee on the Judiciary, sending him a draft of such a bill. Webster, however, in reminding Berrien

[23]Thomas H. Benton, *Thirty Years' View*, p. 416.

[24]Richardson, *op. cit.*, pp. 1907-1908.

[25]"The Diary of Thomas Ewing, August and September, 1841," *American Historical Review*, Vol. XVIII, No. 1 (Oct., 1912), p. 100.

[26]Tyler, *op. cit.*, II, 79.

[27]Richardson, *op. cit.*, p. 1933.

[28]*Ibid.*, p. 1956. The President had the McLeod case specifically in mind.

that the draft of the bill was in response to his request, cautioned the Senator against assuming that it was proposed or recommended by the executive branch. In fact, Webster called it a "private and wholly unofficial act," adding that neither the President nor the Attorney General had seen it. All he could properly say was that the "executive . . . deems some measure quite necessary, but, what that measure ought to be, it leaves entirely to the wisdom of Congress."[29]

Tyler was equally reluctant to deal directly with members of Congress in formulating the second bank bill. Although he had assigned his reasons for vetoing the first bank bill, he did not follow up this action by specifically outlining for Congress what kind of a bank, if any, he would sanction. There followed a series of discussions between Tyler and his cabinet and a conference between Tyler and some congressmen. On August 18, 1841, the President conferred with Representative Sergeant and Senator Berrien, who had professed to come to the President informally as a committee of the Whigs of the two houses to get his views on the subject of a bank. The President, however, did not approve of this method of negotiation, according to Secretary of the Treasury Ewing, who reported in his diary:

> At length the President made his appearance—said he had been conversing with gentlemen who professed . . . to get his views on the subject of a Bank—that he had doubts of the propriety of conferring with them and that he had stated those doubts to them—said that he had his constitutional advisers about him *with whom only* he thought he ought to consult and that having conferred with them, his opinions could be made known to gentlemen on the part of the two houses so far as it was proper to communicate it [*sic*][30].

On two previous occasions the President had conferred with Representative Botts and Representative Stuart, both of Virginia. These consultations resulted in what was either intentional misrepresentation or unfortunate misunderstand-

[29]George T. Curtis, *Life of Daniel Webster*, II, 86.

[30]"The Diary of Thomas Ewing," p. 100. Bell said the President claimed that conferring with congressmen resulted in misrepresentation.

ing on the part of all concerned.[31] Despite his reluctance to "dictate," when the President became convinced that the second bank bill being pushed through Congress would not meet his approval, he made efforts to inform a number of Whig congressmen of this fact. After he left the Presidency Tyler said:

> This opinion was communicated to many members of the House on the very night of the day on which the bill was reported to the House. To Mr. Sergeant I sent a request through Mr. Williams of Connecticut, and Mr. Gregg of New York, expressive of my anxious desire to see him; that I could not sanction the bill he had reported without an amendment. Whether he was informed of my wish, as thus expressed, I know not.[32]

Again faced with a bank bill which he could not approve, the President did not hesitate to use informal means of letting congressmen know what he did *not* want. What is important, however, is that he refused to say unequivocally what he *did* want. The fact was that Tyler was anxious to postpone any further consideration of a bank measure until he could mature plans to present to the regular session of the 27th Congress in December.[33]

Tyler's use of his cabinet members as instruments to negotiate with Congressmen in connection with the second bank bill further evidenced his unwillingness to act positively and directly to assume the legislative initiative. After indicating that he did not consider it either proper or safe to confer with congressmen respecting the projected bank, Tyler asked

[31]Botts had carried to the President a "compromise" amendment to the first bank bill, only to have Tyler claim at a later date that he had not given his consent to it. Botts, however, had returned to Congress claiming that he had the President's assent to it. Tyler, *op. cit.*, II, 70.

Stuart was sent to the President to determine his views before the second bank bill was formulated and carried back to the Whig caucus a measure acceptable to Tyler. This was not, however, included in the final bill without alteration. These incidents served as the grounds on which the Whigs charged that Tyler had broken his word in vetoing the bank bills. See *ibid.*, pp. 74, 76-96; Poage, *op. cit.*, pp. 81-82; Fuess, *op. cit.*, pp. 305-306; Oliver P. Chitwood, *John Tyler, Champion of the Old South*, pp. 222, 239.

[32]Tyler, *op. cit.*, II, 100. Cf. Poage, *op. cit.*, p. 83

[33]"The Diary of Thomas Ewing," p. 103.

his cabinet to aid him in securing the passage of a bill to which he could give his assent. John Bell, in a statement published in the *National Intelligencer*, reported that the President:

> requested that they would take care not to commit him by what they said to members of Congress to any intention to dictate to Congress. They might express their confidence and belief that such a bill as had just been agreed upon would receive his sanction, but it should be as a matter of inference from his veto message and his general views. He thought he might request that the measure should be put into the hands of some friend of his own upon whom he could rely.[34]

The President asked Ewing and Webster to frame a bill which would obviate his objections and requested to see it before it was sent to the House.[35] Whatever may be the facts concerning the negotiations between Webster and Ewing, on the one hand, and some congressmen, including Berrien and Sergeant, on the other, a bill which was represented as meeting with the President's approval was accepted by the Whig caucus for introduction into the House. Tyler and Webster alike claim that the President did not see this bill before it was introduced.[36] It was this measure which Tyler later claimed he earnestly sought to have postponed when he made known his inability to sign it.[37] Whatever may be the true facts in this case, it can safely be concluded that the President failed to avail himself of an opportunity to avoid embarrassment and untold trouble when he declined to state precisely and *publicly* what bill he would support. The climate of opinion was, however, one in which he could have stated his views openly only by acting with the boldness which characterized his use of the veto power. The Whigs had so whipped up the cry against executive dictation to Congress that the *National Intelligencer* was forced to say editorially that the *Richmond Inquirer* was spreading false-

[34]Sept. 25, 1841.
[35]"The Diary of Thomas Ewing," pp. 101-103.
[36]Tyler, *op. cit.*, II, 85-86, 99.
[37]See footnote 31 *supra*.

hoods in saying that "the Executive officers are indirectly mingling themselves with the legislative, directing and dictating the course of Congress."[38]

Tyler's vigorous and unhesitating use of the veto power stands out in amazing contrast to his lack of boldness in proposing legislation. This difference probably reflects both his personality and his constitutional theory. By temperament he was courteous, polished, tactful, and firm, but in his legislative relations with Congress he mimicked Jefferson's deference without possessing his manipulative skill in the cloakrooms.[39] His public career was strongly marked by a great independence of opinion and action which has earned for him a reputation for obstinacy which may not be altogether just.[40] Characteristic of his dogged courage is the statement he made to Judge Beverly Tucker even before vetoing the first bank bill. "I pray you to believe that my back is to the wall, and that while I shall deplore the assaults, I shall, if practicable, beat back the assailants."[41] Tyler's political creed was to a considerable extent summed up in an observation he made in 1832: "Faint heart never won fair lady; and I am sure that submission never won political success."[42] He firmly believed that each department of the government ought to defend itself from the encroachments of the others and that none of them should abdicate its powers to the others. This rather literal construction of the

[38]*National Intelligencer,* Aug. 28, 1841. The charge of indirect influence was, of course, true. Examples of a similar sort in congressional debate abound. The situation so deteriorated that on Feb. 2, 1842, J. Q. Adams introduced two resolutions protesting executive "interference" with Congress. One of these required the President to inform the House whether or not he had authorized Henry A. Wise to state in the House that the President was in favor of the rules or any rule of that body. Neither of these passed. *House Journal,* 27th Cong., 2nd Sess., pp. 298-299, 305.

[39]Poage, *op. cit.,* p. 33. Cf. Frederick J. Turner, *The United States, 1830-1850,* p. 490.

[40]See Chitwood, *op. cit.,* pp. 115, 137-138. Tyler wrote to Judge Tucker, July 28, 1841, decrying the intolerant assaults being made upon him in view of the fact that he hoped his "efforts at compromise would succeed." He had, he said, made efforts to achieve "conciliation and harmony." Tyler, *op. cit.,* II, 53-54.

[41]Tyler, *op. cit.,* II, 54.

[42]*Ibid.,* I, 437.

principle of the separation of powers particularly marked his relations with Congress. The net result could only be to set the President and Congress against each other should there be any material and uncompromised difference between them concerning vital matters of policy.

Senator Henry Clay evinced none of the President's reluctance to plan the work of Congress. When the 27th Congress met in the special session of 1841, Clay outlined, on June 7, the measures of the Whig majority in a resolution embodying a six-point legislative program. This was to include the repeal of the sub-treasury, the incorporation of a bank, an increase in the tariff, the authorization of a treasury loan, and the distribution of the proceeds from the sales of the public lands. Moreover, Clay added to the resolution a statement that the measures proposed as the agenda were ones the postponement of which "might be materially detrimental to the public interests."[43] One of the resolutions also provided for a division of labor between the two houses, so thoroughly did Clay dominate both of them. Moreover, Clay devised a clever stratagem whereby not only he, but also Congress, was committed to his program. The Senate, according to the resolution, resolved that these "subjects ought first, if not exclusively, to engage the deliberations of the Congress at the present session."[44] Let John Tyler, a mere accidental President, think what he might!

The struggle for legislative and party leadership commenced when the Senate agreed to Clay's resolution directing the Secretary of the Treasury to communicate "the plan of such a bank or 'fiscal agent as, being free from constitutional objections, will, in his opinion, produce the happiest results, and confer lasting and important benefits on the country'."[45] Clay, as chairman of a select committee to deal with the bank question, had countered Tyler's deference to

[43]*Senate Journal*, 27th Cong., 1st Sess., p. 24. This, of course, was Clay's answer to Tyler's request in his letter of April 30th that the bank issue be postponed.
[44]*Ibid.*
[45]*Ibid.* The internal quotation is from the President's message of May 31. Cf. Richardson, *op. cit.*, p. 1898.

Congress with a new trap seasoned with the Whigs' own brand of bait.[46] This program aroused the fears of Calhoun, who thought that the old National Republicans were driving under Clay's leadership to effect their program and that they would succeed despite a powerful opposition, especially from the ranks of his own followers. Tyler's course, however, he considered doubtful. "He is no doubt deeply opposed to Mr. Clay, but he is essentially a man for the middle ground, and will attempt a middle position now when there is none."[47] In general, Calhoun was correct in his appraisal of Tyler as a man who favored a middle course. However, Tyler refused, to the near destruction of his political reputation, to take a middle ground on the bank, to which he had devoted his life-long opposition.

The first bill to recreate a Bank of the United States was presented to the President on August 7, 1841. On the 16th he returned the bill to the Senate, assigning his reasons for refusing his assent. Although Tyler intended from the day he received the bill to veto it, he kept the bill the full ten days to permit congressional passions to cool.[48] The veto message was moderate in tone and went directly to the President's grounds for disapproval:

> The power of Congress to create a national bank to operate *per se* over the Union has been a question of dispute from the origin of the Government. Men most justly and deservedly esteemed for their high intellectual endowments, their virtue, and their patriotism have in regard to it entertained different and conflicting opinions. . . . The country has been and still is deeply agitated by this unsettled question . . . It will suffice to say that my own opinion has been uniformly proclaimed to be against the exercise of any such power by this government. . . . I took

---

[46]*Senate Journal*, 27th Cong., 1st Sess., p. 19. The House took a similar step on June 7, when John Sergeant was appointed chairman of a select committee on the currency. *House Journal*, 27th Cong., 1st Sess., p. 24.

[47]"Correspondence of John C. Calhoun" (J. Franklin Jameson, ed.), *Annual Report of the American Historical Association*, 1899, II, 478. (June 13, 1841.)

[48]"Diary of Thomas Ewing," p. 99. Cf. Poage, *op. cit.*, pp. 69-71.

an oath that I would 'preserve, protect, and defend the Constitution of the United States.' Entertaining the opinions alluded to and having taken this oath, the Senate and the country will see that I could not give my sanction to a measure of the character described without surrendering all claim to the respect of honorable men, all confidence on the part of the people . . .[49]

Tyler claimed that while respect was due to the opinions of his predecessors, an equal respect was due to his own opinions.

Especially coming from a Whig President, this portion of the message is significant, for it implicitly states the doctrine of executive independence in the exercise of the veto power and, moreover, bases that doctrine on the oath of office. Tyler was not unmindful of the fact that he could have withheld his assent and permitted the bill to become law at the end of the constitutional ten-day period, as Madison did in approving the rechartering of the Bank of the United States despite his constitutional scruples. But this, he asserted, he was legally as well as morally obligated not to do, since in his judgment, the act was on its face a violation of the Constitution. That is, Tyler conceived it the presidential *duty* to judge the validity of an act of Congress, and if, upon examination of that act, he found it to be an assumption of power not granted, it was equally his duty to refuse his approval.

Tyler found that on two specific grounds the bill before him was invalid. Both offended his strict constructionist's scruples. First of all, he considered it *unnecessary* to vest in the bank power to deal in local discounts. This authority, granted by the bill, was not necessary for the collecting, safekeeping and disbursing of the public revenues. Secondly, the directors of the corporation were granted the power to establish branches in the states with or without their specific consent if objection were not voiced by a state's legislature at its next session after the passage of the bank bill. Moreover, no state could withdraw its assent once given, explicitly or

---

[49]Richardson, *op. cit.,* pp. 1916-1917. Tyler once called the chartering of the first Bank the "primeval sin" against the Constitution. Tyler, *op. cit.,* I, 498.

implicitly. This, the President said, was the language of master to vassal.[50]

Comparison between Tyler's veto of the first bank bill and Jackson's veto of the bank bill of July 10, 1832, is instructive. Jackson claimed for the President the authority to judge, independently of Congress and the courts, the legality of a bill. He did not stop in his veto message, however, at stating merely the formal, legal argument for the doctrine of executive independence. He directed his message at more than Congress; he appealed frankly to the economic interests of the masses who formed the solid foundation for Jackson's political success. As Binkley has pointed out, Jackson made the veto message an instrument of party warfare.[51] Tyler's message, in contrast, lacked any appeal in tone or content to the prejudices of those who stood to lose the most by the rechartering of a national bank of the old-fashioned sort. In picturing the bank as the personified engine of the dreaded centralism of the National Republicans, Tyler was making an appeal which was essentially sectional. Thus it was necessary for him to couch his message in the sophistry of constitutional law. Lurking just underneath the thin veil of legal argument was the understanding of the chief antagonists that the veto was the first maneuver in the political war between Tyler and the Clay Whigs.

In his response Clay, as the spokesman for the Whigs of Congress, enunciated the extreme view of the doctrine of legislative guardianship over the executive. He pointed to the choices which he thought were open to the President when he was faced with the bill. Tyler might have permitted the bill to become law without his signature; he might have been guided by the views of the Supreme Court in *McCulloch*

---

[50]Richardson, *op. cit.*, pp. 1918-1921. Yet the Clay Whigs claimed that this was the very "amendment" to which the President agreed when approached by Representative Botts. Benton, in a speech in the Senate, July 27, 1841, claimed that the 16th article of the act (the state-assent clause) constituted an unlawful delegation of legislative power, since the directors of the Bank, and not Congress, were made the sole judges of the necessity of locating branches of the central bank in the states. *Cong. Globe*, 27th Cong., 1st Sess., p. 212.

[51]Binkley, *op. cit.*, p. 69.

vs. *Maryland*[52] and the action of Madison in signing the bill
for the second Bank of the United States; he might have
been guided by the wisdom of his party and his cabinet, who
favored a bank; he might have been guided by Congress
where the majority in favor of the bill had been 131 to 100
in the House. Lastly, and most important of all, the President might have *resigned his office,* since the immediate representatives of the people, the members of Congress, surely
spoke the will of the people. In accepting this last alternative,
Clay said, Tyler would only be following his own previous
action of resigning his seat in the Senate when he could not
conscientiously obey the instructions of the Virginia General
Assembly to vote for the expunging resolution.[53] Thus, according to Whig doctrine, Congress spoke as the authoritative voice of the people and it was the duty of the President
to obey it. To put the matter simply, the President was to
be guided by everybody's judgment but his own.

In his veto of the second bank bill, September 9, 1841,
Tyler found himself constrained again to refuse his assent
"by the duty faithfully to execute" his office.[54] He added to
the view expressed in the first bank veto message a statement that the veto power was a "great conservative principle of our system."[55] Without this principle "a mere representative majority might urge the Government in its legislation beyond the limits fixed by the framers or might exert
its just power too hastily or oppressively."[56] Retorting obviously to Clay's suggestion that he resign his office rather
than oppose Congress, Tyler added:

---

[52] 4 Wheaton 316.

[53] *Cong. Globe,* 27th Cong., 1st Sess., Appendix, pp. 364-365. Clay avoided men-
tioning the slim margin by which the bill passed the Senate (26 to 23). Benton
called the 27th Congress a "minority assembly, formed on the census of 1830,
and . . . soon to be superseded by a new body, representing the census of 1840.
The present Congress represents but thirteen millions of people; the new one
will represent near seventeen millions. . . ." *Ibid.,* p. 199.

[54] Richardson, *op. cit.,* p. 1921.

[55] *Ibid.*

[56] *Ibid.*

It is a power which ought to be most cautiously exerted, and perhaps never except in a case eminently involving the public interest *or* one in which the oath of the President, acting under his convictions, both mental and moral, imperiously requires its exercise. *In such a case he has no alternative. He must exert the negative power* ... or commit an act of gross moral turpitude. Mere regard to the will of a majority must not in a constitutional republic like ours control this sacred and solemn duty of a sworn officer ... It must be exerted against the will of a mere representative majority or not at all. It is alone in pursuance of that will that any measure can reach the President, and to say that because a majority in Congress have passed a bill he should therefore sanction it is to abrogate the power altogether and to render its insertion in the Constitution a work of absolute supererogation. *The duty is to guard the fundamental will of the people themselves* from ... change or infraction by a majority in Congress; and *in that light alone* do I regard the constitutional duty which I now must reluctantly discharge.[57]

Again Tyler asserted the doctrine of presidential guardianship over the Constitution while at the same time pointing out the obvious truth (taken for granted today) that a President can exercise his veto power only in opposition to the majority will of Congress. In light of Whig fulminations against Jackson's use of the veto power, Tyler had little choice but to undergird his opposition to the bank in terms which would appear to put him in a strong moral position. Hence, he laid great stress on the doctrine that he was compelled by his oath to prevent what he considered to be subversion of the Constitution. The veto power was viewed with

bid., pp. 1922-1924 (italics added). Hamilton's comments regarding the use of the veto are pertinent here. "The superior weight and influence of the legislative body in a free government, and the hazard to the Executive in a trial of strength with that body, afford a satisfactory security that the negative would generally be employed with great caution; and there would oftener be room for a charge of timidity than of rashness in the exercise of it. ... [The President] would not fail to exert the utmost resources of that influence to strangle a measure disagreeable to him, in its progress to [him], to avoid being reduced to the dilemma of permitting it to take effect, or of risking the displeasure of the nation by an opposition to the sense of the legislative body." *The Federalist*, p. 478.

such fear and suspicion that he was probably wise to sublimate his real objections to the bill in a cloud of constitutional jargon. Tyler must have been aware of the obvious
and very great hazards of an open struggle with a Congress
lead by a politician as skilled and popular as Clay. In this
instance Tyler's opposition to the financial legislation dear
to Clay was so great that he preferred no action at all to a
rechartering of the old Bank of the United States. In such
a case the veto was an ideal weapon in presidential hands.

The classic Whig retort of Representative Mason of Ohio
scaled the heights of impassioned but fruitless oratory:

Who could have believed that the condemned and repudiated doctrines and practices of the worst days of Jackson's rule would have been revived within the first half
year of a Whig administration? . . . Is it not calculated to
excite astonishment that one of the cast-off, disgraced,
and obsolete prerogatives of the Crown of Great Britain
should have been dug up from a dishonored grave, to
which the indignant voice of that nation had consigned it,
and borne across the Atlantic, to be transplanted in the
soil of Republican America—here to be nourished and
defended as 'the tree of life' in our garden of Eden? . . . Is
it not, however, strange, and humiliating as it is strange,
that the exercise of this monarchical power by a President
of the United States, condemned and repudiated as it has
been . . . in the land of its birth, should here be hailed
with rejoicings and celebrated with bonfires and proces-
sions by men calling themselves Democrats? What kind
of Democracy is that which makes itself frantic with joy
to see one man thwart a nation's will, spoken through the
chosen representatives of a mighty people? [58]

[58]*Cong. Globe*, 27th Cong., 1st Sess., pp. 391-392. This veto, of course, killed the
Bank of the United States for all time and seriously damaged the financial program of the Whigs. The political undertones of the counter-moves between President and Congress were not lost on knowing heads. Representative John Minor
Botts of Virginia made a vitriolic attack on Tyler, charging him with perfidy
for his veto of what Botts called the President's own bill—with the *title* written
in his own hand. Representative Profitt made a lengthy reply which included
the following pertinent observation: "The first bill that passed all acknowledged
to be a most contemptible affair. I voted for it reluctantly; several of the most
prominent Whigs in this House voted against it. . . . It was, therefore, necessary

The heavy skirmishes between Tyler and Congress over the bank issue in 1841 gave way to the cannonades of trench warfare over the tariff and the distribution of the proceeds from the sale of public lands in 1842. Once again the President used the veto vigorously and with telling effect on the financial plans of the Whigs. Congress passed the provisional tariff act of June 25, 1842, which sought to postpone certain reductions in duties provided in the Compromise Act of 1833 and to continue, after August 1, 1842, the distribution of the proceeds from the sales of the public lands. The latter feature abrogated the distribution act of September 1, 1841, since that measure provided that distribution should cease if the duties were raised above twenty per cent. The act obviously sought to continue distribution because it was politically attractive to many of the Western states then deep in debt and sought to maintain the government's revenues, while giving to the manufacturing interests the higher tariffs they sought.[59]

---

to frame another. And even long before it went to the Executive, the gentleman from Virginia [Botts] predicted confidently that it would be vetoed. . . . But how came that gentleman to know that The President would veto this bill? . . . Sir, was it framed with a view to 'heading' the President? Sir, if the gentleman will not dispel the mystery hanging over all this Bank business, I will. The whole session has been passed in 'President-making.' I told you so a few days hence. I tell you so again. And I repeat that from the first meeting of Congress up to this hour there has been a determination on the part of some gentlemen to create an issue with the President. . . . I tell the gentleman, 'Beware of the people!'. . . They, sir, are not willing that, while you play this desperate political game, their interests, their principles, their honesty of purpose, shall be sacrificed or forgotten in the heartless schemings of ambition. They did not send us here, sir, to plot and counter-plot—to mine and undermine—for political purposes. . . . And I think when we return home they will inform us that it is not a fitting employment for legislators and statesmen. . . . I fear not their verdict . . ." *Cong. Globe*, 27th Cong., 1st Sess., pp. 385-391 *passim*. Tyler was burned in effigy and insulted by a mob in front of the White House, but neither the House nor the Senate would take action on resolutions to investigate the incident. In time several persons were prosecuted, but they were saved at Tyler's request. See *House Journal*, 27th Cong., 1st Sess., p. 412; Sargent, *op. cit.*, pp. 125-131; Chitwood, *op. cit.*, pp. 228-229.

[59]Opponents of distribution claimed that it was a device which was intended to drain money from the Federal Treasury at a time when it suffered from a deficit. This further draining of an empty treasury made an increased tariff necessary, they said. See Chitwood, *op. cit.*, pp. 297-299. Cf. Turner, *op. cit.*, pp. 503-508.

The President promptly vetoed the bill. Moreover, this veto marked a distinct change in his use of that power. He had refused his approval of the two bank bills in 1841 on the ground that neither one was a measure which Congress had the power to pass. He vetoed the tariff measure, however, frankly because he considered it to be unsound policy. Again assuming a deferential tone toward Congress, Tyler regretted the "embarrassments" he would suffer in the absence of "the superior wisdom of the legislature" but he could not convince himself that "the exigency of the occasion" would justify his signing the bill in the light of "my present views of its character and effects."[60] Tyler further confounded Congress by directing that the revenue continue to be collected under the act of 1833. In doing this he was guided by an opinion of Hugh Legaré, his Attorney General, who concluded that the act of 1833 could be executed without further legislation. "This act," he said, "must be read with all other statutes . . . as a part of a consistent and systematic whole."[61] Although the question of the basis of the Secretary of the Treasury's action in this instance was raised in the House, the only action taken by that body was to print the report of the Committee on the Judiciary.[62] The attempt to raise again the cry of executive usurpation was made by this maneuver, but it achieved nothing.

Through the heat of July a sullen and vengeful Whig majority labored again to trap the President on the tariff and distribution questions.[63] On August 5, 1842, the second tariff and distribution bill was passed and sent to the President. In principle it did not differ from its June predecessor; it still united an increase in the tariff rates with continued dis-

[60]Richardson, *op. cit.*, pp. 2033-2036. The vote to reconsider in the House failed to carry; it was 114 to 97. *House Journal*, 27th Cong., 2nd Sess., p. 1051.

[61]4 *Opinions of the Attorneys General* 56 (Benjamin F. Hall, ed.). The opinion of Legaré and the action of the President were upheld by the Supreme Court in *Aldridge* vs. *Williams*, 3 Howard 9 (1845). Tyler precipitated the storm over this action by saying in his first Annual Message that he thought no duties could be collected after June 30, 1842, unless Congress enacted a new tariff law.

[62]*House Journal*, 27th Cong., 2nd Sess., pp. 1036-1037.

[63]Chitwood, *op. cit.*, pp. 297-299.

tribution. There was no reason for the Whig leaders to believe that the President would sign this measure after vetoing that of the previous June. He did not disappoint them—his veto message was sent to the House in four days. Again he refused his assent solely on the ground that the measure embraced a policy which he thought to be wholly unwise. It united two totally incongruous proposals—one a revenue measure, the other an appropriation bill. In addition, Tyler added, Congress did this in full view of his opinions "communicated in advance of any definitive action of Congress on the subject either of the tariff or land sales" and contained in his messages to the regular session, in his special messages of March 25, and in his veto message of June 29.[64] Thus, he concluded, the undesirable collision which had occurred between the President and Congress clearly did not arise out of any "capricious interference" or any "want of a plain and frank declaration of opinion on the part of the former."[65] By the summer of 1842 John Tyler apparently had learned the very necessary lesson that a President must lead, not follow, Congress.

The fury of the Whigs in Congress knew no bounds after this fourth veto of an important measure. When the President's message was returned to the House for reconsideration, John Quincy Adams moved at once that the veto message be referred to a select committee of thirteen members, with instructions to report thereon.[66] Representative Foster of Georgia immediately challenged this motion as being a plain violation of the Constitution, which he understood to require that the House enter on the Journal the President's objections to a bill and proceed to reconsider them at once. The Speaker, John White of Kentucky, refused to settle Foster's point of order and bound himself by the decision of the House; but this was to accept Adams' motion for reference. Adams then modified his motion so as to refer only the President's message, not the bill, to the select com-

[64]Richardson, *op. cit.*, p. 2037.
[65]*Ibid.*
[66]*House Journal*, 27th Cong., 2nd Sess., p. 1252

mittee; and this move was accepted. Despite further parliamentary maneuvers to force immediate reconsideration of the bill, the motion for reference prevailed and was voted affirmatively, 108 to 84.[67] Needless to say, Adams was appointed chairman of the committee.

The majority of the committee brought forth a jeremiad which excoriated the entire course of the President's actions since the start of the special session of 1841. More particularly, it concerned itself with the question of the proper relationship of the President and Congress in the legislative process. Raising by inference the old Whig cry of executive dictation, the committee observed:

In the spirit of the Constitution . . . the Executive is not only separated from the Legislative power, but made *dependent upon and responsible to it.* Until a very recent period of our history, all reference, in either House of Congress, to the opinions or wishes of the President, relating to any subject in deliberation before them, was regarded as an outrage upon the rights of the deliberative body, among the first of whose duties it is to spurn the influence of the dispenser of patronage and power. Until very recently, it was sufficient greatly to impair the influence of any member to be suspected of personal subserviency to the Executive; and any allusion to his wishes in debate, was deemed a departure not less from decency than from order.[68]

The report then dealt with the President's conception of the extent and nature of the veto power. Here the committee chose to arraign Tyler for the view he expressed in a letter made public on July 4, 1842, by some of his supporters in Philadelphia. It said: "Each branch of the government is independent of every other, and heaven forbid that the day should ever come when either can *dictate to the other.* The Constitution never designed that the executive should be a mere cipher. On the contrary, *it denies to Congress the right to pass any law without his approval,* thereby imparting to it,

---

[67] *Ibid.,* pp. 1253-1254.
[68] *Ibid.,* p. 1348 (italics added).

for wise purposes, an active agency in all legislation."[69] Although this view ignored the provision whereby a bill becomes law without the President's signature in the ten-day period, the letter did clearly reveal Tyler's view that the President's *active* part in the legislative process consists in using the veto power to prevent unconstitutional or unwise legislation. It was this thesis in the letter of July 4 that infuriated the select committee much more than did the President's rather conciliatory and mild tone in the veto message of August 9.[70] Sneering at Tyler's mild claim of the right to submit hasty legislation to Congress for the reconsideration of the two houses, the committee suggested that the difference in tone between this view and that expressed in the Philadelphia letter was due to the President's awareness that the House possessed the power to impeach him. But, the committee admitted, "they are aware that the resort to that expedient might, in the present condition of public affairs, prove abortive,"[71] Then, with what Binkley has called "the fatuity of reactionaries,"[72] the committee piously intoned its benediction:

> In the sorrow and mortification under the failure of all their labors to redeem the honor and prosperity of their country, it is a cheering consolation to them that the termination of their own official existence is at hand; that they are even now about to return to receive the sentence of their constituents upon themselves; that the Legis-

[69]Tyler, *op. cit.*, II, 171.

[70]In that message Tyler said: "Nothing can be more painful to any individual called upon to perform the Chief Executive duties under our limited Constitution than to be constrained to withhold his assent from an important measure adopted by the Legislature. Yet he would neither fulfill the high purposes of his station nor consult the true interests of the solemn will of the people—*the common constituents of both branches* of the Government—by yielding his well-considered, most deeply fixed, and repeatedly declared opinions on matters of great public concern to those of a coordinate department without requesting that department seriously to re-examine the subject of their difference. The exercise of *some independence of judgment in regard to all acts of legislation is plainly implied in the responsibility of approving them.*" Richardson, *op. cit.*, p. 2036 (italics added).

[71]*House Journal*, 27th Cong., 2nd Sess., p. 1351. See further this chapter respecting impeachment.

[72]Binkley, *op. cit.*, p. 69.

lative power of the union, crippled and disabled as it may
now be, is about to pass, renovated and revivified by the
will of the people, into other hands, upon whom will devolve the task of providing that remedy for the public
distempers which their own honest and agonizing energies
have in vain endeavored to supply.[73]

The task was, indeed, to pass to other hands. In the elections which followed in the fall of 1842 the Whig majority
of twenty-five in the House of Representatives was replaced
by a Democratic majority of sixty.[74]

The President, thoroughly nettled by this extraordinary
proceeding on the part of the House, responded the next day
with a "Protest Message" which bitterly denounced the
House for a proceeding which he called extra-legal. After
pointing out that he had refused his assent to the tariff bill
in "compliance with the positive obligation of the Constitution," he stated his reasons for this Jacksonian protest:

I would not have been so far forgetful of what was due
from one department of the Government to another as to
have intentionally employed in my official intercourse with
the House any language that could be in the slightest
degree offensive to those to whom it was addressed. If in
assigning my objections to the bill I had so far forgotten
what was due to the House . . . as to impunge its motives
in passing the bill, I should owe, not only to that House,
but to the country, the most profound apology. Such
departure from propriety is, however, not complained of
in any proceeding which the House has adopted. It has,
on the contrary, been expressly made a subject of remark,
and almost of complaint, that the language in which my
dissent was couched was studiously guarded and cautious. . . .

But that committee, taking a different view of its duty
from that which I should have supposed had led to its
creation, instead of confining itself to the objections urged
against the bill, availed itself of the occasion formally to
arraign the motives of the President for others of his acts

[73]*House Journal*, 27th Cong., 2nd Sess., p. 1351.
[74]John Fiske, *Essays, Historical and Literary*, I, 357-358.

since his induction into office. In the absence of all proof
and, as I am bound to declare, against all law or precedent
in parliamentary proceedings, and at the same time in a
manner which would be difficult to reconcile with the
comity hitherto sacredly observed in the intercourse between independent and coordinate departments of the
Government, it has assailed my whole official conduct
without the shadow of a pretext for such assault, and,
stopping short of impeachment, has charged me . . . with
offenses declared to deserve impeachment. . . .[75]

Noting that the House had adopted the report of the committee almost without discussion, he called this action an
invasion of his constitutional powers as "Chief Magistrate
of the American people" and further claimed that he stood
charged without evidence of violating pledges which he had
never given and of usurping powers "from corrupt motives
and for unwarrantable ends."[76] He then revealed his sensitivity to this proceeding by asking why it was adopted at
this time. Could it be because he was the first Vice-President
to succeed to the Presidency and thereby to test a contingent
political institution? "I have been made to feel too sensibly
the difficulties of my unprecedented position not to know all
that is intended to be conveyed in the reproach cast upon a
President without a party."[77] But, he added, he had not
asked for the office, although once in it he was responsible
only to the people as a moral agent for a free and conscientious exercise of his powers. His protest was not in his name
alone: "I represent the executive authority of the people of
the United States, and it is in their name . . . that I protest
against every attempt to break down the undoubted constitutional power of this department without a solemn amendment of that fundamental law."[78] This was his unequivocal

[75]Richardson, *op. cit.*, pp. 2043-2046. Cf. Binkley, *op. cit.*, p. 78.

[76]The committee had given official voice to the Whig claim that Tyler had pledged
himself to accept both the first and second bank bills while they were in Congress, only to veto them when they were presented to him.

[77]The committee had accused Tyler of using the veto power to break up the Whig
party.

[78]The cabinet supported this message. Tyler, *op. cit.*, II, 180. Preston of South
Carolina said in debate on Clay's proposed amendment to the Constitution

answer to the Whig claim of the House that the President is "dependent upon and responsible" to Congress. When the President exercises the veto power, he said, he does so in the name of the nation, conscientiously fulfilling his obligation to judge both the validity and the wisdom of acts of Congress. His responsibility for such acts is then one owed to the nation, not to Congress. The veto power is to be used, he added, to prevent the encroachments of the legislative upon the executive branch. Should the President and Congress be at opposite poles, it is for the nation to decide who is responsive to the popular will.

From this date forward, the Whigs were beaten at their own game. With more than one hundred of the members of the House absent, a slim Whig majority refused to accept the protest because it was a violation of the privileges of the House. They failed, however, in their effort to return the message to the President.[79] A resolution, proposed by Adams' select committee, to amend the Constitution to reduce the requirement of a two-thirds majority to override the President's veto to a simple majority, was defeated when it failed to obtain a two-thirds majority.[80] With the President's dramatic stand in the protest message before them, Congress passed separate tariff and distribution measures. Having used the veto to get the legislation he wanted, Tyler signed the tariff bill and pocket-vetoed the distribution bill.[81]

Seeking to immolate Tyler on the altar of party loyalty, the extreme Whigs in the House suffered one final defeat

---

reducing the vote necessary to override the veto to a majority: "The Executive was elected by the people of the United States; and was the only representative that was not, in the nature and design of the Constitution, elected with regard to any particular section . . . and, in one sense, was voted for by the whole people." *Cong. Globe,* 27th Cong., 2nd Sess., p. 167.

[79]*House Journal,* 27th Cong., 2nd Sess., pp. 1458-1463. The vote was 87 to 49 The vote on the constitutional amendment was lost 69 to 63.

[80]*Ibid.,* p. 1352. On Jan. 24, 1842, Clay moved a constitutional amendment to reduce the majority necessary to override a veto to a majority of the two houses. This proposal was obviously a political gesture aimed at the nation, not Congress; it was never even voted upon in the Senate. *Cong. Globe,* 27th Cong., 2nd Sess., p. 164.

[81]*House Journal,* 27th Cong., 2nd Sess., p. 1582. Cf. Fiske, *op. cit.,* p. 358.

which demonstrated more than anything else their impotence. The following January a lame-duck House permitted John Minor Botts to move his resolutions of impeachment. The doctrine of legislative guardianship suffered a sobering defeat by the overwhelming vote of 127 to 84 against the Botts resolutions.[82]

Tyler's vigorous and effective use of the veto power has been clouded with an avalanche of personal abuse and defamation heaped upon him by a Whig press and Congress. Charged with treason to the party in vetoing the bank bills and damned out of anger for his tariff vetoes, Tyler has stood in the pages of history more to be pitied than censured. Given the climate of opinion during the first two years of his administration, it would seem that Tyler really acted with considerable boldness in taking a stand which paralleled, to a remarkable degree, Jackson's course. In fact, in destroying the legislation creating a bank and continuing the distribution of the proceeds from the sale of public lands (and an internal improvements bill later), he was only taking the positive action which he most wanted from Jackson when he supported him a decade earlier.[83] Since Tyler preferred no legislation to Clay's bank bills, it exactly suited his conception of the President's role in the legislative process to avoid taking the initiative while reserving to himself the

[82]*Cong. Globe*, 27th Cong., 2nd Sess., pp. 157-159, 163 (Jan. 10, 1843). Apparently the Whigs even thought of attempting a vote of no confidence in the President in July, 1842. Clay, in writing to Crittenden (Clay's successor in the Senate), said that if this "English usage" were attempted John Tyler would "laugh in your face." He thought that impeachment might be tried "if it can be carried in the House without splitting our party, and nothing better can be done." Tyler, *op. cit.*, II, 186.

[83]Of Tyler's two other major vetoes, one of an internal improvements bill and the other of a naval construction bill, only the latter was passed over his veto; Richardson, *op. cit.*, pp. 2183-2186; *House Journal*, 28th Cong., 1st Sess., pp. 1085-1086; *ibid.*, 2nd Sess., pp. 567-568. There were several other vetoes, ten in all, but they came about as a result of Tyler's strict construction of the constitutional provisions dealing with the technicalities of the veto and not because of divisions between him and Congress. He refused his assent to H.R. 210 of the 27th Congress because it was presented to him on the last day of the second session despite a House rule which forbade presenting a bill to the President on the last day of a session. He claimed a lack of time to consider its numerous provisions. In 1843 he refused to sign a joint resolution presenting the thanks of Congress to Samuel T. Washington for the service sword of George Washington,

power to prevent objectionable bills. In addition, since Tyler was anxious to secure the support of moderates on these questions, he thought it expedient to demonstrate his opposition to the extremists by his use of the veto power. Once Clay's plan was dead, he reasoned, he was forced by public opinion to step into the breach with his own proposals which, of course, died "abornin' " in Congress. With the revival of business after the summer of 1842, however, Tyler could feel that the wisdom of his vetoes had been confirmed, and that a positive legislative program was unnecessary. The overthrow of the Whigs in the elections of 1842 only served to strengthen his conviction that his defense of the dignity and powers of the Presidency was thoroughly justified. The President, even an "accidental" one, had not been reduced to the level of a handmaid of Congress, although he had lost the support of a party in the process.

---

although he communicated a copy of the resolution to Washington. His refusal to sign was based solely on the fact that the resolution did not reach him until after the adjournment of Congress. In the following year he refused to receive two bills because the House had already adjourned before Mr. Atherton of the Senate Committee on Enrolled Bills could reach him with the measures. More recently the Supreme Court rejected this rather too literal interpretation of the President's power to receive bills at the end of a session. See *The Pocket Veto Case*, 279 U.S. 655 (675) and *Edwards* vs. *United States*, 286 U.S. 482 (492). Tyler's vetoes here mentioned may be found in Richardson, *op. cit.*, pp. 2109, 2126, 2182-2183; and in *Senate Journal*, 28th Cong., 1st Sess., p. 403. Tyler, like Madison and Jackson before him, gave Congress the reasons for his pocket vetoes, but this practice appears to have died out after his administration. See Richardson, *op. cit.*, II, 508; III, 1071, 1200, 1201, 1275, 1337.

Tyler's action in signing a congressional apportionment act on June 25, 1842, was unprecedented. This act, which required members of the House to be elected from single districts, aroused the ire of all States' Rights advocates and the Democratic party particularly. Since Tyler did not wish to face the ridicule of Democrats by signing such a nationalist bill—nor did he need to stir the wrath of the Whigs any further by refusing both the apportionment act and the "provisional tariff" act then in Congress (and soon, he knew, to be vetoed)—he decided to sign the apportionment act and to *give his reasons for doing so!* He claimed that since he had no clear and certain doubt of the validity of the act, he had signed the bill "from respect for the declared will of the two Houses of Congress." He said that he was following "the advice of the first Secretary of State [Treasury?] to the first President . . . and the example set by that illustrious citizen upon a memorable occasion." He concluded that "I have not been able to bring myself to believe that a *doubtful* opinion of the Chief Magistrate ought to outweigh the solemnly pronounced opinion of the representatives of the people and the States." Richardson, *op. cit.*, pp. 2012-2013; cf. Charles Warren, *The Supreme Court in United States History*, I, 101.

Chapter III

CABINET CRISES

ONE OF the first decisions Tyler made after arriving in Washington was to retain Harrison's cabinet. Every President must make an early choice of his principal executive assistants and it is the usual practice for him to announce his selections before he has entered upon his official duties. Since the Constitution only anticipates, but does not direct, the appointment of the department heads, in the eyes of the law the President has a free hand.[1] Only on those rare occasions when the Senate has rejected a presidential nomination is any barrier interposed within the framework of the constitutional system.[2] Limitations of a highly practical and compelling nature, however, have as a rule materially affected each President's selection of his subordinate department heads. Such matters as factional alignments within the President's party, geographical distribution of the members, religion, and administrative ability are commonly assumed to be factors influencing a President. In the case of Tyler there were at least two other considerations controlling his decision to keep Harrison's appointees. To begin with, in succeeding to the Presidency, Tyler was faced with a ready-

[1]Except, of course, for the constitutional prohibition against appointing a member of either house of Congress in certain instances; *Const. of U.S.*, Art. I, Sec. 6, Cl. 2.

[2]Prior to Tyler's administration the only such rejection which had occurred was that of Roger B. Taney, nominated by Jackson to be Secretary of the Treasury in 1834. Corwin, *op. cit.*, p. 416.

made cabinet, and any decision, either to retain the members or to shed them at the outset, was bound to have complications. Moreover, the Whigs were not unmindful of the practice followed from Jefferson to Jackson whereby cabinet officers had frequently outlasted Presidents in their posts. It was at this time by no means an established rule that the members of the cabinet should always be men of the President's free choice. Nor, for that matter, was the President necessarily presumed to be free to consult with the members and accept or reject their advice on his own responsibility. The Whigs were especially fond of referring to the cabinet as the President's "constitutional advisers."[3]

There was some newspaper speculation to the effect that Tyler could not continue Harrison's cabinet without again commissioning the members. It was argued that since the members held their commissions at his pleasure, the President had a legal basis for making a completely free choice.[4] Tyler claimed the Presidency in his own right and was not merely acting in place of Harrison; therefore, he was presumed to have a measure of freedom which would not have been accorded a mere "acting" President. Contrariwise, the extreme Whig view was that the members would not resign. "This is the practice in monarchies, where ministers are the King's servants. In our republic they are the servants of the people, and commissioned by the consent of the Senate to offices created by law."[5] It may reasonably be concluded from this Whig view of the President's relations with the cabinet that he could remove members only with the consent of the Senate.[6] It was noted editorially that "when J. Q. Adams succeeded Mr. Monroe, Mr. McLean . . . Mr. Southard . . . and Mr. Wirt retained their commissions without any new appointment or intermediate resignation."[7]

The theory and practices affecting the President's cabinet

[3]Corwin, *op. cit.*, pp. 378, 516-519 *passim*.
[4]*Niles Register*, LX, 88 (from the *Pennsylvanian*).
[5]*Ibid.* (from the New York *American*).
[6]This is not the prevailing view. See *Myers* vs. *United States* 272 U.S. 72.
[7]*Niles Register*, LX, 88.

were not the same in 1841 as they were before or have been
since that time. Or, to state the truth, these matters have
been settled by individual Presidents as a highly personal
matter. John Adams, for example, retained Washington's
cabinet only to discover perfidy among the members who
were secretly serving Hamilton, so that in time Adams had
to turn them out of office. Jefferson, in claiming that he
relied on cabinet advice in reaching important decisions, said
that in taking a vote "the President counts himself but one,"
although he might certainly control if the occasion arose to
do so.[8] From Jefferson's time forward no President had appointed a completely new cabinet until Jackson came to
power. With all the startling innovation which marked his
Presidency, "Old Hickory" unequivocally expounded the
principle that a cabinet must yield to the President's views
when he drove Duane from his post as Secretary of the
Treasury and replaced him with the more cooperative Roger
Taney. Nor did it soothe Whig paroxysms of anger to note
that the President asserted full supervisory and removal
authority over a department head who was thought to be
peculiarly subject to congressional direction. The Whigs were
no less exacerbated by the fact that Jackson rarely, if ever,
relied on the advice of his cabinet and lent his ear instead
to the suggestions of unofficial advisers, derisively called the
"Kitchen Cabinet" by his political enemies.[9]

In reaching his decision regarding cabinet personnel Tyler
was faced with several problems, some which were evident
to him at the outset of his administration and others which
emerged in the passing years. At the outset there was the
question: what does an "accidental" President do with an
inherited cabinet? Before many months had passed he was

[8]Quoted in Corwin, *op. cit.*, p. 378. There is a story attributed to John Tyler, Jr.,
the President's private secretary, that his father emphatically rejected the view
that decisions were to be reached by majority vote in cabinet meetings. Webster
is said to have told the President that this was Harrison's practice, only to have
Tyler rejoin with the assertion: "I am the President, and I shall be held responsible for my administration." Whether the story is literally true or not, in effect
it reflects Tyler's practice. See Binkley, *op. cit.*, pp. 92-93.

[9]Binkley, *op. cit.*, pp. 46, 64-65; Corwin, *op. cit.*, pp. 97-101, 516-517.

faced with the choice of yielding to the views of the members on a major policy question or of witnessing the destruction of his cabinet. Tyler, then, like every other President, had to determine to what extent he would consult with his subordinates and to what extent he would heed their advice. There was also a unique problem involved in the political relationships of some of the original cabinet members to Senator Henry Clay, the most powerful figure in the Whig party. Tyler, like John Adams, was tormented by the problem of possible disloyalty among his department heads and was forced to ask himself how much he should trust them or turn instead to a "Kitchen Cabinet." Moreover, the effect of cabinet selections on factional or partisan alignments posed a vexatious puzzle from the outset of his administration. The crux of Tyler's problems was this: is the President merely one among equals in his cabinet or is he the master? If he is the master, does he consult with the members fully and freely or just incidentally and discontinuously with reservations revealed only to personal, "unofficial" advisers? Should the latter be the case, are the Secretaries mere presidential mammets serving solely to direct the administration of their departments, and not his "constitutional advisers"?

The first difficulty Tyler faced in regard to the cabinet— one peculiar to his administration—was that a Senator had exerted a powerful, if not controlling influence over Harrison in the selection of cabinet members. Clay had apparently rejected the offer of a post, preferring to remain in the Senate as the leader of the Whig party.[10] With several of his loyal lieutenants in the cabinet Clay was prepared to make that body the nexus between the inexperienced President Harrison and a Congress which he dominated from his seat in the Senate. If Clay and the other leading Whigs could forge such a link and reinforce it with the doctrine that the President must heed his "constitutional advisers" on policy issues, they reasoned that the stage would be set for the regeneration of legislative control of the executive. The constitutional system was to be restored to the "pure Republican prin-

[10]Poage, *op. cit.*, p. 18.

ciples" so dear to the Whigs. This plan, like Clay's legislative program, was wrecked on the independence and courage of "His Accidency," John Tyler.

Tyler was alert to the fact that Harrison's cabinet choices had been made with a view to Whig factionalism and the presidential aspirations of Clay and Webster in 1844. As early as December 20, 1840, Tyler had written to his friend Wise:

> I agree with you fully in the importance you attach to General Harrison's first step. It is one, however, of great difficulty. I hope he may meet and overcome it. His language should be firm and decisive to one and all. There should be no caballing, no intriguing in his Cabinet. Every eye should be fixed upon the official duty assigned and never once lifted up to gaze at the succession.[11]

Writing to T. G. Clemson a week earlier Calhoun had said that the composition of the new cabinet was not yet certain but "the impression is that the influence of Mr. Clay will prevail."[12] It had been well known that Webster would probably be Secretary of State and that John J. Crittenden, Clay's principal handyman, would be the Attorney General. Rives, in writing to Legaré in the same month, had expressed the view that the composition of the cabinet was to serve the interests of Clay and Webster in the Whig nomination for the Presidency in 1844. He thought, however, that an even distribution would be made of the posts between the two.[13]

This state of affairs meant that the cabinet as a policymaking body was now a probable focal point of trouble, since it was well known that both Clay and Webster were quite unsympathetic to the strict States' Rights views entertained by Tyler. Despite these circumstances, Tyler asked the members of the cabinet to stay, hoping to conciliate the

---

[11]Tyler, *op. cit.*, III, 86. Cf. letter to T. W. Gilmer, Jan. 7, 1841, to the same effect; *ibid.*, II, 14.

[12]"Correspondence of John C. Calhoun," p. 468; cf. Calhoun to J. E. Calhoun, p. 470.

[13]Tyler, *op. cit.*, III, 87-88. This view apparently was correct. See Poage, *op. cit.*, pp. 18-20.

two factions of the Whig party.[14] Had he taken any other
course, he would have precipitated immediate and possibly
unnecessary party strife.

Tyler was almost immediately faced with the problem
of controlling his cabinet. The special session of Congress
brought about a party struggle which was not long in reaching into cabinet circles. Once Clay was apprised of Tyler's
inflexible views toward such a step,[15] it became expedient
for him to act through the cabinet as much as possible.
Meanwhile, the President's lack of accord with the views
of his cabinet was revealed publicly in the first of three
articles published by Webster in the *National Intelligencer*
in June, 1841:

> The sentiments of the President ... as they have been
> well known, and constantly maintained, for the last fifteen
> years, are not, in all respects, such as the Secretary of the
> Treasury and other members of the Cabinet are equally
> well known to have entertained and expressed. These dif-
> ferences chiefly respect the extent of the constitutional
> authority of Congress in the creation of a Bank, and
> clothing it with powers.[16]

When the first bank bill had run its stormy course in Congress, it was presented to the President on the 7th of August,
1841. On the next day Webster wrote to his wife that the
President—

> keeps his own counsel as to approving or disapproving.
> Opinions differ very much as to what he will do. A great
> commotion will doubtless follow, if he should veto the
> bill. By agreement I say nothing to him on the subject,
> and have therefore no better means of judging than others.

[14]Henry A. Wise, *Seven Decades of the Union*, p. 182. Wise claimed that Tyler was
advised to revise his cabinet at once, leaving only Webster in it to settle the
Maine boundary question. Wise did not say who so advised the President, but
events were soon to prove that he was surrounded by his own "cabal" who
became the objects of Clay's mordant criticism. Cf. Tyler to Judge Tucker (July
28, 1841). Tyler, *op. cit.*, II, 53-54.

[15]Tyler to Clay (April 30, 1841), Tyler, *op. cit.*, III, 94.

[16]*The Writings and Speeches of Daniel Webster*, National Edition, XV, 124-125.
This statement was published on June 16, 1841, four days after Ewing had submitted his bank plan to the Senate at the call of that body.

But the inclination of my opinion is that he will sign the bill.[17]

Webster was wrong in his opinion, but it was not until August 16 that he and the other members of the cabinet learned with certainty that the President would veto the bank bill.[18] As far as the cabinet was concerned, the President had kept his own counsel. However, he hardly came unaided to this decision. T. W. Gilmer wrote on August 7, the day the bill was sent to the President, that:

> now it is confidently anticipated by the President's friends that there will be, as I think there should be, a new cabinet. The bill passed yesterday and will be vetoed next week.[19]

On August 12 an editorial entitled "Truisms" was published in the *Madisonian*, to the consternation of Clay's paper, the *Intelligencer*. Apparently the *Madisonian*, a Whig paper in the campaign of 1840, was already being converted into Tyler's unofficial paper, and its editorial policy reflected the views of the President. Considering the rumored discord between the President and his cabinet over a vital matter of policy, the editorial was most instructive:

> This government is divided into three departments, viz; the Executive, the Legislative and the Judiciary departments. The Executive is as independent of the two houses of Congress, and of the Judiciary, as either of these branches are [*sic*] of it, and of each other.
>
> The Executive branch consists of the President and his Cabinet, and their bureaux and subordinates. But the President is the head, being the only one elected by the people, and the others are chosen by him, and are removable at his will. The Cabinet, unlike the ministry of England, is supposed to conform to the views of the head of the Executive branch, and are selected by him to carry out practically his official views. This is clear from the

---

[17]*The Private Correspondence of Daniel Webster* (Fletcher Webster, ed.), II, 108.

[18]*The Letters of Daniel Webster* (C. H. Van Tyne, ed.), p. 235. Cf. "The Diary of Thomas Ewing," p. 99. For the statement of Webster to the effect that the cabinet unanimously recommended that the President sign the bill, see J. H. Parks, *John Bell of Tennessee*, p. 183.

[19]Tyler, *op. cit.*, II, 707.

fact that the President is alone responsible for all their
official acts. To suppose, as rumor does, any discrepancy
of views or opinions on fundamental subjects, or of administrative policy, between the President and the members of this Cabinet, is to suppose the inherent existence
in the Executive government of the elements of its own
weakness and destruction.

The necessary independence and force of the Executive
branch of the Government absolutely requires that it
should be a whole, a unit; for unless the members of the
Cabinet are sincere and willing exponents of the President's deliberate convictions, the absurd spectacle is presented of a necessary power divided against itself, neu-
tralized by its own refractory members, defeating its own
objects, shorn alike of its dignity, its moral influence, and
an unembarrassed exercise of its legal authority.[20]

The *Intelligencer* recoiled at this "Jacksonian pretension to
executive infallibility":

It is one of the most odious of those Jacksonian preten-
sions upon which the People set the seal of condemnation
at the Presidential election in November last; and it does
not diminish the public astonishment at its early appear-
ance that the columns of the *Madisonian* should have been
selected for it.[21]

This assertion that the President must be master in his
official household and independent of the other two branches
was merely a prelude to the President's veto. When his veto
message was finally received in the Senate, debate on reconsideration was delayed for three days. By the end of that
time Clay was ready with his charge that the President had
refused to heed the advice of his cabinet and that he had
yielded to the intrigues of a cabal. Crying out that the public
ills of the past twelve years had been inflicted upon the people through the maladministration of the executive branch,
Clay went directly to his doctrine of cabinet control. The
President might well have been guided in his consideration
of the bank bill "by the judgment of the party which brought

[20]Quoted in the *National Intelligencer*, Aug. 14, 1841.

[21]*Ibid.* The parallel between the doctrine of the "Truisms" editorial and that in
Jackson's veto of the bill for the Bank of the United States is striking.

him into power . . . and, if public fame speaks true, of the
Cabinet which the lamented Harrison called around him,
and which he voluntarily continued."[22] This the President
was not content to do, Clay charged. After Senator Rives
of Virginia had intervened in the debate, Clay returned to
the fight, raising the cry of kitchen cabinet intrigue:

> Although the honorable Senator [Rives] professes not to
> know the opinions of the President, it certainly does turn
> out in the sequel that there is a most remarkable coin-
> cidence between those opinions and his own; and he has,
> on the present occasion, defended the motives and the
> course of the President with all the solicitude and all the
> fervent zeal of a member of his privy council. There is a
> rumor abroad that a cabal exists—a new sort of kitchen
> cabinet—whose object is the dissolution of the regular
> cabinet—the dissolution of the Whig party—the disper-
> sion of Congress, without accomplishing any of the great
> purposes of the extra session—and a total change, in fact,
> in the whole face of our political affairs. I hope . . . that
> the honorable senator is not, cannot be, one of the com-
> ponent members of such a cabal . . .[23]

Rives immediately denied being a member of such a group,
adding that he knew nothing of it. However, he thought
that:

> the President himself was the best judge of these matters.
> He knew best the sentiments of the distinguished gentle-
> men around him, and knew how far their opinions coin-
> cided with his, and the harmony of the Cabinet could be
> preserved.[24]

Senator Archer of Virginia, however, rather let the truth out
by challenging Clay's language in referring to a "low, vulgar
and profligate cabal. Who," he queried, "were the members
of this group, then, but the representatives of the people of
the United States?"[25] The "cabal" included three House

[22]*Cong. Globe*, 27th Cong., 1st Sess., Appendix, p. 364.

[23]This is the version of Clay's speech in Benton, *op. cit.*, II, 324. The version in
the *Cong. Globe* differs slightly from this but does not purport to be a verbatim
report; see Appendix, p. 364.

[24]Benton, *loc. cit.*

[25]*Ibid.*

members from Virginia—Wise, Thomas W. Gilmer, Francis
Mallory—and Caleb Cushing of Massachusetts, all staunch
Tyler advocates.

Clay could milk little nourishment from his knowledge
that Tyler, as charged, had ignored the views of his cabinet
on the bank question and had turned instead to a coterie of
unofficial advisers hostile to the Kentucky Senator. In addition to the congressmen included in this group Tyler turned
to Judge Beverly Tucker and to Thomas Dew of the College
of William and Mary. Duff Green, a former member of
Jackson's "Kitchen Cabinet" who was close to Calhoun, was
a frequent visitor at the White House from the beginning of
the Tyler Administration and later served as a special
diplomatic agent for the President. In time Tyler fell out
with Judge Tucker and Rives, but the others remained close
to the President and eventually were rewarded with cabinet
or diplomatic posts for their loyalty. Tyler's *éminence grise*,
however, at least in the first two years of his administration,
was Littleton W. Tazewell of Virginia. Writing one of his
numerous letters to Tazewell at the close of the sulphurous
second session of the 27th Congress, the President threw
himself upon the judgment of his old friend, a former Whig
returned Democrat:

> You will perceive in this, My Dear Sir, the great weight
> which your opinions are destined to produce with me—
> and I shall always be the loser whenever you withhold
> them. Nor is the frankness with which you have confessed
> them upon this occasion in the least degree unacceptable
> to me. I have been so long surrounded by men who have
> worn smiles on their eyes and honey on their tongues, the
> better to cajole and deceive, that to be shown the error
> of my ways whenever I do err, often in a plain and down-
> right fashion, is a positive relief . . . I could sincerely wish
> that the 4th of March was more nearly at hand, but even
> if it was here present, the future would be by no means
> certain. The country is torn by faction, and everything is,
> therefore, in an unsettled state. I shall ere long have occa-
> sion to apply to you once more to consult for me your
> Sibylline oracle.[26]

[26]Tyler Papers, Vol. II, No. 6429. Tyler's close association with Tazewell appears,

The President's veto of the second bank bill served as the direct instrument of cabinet destruction. On September 4, 1841, the President and his cabinet were meeting when the bill was presented to him. He immediately made known to the cabinet members his intention to veto the bill. The members of the cabinet were solidly against this course of action and told the President so.[27] He persisted in his view, nevertheless, and returned the bill to the House with his objections. This action appeared to Ewing to be most undesirable in view of the role the cabinet had played in the formulation and passage of the bill. Whatever may have been the wishes of the various cabinet members to remain at their posts, with the exception of Webster, they resigned *en masse* on the afternoon of September 11, charging the President with bad faith in his dealings with them.[28]

The cabinet breach could not have come as any great surprise to knowing heads in Washington—or throughout the country, for that matter. On July 28 Abel P. Upshur, who was not then in Washington, wrote to Judge Beverly Tucker in appraising the members of the cabinet:

He [Tyler] has not a sincere friend in it. Webster will adhere to him till he kills Clay, and no longer. Ewing, Bell, Crittenden and Granger will sacrifice him to Clay. Badger is too generous to betray him—but Badger is a Federalist, and will not aid him in shaking off National Republican centralism.[29]

Calhoun, writing to J. H. Hammond on August 1, 1841, predicted that "the loss of the bank bill would probably break up the Whig party and lead to a remodeling of the Cabinet."[30] On August 24 Representative Reynolds of Illinois, while speaking on the Post Office appropriation bill, said:

---

on first sight, to be startling in view of the fact that the latter had been one of several Democratic candidates for Vice-President in opposition to Tyler in 1840. This matter is further discussed in chapter vi. Cf. Chitwood, *op. cit.*, p. 271; Poage, *op. cit.*, pp. 96-97.

[27]"The Diary of Thomas Ewing," p. 109.

[28]Clay gave his orders to the cabinet members to leave at a party at Badger's home on Sept. 9. Webster was absent from this meeting. Poage, *op. cit.*, p. 101.

[29]Tyler, *op. cit.*, II, 115.

[30]"Correspondence of John C. Calhoun," p. 484.

I am satisfied that the head of the Postmaster General
himself will soon be taken off; he himself will soon experience the pleasures of the *guilotine* [*sic*], if I am not greatly
mistaken in the signs of the times. He will be like the rude
boy up the old man's apple tree. He will have to come
down and ask the old man's pardon. I have no means of
knowing this event more than any other citizen. I am in
no cabinet secret, and I am quite glad of it. I never, to
my knowledge, saw President Tyler, but I presume he is
influenced by reason, and the same considerations which
would operate on other individuals in similar situations.
Common rumor, and the reasonableness of the thing itself,
induce all to believe that a dissolution of the cabinet must
and will take place . . . It is an impossibility for an administration to produce prosperity and happiness for the people, when the President and Cabinet are divided. . . . The
President is the responsible officer to the people for his
administration. He was selected and made responsible for
this high trust. It is to him the people look for the correct
administration of the public affairs of the nation.[31]

The members of the cabinet were not unanimously desir-
ous of resigning. Webster excepted, however, they could not
cut their ties with Clay. Ewing complained that Clay demanded much more of his friends then he was willing to
return to them. Ewing even thought that the cabinet could
remain in office as long as Crittenden stayed on, since "the
presence of Mr. Crittenden as a member of the Cabinet
would serve to avert attacks, in the mischief of which, if
made, he must share."[32] Webster considered resigning, but
he decided against it at the last moment.[33] Granger, too,
hesitated, but he finally received his walking orders from
Millard Filmore and the New York delegation in the House.[34]
A final move to prevent cabinet disruption was made by

[31]*Cong. Globe,* 27th Cong., 1st Sess., p. 262.
[32]"The Diary of Thomas Ewing," p. 110.
[33]Mrs. Chapman Coleman (ed.), *The Life of John J. Crittenden,* I, 147; cf. Poage,
op. cit., p. 101.
[34]Fillmore to Granger (Sept. 9, 1841), Francis and Gideon Granger Papers, Library
of Congress. Fillmore was more or less a Clay adherent at this time. For party
reasons the President regretted Granger's resignation; see Chitwood, *op. cit.,*
p. 274.

attempting to secure from the President a pledge that he would not turn out his cabinet, with the promise in return that the bank issue would be postponed until the regular session of Congress in December. This proposal, aimed at securing control of the President, failed.

> This proposition was made to me; I need not add that it was indignantly rejected. I answered that I would or would not discard them, as I thought proper. The Constitution gave me full power over the subject, and I would not part with my control over the members of my political household. Mr. Ewing can now be plainly understood when he says that I 'would not agree to give the assurance that no hostile movements would be made' . . .[35]

Whatever partisan advantage the Clay element of the Whig party may have sought to gain through either forcing the President's compliance with its views on the bank issue or forcing the resignation of the cabinet, the fact remains that the President courageously refused to be cowed. In fact, he wished to rearrange his cabinet and he chose this means of doing so.[36] Indeed, negotiations had been under way for some time for the formation of a new cabinet, so that the President was able to submit to the Senate the names of new heads of the departments (except for Webster) on Monday, September 13, the day Congress had set for adjournment.[37] In acting so promptly to fill these vacancies Tyler was mindful of one of the chief criticisms he had of Jackson's conduct in failing to nominate to vacancies while the Senate was in session and in making diplomatic appointments without its consent.[38] The nominations were immediately confirmed, so that Tyler was able to report to his confidant, Tazewell:

[35]Tyler, *op. cit.*, II, 102.

[36]Mary Hinsdale, *A History of the President's Cabinet*, pp. 112-113.

[37]See Poage, *op. cit.*, p. 96; Coleman, *op. cit.*, I, 164.

[38]In 1834 Tyler complained that under Jackson the appointing power was exercised without the consent of the Senate: "The conclusion, then, is obvious, that as soon as may be after the Senate meets the President should nominate all whom he has appointed in the recess. The appointing power is *with him and the Senate;* and yet under the new practice, if the Senate continues in session the whole year round, the President's minions might be continued in office upon his mere appoint-

I know that it entered into the belief of all the conspirators that I could not surround myself with a Whig Cabinet in which they have been most grievously deceived. I have in my new organization thrown myself upon those who were Jackson men in the beginning and who fell off from his administration for very much the same reasons which influenced you and myself. They are men of acknowledged ability, and conform to my opinions on the subject of a national Bank.

In referring to the "conspiracy" Tyler was reminded of Tazewell's prediction ventured in December, 1840: "Your early prophecy was of infinite service to me from the moment of my assuming the helm, as without it my ship, already tempest tost, might ere this have been stranded."[39]

---

ment until the last day without the Senate being consulted. The provision that the person appointed during the recess shall continue in office until the end of the session, is a provision necessary in itself to enable the Senate to deliberate thoroughly. Now the President is indeed a unit. He has in very truth *his* Secretary of State, *his* Secretary of the Treasury, *his* Attorney General,—as who should say *his* grace and majesty." Tyler to Dr. Henry Curtis (April 6, 1834), Tyler, *op. cit.*, I, 493.

[39] *Ibid.*, II, 131; cf. Tyler Papers, Vol. II, No. 6409. In September, 1844, Tyler said that he had, under the Constitution, only a few hours to choose his new cabinet. "Let it be borne in mind that all vacancies occurring during the session of the Senate must be filled before its adjournment, and cannot be afterwards." This is a discredited construction of Art. II, Sec. 2, Cl. 3, which says, "The President shall have power to fill up all vacancies that may happen during the recess of the Senate, by granting commissions which shall expire at the end of their next session." Tyler, *op. cit.*, II, 94.

When Hugh Legaré became Tyler's Attorney General, he reinforced this view of the President's power to make recess appointments, saying, "I am very clear the President has no right to make or leave a vacancy during the sitting of the Senate, without nominating a successor to it, and then to fill it up after the adjournment of the session." The opinion is dated May 11, 1842. 4 *Opinions of the Attorneys General* 27-28.

Even though he was ready with his cabinet choices, Tyler was heavily burdened with administrative duties. He told Thomas Cooper: "The greatest mass of business has devolved upon me during the last fortnight which I have had yet to bear ... I bethink me of a flight to the country in order to repair some waste of physical and mental strength which a continuous severe service of now six months has served in some measure to impair. I need scarcely say to you at this late day that the report as to my illness was of the character which you described. Thank heaven I have no brain fever nor have I had, and instead of experiencing weariness at the course of the vile conspirators, my health is now decidedly improved, and I have a hope that neither the assaults made, or the *still more violent assaults to be made*, can in any manner disturb me. My friends the Clay Whigs, if they have not already made the discovery, will ere long I hope find it out." Tyler Papers, Vol. II, No. 6405 (italics added).

It is not clear whether Clay expected Tyler to yield to the wishes of his cabinet regarding bank legislation or to resign his office in the face of his presumed inability to recast his cabinet in such a short period of time. Since Tyler claimed that he could make no cabinet appointments after the adjournment of the Senate, he could not, according to one theory, carry on the business of the government. In such a case he would practically be forced to resign and permit the temporary succession of the President *pro tempore* of the Senate. The special election which then would have been held might have given Clay his chance for the Presidency. Instead, Tyler rejected the Whig doctrine of cabinet guardianship of the President and surrounded himself with a group in which his "greatest objective should be to have no more jarring. . . . I would have each member to look upon every other in the light of a friend and a brother."[40] Clay's further efforts to limit the President's control of his cabinet met with similar failure.[41]

Tyler was one President who relied heavily on the advice of his cabinet in the formulation of policy once he had secured control of his official household and had established a measure of harmony between himself and the heads of the departments. For example, immediately after his new cabinet was formed in September, 1841, Tyler called upon the members for advice before authorizing Webster to send instructions to Commodore Morriss at Montevideo. He told Webster:

> I have deemed it proper to call the attention of the cabinet to the instructions prepared by you for Commodore Morriss, in relation to the case of Johnson at Montevideo: They concur in suggesting to you the propriety of so modifying the instructions as to direct the Commodore to ascertain the facts . . . and to report. . . . What think you of

[40]Tyler, *op. cit.*, II, 123.
[41]On Jan. 24, 1842, Clay again raised the cry of "executive usurpation" and introduced three resolutions to amend the Constitution intended to secure congressional control of the Secretary of the Treasury, limit the President's veto power, and deny him eligibility for re-election. Clay would have had the Secretary of the Treasury and the Treasurer chosen by a joint vote of the two houses and removable by them but not by the President. *Cong. Globe*, 27th Cong., 2nd Sess., p. 164.

appointing an agent to Holland? . . . The subject has been much spoken of in cabinet meeting.[42]

The President's first Annual Message to Congress in December, 1841, had the support of the entire cabinet, according to Upshur, then Secretary of the Navy, who wrote to Tucker:

> I sent you the President's message Tuesday. . . . For my part I think highly of it. . . . I also think very highly indeed of the modest and candid spirit in which it was submitted to the criticism of the cabinet. If you condemn it, you will have the high authority of the whole cabinet against you.[43]

Tyler had discussed several of his problems with the inherited cabinet even during the time when his break with the members was imminent.

Adams reported that the President deferred the removal of Nicholas P. Trist from the consulship at Havana until he had received the views of the cabinet members on the matter. During the bank bill crisis in September, 1841, when the President lacked the members' support for his policy, he met them almost daily until their resignations were given.[44]

The President apparently never wholly discarded this practice of submitting most of his major policy decisions to the test of cabinet criticism.[45] He told his brother-in-law, Alexander Gardiner, that his last Annual Message, "which is highly approved by the cabinet, will probably go in on Tuesday."[46] A most important decision made by Tyler to act on the joint resolution for the annexation of Texas was taken only after careful consideration had been given the matter by the cabinet. Writing in 1848, Tyler said, "the whole cabinet assembled; every member gave a decided preference to the House resolution over that of the Senate. . . . All concurred in the necessity of immediate action."[47]

[42]Tyler, *op. cit.*, II, 127.

[43]Upshur to Tucker (Dec. 12, 1841), *ibid.*, p. 153.

[44]Adams, *op. cit.*, X, 482. Cf. "The Diary of Thomas Ewing," pp. 107-110.

[45]Wise, *op. cit.*, p. 207. Wise said, however, that Tyler sent in his veto of the second tariff bill in 1842 without prior consultation with his cabinet.

[46]Tyler, *op. cit.*, II, 358.

[47]*Ibid.*, p. 364; cf. pp. 201, 241-242.

The conduct of foreign relations occupied much of Tyler's energies and attention throughout his administration and it is perhaps not surprising, therefore, that he elevated his various Secretaries of State (Webster, Upshur and Calhoun) to a position of first among equals in the cabinet. He customarily referred to the Secretary of State as his "premier" and vested him with special dignity by directing him to call cabinet meetings and to remind the heads of the other departments of pending duties to be performed.[48]

Tyler's cabinet was somewhat notable for the great number of cabinet appointments he made—nineteen to head the five departments (State, Treasury, War, Navy, Post Office) and that of Attorney General.[49] Aside from the deaths of Upshur, Gilmer and Hugh Legaré in office, the refusal of Judge John McLean of the Supreme Court of the United States to accept his appointment as Secretary of the Treasury, and the failure of James Porter and David Henshaw to receive confirmation by the Senate after serving by virtue of recess appointments, the vacancies were caused by resignations. Moreover, these resignations directly reflected Tyler's desire to surround himself with subordinates who were competent and willing to execute his policies without important reservations.

Aside from the explosion which blew the inherited cabinet out of the White House, there was one other major revision which registered Tyler's determination to mold his executive

[48]*Ibid.*, pp. 388, 395, 397. Cf. *Domestic Letters*, Department of State, National Archives. (Webster to department heads, Sept. 23, 1841.) Typical of his practices is the order in a note to Webster, July 10, 1842: "I send you your admirable letter with one or two suggestions, which you may incorporate or not. These Mexicans mean mischief. Do summon a cabinet for nine o'clock this evening. . . . Will it not be well to feel Lord Ashburton's pulse in this matter, so as if possible to ascertain whether Great Britain has anything to do with it?" The Mexican Foreign Minister had sent Webster a note violently critical of our policy respecting Texas and Mexico. Tyler, *op. cit.*, II, 258.

[49]The number nineteen includes the six members of the cabinet inherited from Harrison. That is, nineteen men actually served Tyler in the cabinet. The nomination of Judge John McLean to be Secretary of the Treasury is not included in this total figure, since he declined appointment despite confirmation by the Senate. Neither is the nomination of Caleb Cushing to the same post included, as the Senate refused its consent in his case.

chiefs into a unified council which would enthusiastically aid his drive to annex Texas. Rumors of cabinet reform seeped out nearly a year before the change occurred. In April, 1842, one of Tyler's New York supporters, Alexander Hamilton, urged the President to drop the two important Whigs, Webster and John C. Spencer (Secretary of War).[50] In August of the same year Calhoun wrote Duff Green, one of his close associates who frequented the White House, saying that there was "no foundation for the rumor of my going into Mr. Tyler's Cabinet."[51] The rumors of discord and impending change were correct, however, for in April, 1843, Van Zandt, Texas' minister in Washington, confidentially told Anson Jones, Texas' Secretary of State, that there was not the best understanding among all the Secretaries at that time and that "Mr. Tyler certainly feels embarrassed from the opposition which surrounds him, and any attempt to force matters too strongly would possibly produce an explosion which is certainly much to be dreaded."[52] An open schism was avoided when, in May, 1843, Webster bowed out of the administration after successfully negotiating the Webster-Ashburton Treaty with the British. An intransigent Senate denied him a graceful retirement to the Court of St. James, and thereby spoiled Tyler's plans in a minor way. Upshur, the Secretary of the Navy and one of Tyler's Virginia friends of long standing, became Secretary of State to undertake the Texas negotiations for which Webster was politically unfit. With the death, a month later, of Hugh Legaré, the Attorney General from South Carolina, Tyler immediately turned to another Southerner, John Nelson of Maryland, for a replacement. Significantly, Tyler told Nelson that aside from his legal attainments "your familiarity with the forms and substance of diplomatic intercourse renders your accession to the Cabinet not only of deep interest to myself but to the country."[53] The recasting of his cabinet

[50]Alexander Hamilton to Tyler (April 23, 1842), Tyler Papers, Vol. II, No. 6423.
[51]"Correspondence of John C. Calhoun," p. 515.
[52]Tyler, *op. cit.*, III, 130.
[53]Tyler Papers, Vol. II, No. 6438.

was completed when Tyler encouraged the resignation of Walter Forward, the Secretary of the Treasury from Pennsylvania, because of his alleged incompetence, replaced him by shifting Spencer from the War Department to the Treasury, and replaced Spencer with a Pennsylvania Democrat, James Porter, in a move to keep his political fences in that pivotal state in good order.[54] The appointment of David Henshaw, one of Jackson's old wheelhorses in Massachusetts, to fill Upshur's former post in the Navy Department gave the President the balance of partisan and policy support which he considered necessary for the task at hand.[55]

Aside from policy considerations, the President's selection of his principal executive subordinates seems inevitably to have been colored by factional alignments in his party and by geographical distribution. The last three cabinet choices made by Tyler further emphasized the importance of these factors which had so greatly influenced his earlier appointments. Upon the deaths of Gilmer and Upshur in February, 1844, he added John C. Calhoun and George Y. Mason, another States' Rights Virginian, to the inner circle.[56] When Spencer resigned in May, 1844, in fruitless anticipation of an appointment to the Supreme Court, Tyler found his replacement in George Bibb, an old-school Republican from Kentucky. It is significant that the cabinet as it was finally reconstituted contained one Northerner (Wilkins of Pennsylvania) among five Southerners. Tyler had groped his way through the thicket of policy and partisanship and had emerged with a sectional cabinet dedicated to a grand assault intended to bring Texas into the Union.

By driving out the members of Harrison's cabinet Tyler settled two issues which were peculiar to his administration, although they are not ordinarily related. For one thing, he rejected Clay's efforts to subordinate the President to infor-

[54]Tyler, *op. cit.*, III, 104; Tyler Papers, Vol. II, No. 6430.

[55]When the Senate refused to confirm Porter and Henshaw, Tyler successfully appointed William Wilkins, a Buchanan Democrat from Pennsylvania, and Thomas W. Gilmer, a States' Rights Virginian, in their respective places. Further political implications in cabinet shifts are discussed in chapter vi.

[56]Calhoun's selection is discussed in more detail in chapter vi.

mal congressional control through the cabinet. Secondly, Tyler rejected the doctrine that in cabinet councils the President is merely one among equals. Instead he took the view that the President alone is responsible for executive decisions, even though he may subject his proposed actions to the crucible of cabinet criticism. So seriously did Tyler accept the doctrine of executive unity that in 1843 he effected a second major revision of his cabinet in order to insure himself of harmonious support for his plan to secure the annexation of Texas. He had proved that the mere accident of his succession to the Presidency was not a sufficient ground for the claim that the President is anything less than master of his political subordinates.

Chapter IV

PROBLEMS OF THE PREROGATIVE

WHEN THE framers opened Article II of the Constitution by vesting "the executive power" in the President, they raised, rather than settled, one of the most persistent and troublesome of all our constitutional questions: what is the nature and extent of the President's powers? Some anonymous wit has observed that the scope of the President's authority under the Constitution is as definite as a bucket that has neither sides nor bottom. This is to say that if the opening clause is, as Hamilton contended, a grant of power, its limits seem nowhere to be clearly defined. Should the Madisonian view prevail, however, our epigram becomes mere exaggeration and the vesting clause conveys no undefined grant of power but serves only to name the kind of power possessed by the President. According to this Madisonian (or Taftian) view, the President's powers are particularized, especially in the second and third sections of the article, and he is restricted to the exercise of those alone.[1] He may not, accord-

---

[1] William Howard Taft, *Our Chief Magistrate and His Powers*, pp. 139-140. The Hamiltonian theory was given embellishment by Theodore Roosevelt in his autobiography and is quoted at length in Corwin, *op. cit.*, p. 189. Let it be noted that even Taft conceded to the President powers which could be reasonably implied from the specific grants in Article II. If that is the case, the only limit on a President is his own self-restraint. See further chapter v.

ingly, conjur up visions of unspecified, or inherent, powers to meet a situation which in reality or fancy demands that the President act in the national interest. It is really quite correct to say that we have had as much difficulty determining the extent of presidential inherent powers as we have had with the implied powers of Congress. It is probably true also that few, if any, Presidents have accepted either of these views literally.

Jackson's emphatic contribution to the many aspects of the prerogative was his claim to a broad removal power which could be inferred from the grant of executive power and his constitutional injunction to "take care that the laws be faithfully executed," together with an assertion that his power of political supervision over his subordinates knew no limits which could properly be imposed by Congress. Also, he asserted for the President the power to judge, on the basis of his oath and independent of Congress and the courts, the meaning of the Constitution. Of no less importance was the Jacksonian tenet that the executive was one of three *equal* branches of the government.[2] Such constitutional doctrines, used to thwart Jackson's opponents, gave them a unity on the issue of presidential power which they utterly lacked on political questions. The Whig view was ably expounded by Tyler's friend and cabinet officer, the States' Rights Virginian Abel P. Upshur. In 1840, one year before entering Tyler's cabinet, Upshur lamented that:

> The most defective part of the Constitution beyond all question, is that which relates to the Executive Department. It is impossible to read that instrument without being struck with the loose and unguarded terms in which the powers and duties of the President are pointed out.[3]

The nationalist Whigs sanctioned a liberal interpretation of congressional powers and damned the executive prerogative, while the States' Rights members of the party excoriated liberal construction by either branch. As a member of the latter (or lesser) school of Whigs, Tyler was confounded by

[2]Binkley, *op. cit.*, pp. 66-85 *passim;* Corwin, *op. cit.*, pp. 22-24, 76, 99-100.
[3]Quoted in Corwin, *op. cit.*, p. 25.

this dogma once he became President. In several matters involving the prerogative he accepted Jacksonian views just as he was constrained to mimic Jackson in his legislative struggles with Congress. Tyler certainly assumed that the removal power was the President's and he used it frequently to wring howls of protest from evicted Democrats, even while he denounced purely spoils removals on the lower levels of the civil service. His contribution to the appointing power was the novel practice of renominating rejected nominees until the Senate made clear the fact that its repeated refusals of consent were meant to be final. Interpreting the "take care" clause and his oath of office, Tyler emphatically reaffirmed the doctrine of executive autonomy expounded by Jackson. His claim of an executive investigative power appears to have been a novel one, although the congressional reaction to his assumption did little to help succeeding Presidents. Tyler's refusal to give Congress information relating to matters under legislative scrutiny was not a novel practice, but he acted in defense of the executive power, upon which, according to his theory of the Constitution, Congress could not encroach. His claim of executive discretion as Commander-in-Chief in dealing with Dorr's Rebellion in Rhode Island once again reasserted the theory that the President possesses a vast and not always well-defined executive power.

Few of the Jacksonian policies had infuriated the Whigs more than the introduction of the spoils system and the Jacksonian claim to a broad and unlimited executive power to remove from office.[4] It was the very essence of Whiggery to resist these instruments of executive autocracy and to call for a restoration of pure Republican principles in the

[4]The removal rule in 1841, in so far as it was accepted as authoritative, was the "decision of 1789" by Congress (in acts establishing the Departments of State, Treasury and War) and Jackson's assertion of 1834 to the effect that the President had complete authority to remove executive subordinates as a necessary inference from his possession of "the Executive power" and the clause requiring him to "take care that the laws be faithfully executed." That is, the power accrued to him by implicit rather than explicit constitutional grant. Corwin, *op. cit.*, pp. 102-112. Cf. James Hart, *The American Presidency in Action, 1789*, pp. 247-248; the "decision of 1789" is discussed pp. 155-248 *passim*.

government.[5] Sensitive to Whig orthodoxy, in his Inaugural
Address Tyler deprecated the effects of spoils removals:

> So long as the President can exert the power of appointing
> and removing at his pleasure, the agents selected for their
> custody [the public funds], the Commander-in-Chief of the
> Army and Navy is in fact the treasurer. A permanent and
> radical change should therefore be decried. The patronage
> incidental to the Presidential office, already great, is con-
> stantly increasing. Such increase is destined to keep pace
> with the growth of our population, until, without a figure
> of speech, an army of officeholders may be spread over the
> land. The unrestrained power exerted by a selfishly ambi-
> tious man in order either to perpetuate his authority or to
> hand it over to some favorite as his successor may lead to
> the employment of all the means within his control to
> accomplish his object. The right to remove from office,
> while subjected to no just restraint, is inevitably destined
> to produce a spirit of crouching servility with the official
> corps, which, in order to uphold the hand which feeds
> them, would lead to direct and active interference in the
> elections, both State and Federal. . . . I will at a proper
> time invoke the action of Congress upon this subject, and
> shall readily acquiesce in the adoption of all proper meas-
> ures which are calculated to arrest these evils, so full of
> danger in their tendency.

Tyler, nevertheless, whetted Whig appetites and dismayed
the Jacksonian Democrats by laying down the broad rule
that:

> I will remove no incumbent from office who has faithfully
> and honestly acquitted himself of the duties of his office,
> except in such cases where such officer has been guilty of
> an active partisanship or by secret means . . . has given
> of his official influence to the purposes of party, thereby
> bringing the patronage of the Government in conflict with
> the freedom of elections.[6]

At the same time, it is interesting to note that the practical standard used to determine what constituted active
partisanship on the part of a government officer was not very

[5]Cf. Binkley, *op. cit.*, p. 88.
[6]Richardson, *op. cit.*, pp. 1890-1891.

sharply drawn. On April 30, 1841, before Tyler had broken
with Clay he assured him that "my attention is turned to
the removals from office after the manner that you suggest,
and I hope that to the recent appointments you have nothing
to object. The P. Office at Lexington shall be attended to." [7]

Despite this concession to the exigencies of practical politics, the President's professed aim was to discourage active
partisanship on the part of government employees. Nevertheless, he did not suggest that limits be placed upon his
power to remove those subordinates who refused otherwise
to comply with his instructions. In his first Annual Message
to Congress in December, 1841, the President again alluded
to the problem:

> I feel it my duty to bring to your consideration a prac-
> tice which has grown up in the administration of the
> Government which, I am deeply convinced, ought to be
> corrected. I allude to the exercise of the power which usage
> rather than reason has vested in the Presidents of remov-
> ing incumbents from office in order to substitute others
> more in favor with the dominant party. . . . In respect to
> the exercise of this power nothing should be left to dis-
> cretion which may safely be regulated by law, and it is of
> high importance to restrain as far as possible the stimulus
> of personal interest in public elections . . . I shall cordially
> concur in any constitutional measures for regulating and,
> by regulating, restraining the power of removal. [8]

Although the President indicated more than a usual willing-
ness to see his power of removal limited in this respect, Congress failed to act on his suggestion. [9]

---

[7] Tyler, *op. cit.*, III, 94. Apparently in this case Tyler thought it best to apply the
rule which says that a little grease applied to the axle will keep the whole wheel
from squealing.

[8] Richardson, *op. cit.*, pp. 1941-1942.

[9] On July 27, 1842, a select committee reported H. R. 549, a bill to prescribe the
method of removing certain officers, to include the requirement that the person
removed be furnished with reasons in writing and that all removals should be
publicly reported. *House Journal*, 27th Cong., 2nd Sess., p. 1171. This bill was
never further acted upon. Similar attempts to limit or prescribe the method of
removal from office were equally fruitless. See *House Journal*, 28th Cong., 1st
Sess., pp. 369-370.

The special session which commenced May 31, 1841, was
barely under way when the Democrats in the House and
Senate raised the cry that Whig theory and practice were
not in complete accord regarding removals from office. In
both the houses resolutions intended to embarrass the President were proposed. In the Senate Buchanan moved a resolution requiring the President to send to the Senate a list
of all removals from office since the 4th of March, 1841,
along with the names of those appointed to fill these vacancies.[10] On the same day Watterson introduced substantially
the same resolution in the House.[11] The Whigs, still aligned
with the President, smelled trickery and amended the resolutions in both houses so as to require the President to list
all removals since March 4, 1829. This effectively silenced
the Democrats. The President welcomed the opportunity to
comply with the request.[12] Tyler was aware that as long as
no new bank legislation was enacted to care for the public
funds (after the repeal of the sub-treasury), he was expos-
ing himself to charges that the "purse and the sword" were
united in presidential hands. He wrote to Tazewell of his
difficulties: "That unfortunate concession to the President
of the power to remove stands in the way of everything."[13]
A tender regard for his position in this case did not deter the
President from removing from the Collectorship at Philadelphia a Jonathan Roberts, who had refused, after conference
with the President, to remove the deputy collector, Calvin
Blythe, an active anti-Tyler man in the customs house. The
House of Representatives assumed the burden of investigating this removal with no more result than to demand of the

[10]*Senate Journal*, 27th Cong., 1st Sess., p. 47. In support of his resolution, in debate
on June 24, Buchanan said that before leaving home he was informed that the
Postmaster General was making removals at the rate of 130 per day. In fact,
he had heard that in one case the post office itself was moved to an area where
a deserving Whig lived. *Cong. Globe*, 27th Cong., 1st Sess., p. 101.

[11]*House Journal*, 27th Cong., 1st Sess., pp. 147-150.

[12]*Ibid.*, p. 365.

[13]Tyler, *op. cit.*, II, 131. The reference is to the board of control in Tyler's exchequer plan presented to the Congress at the start of the regular session. With
neither the sub-treasury nor a national bank, the President could deposit national
funds in such banks as he saw fit.

Secretary of the Treasury the reasons for the action. The President saw fit to permit the House to know his reasons for removing Blythe and Roberts, since they were in complete accord with his announced policy.[14] The House did not further challenge the President with respect to this matter.

On the whole it was the President's policy to delegate to his Secretaries discretion to appoint and remove. However, in July, 1841, he interposed himself between Ewing and several office holders in the Treasury Department, forbidding their removals on purely partisan grounds.[15] Late in his administration, with the shift in party tides, he changed this policy. In July, 1844, Calhoun reported that:

> the claims on the part of Mr. Tyler's political and personal friends are pressing; and it is naturally to be expected that he would give them a preference, especially as many of them have had their expectations for a long time[!]. It is difficult under such circumstances to press any one of my friends on him successfully however great his qualifications. Acting, as I suppose, under the force of the circumstances alluded to, he makes most of his appointments on his own responsibility, without consulting the appropriate Department. This, however, is in strict confidence.[16]

Cheerfully thrusting his head in the lion's mouth, the President told Congress in his first message to the special session of 1841:

> The power of appointing to office is one of a character the most delicate and responsible. The appointing power is ever more exposed to be led into error. With anxious solicitude to select the most trustworthy for official station, I can not be supposed to possess a personal knowledge of the qualifications of every applicant. I deem it, therefore, proper in the most public manner to invite on the part of the Senate a just scrutiny into the character and pretensions of every person I may bring to their notice in the regular form of a nomination to office . . . I shall with the greatest cheerfulness acquiesce in the decision of that body,

[14]*House Journal*, 27th Cong., 3rd Sess., pp. 361, 397-398.
[15]Chitwood, *op. cit.*, p. 368.
[16]"Correspondence of John C. Calhoun," p. 602.

and regarding it as wisely constituted to aid the executive department in the performance of this delicate duty, I shall look to its "consent and advice" as given only in furtherance of the best interests of the country.[17]

Nothing could have pleased the Whigs in Congress any more than this presidential deference to the Senate. This was, indeed, balm to soothe the wounds inflicted on the dignity of the Senate in the long years of Jacksonian "executive usurpation." Time and the dictates of party ambition, however, soon gave Tyler reason to rue his genuflection to the Senate. On February 27, 1843, the President nominated Henry A. Wise, his co-Virginian who had labored so long in the fields for him, to be minister to France. On March 3, the Senate refused its consent by a vote of 24 to 12.[18] On the same day the President renominated Wise, saying:

In submitting the name of Henry A. Wise to the Senate . . . I was led to do so by considerations of his high talent, his exalted Character, and great moral worth. The country, I feel assured, would be represented at Paris in the person of Mr. Wise by one wholly unsurpassed in exalted patriotism and well fitted to be the representative of his country abroad. His rejection by the Senate has caused me to reconsider his qualifications, and I see no cause to doubt that he is eminently qualified for the station. I feel it, therefore, to be *my duty to renominate him.*[19]

Whatever may have been Tyler's belief in 1841 that he ought to bow to the Senate's searching scrutiny of his nominations, he saw in 1843 some higher duty. He apparently viewed the Senate's power to accept or reject presidential nominations to be in the nature of advice which became authoritative only with repeated refusals. The Senate again rejected Wise —this time by a vote of 26 to 8. Once more the determined

[17]Richardson, *op. cit.*, p. 1903.

[18]*Senate Journal,* 27th Cong., 3rd Sess., p. 312. Tyler's sensitivity towards the Senate's share of the appointing power stemmed, no doubt, from his own criticism of Jackson, who made several recess appointments to thwart the Senate and failed to nominate when the Senate was in session. Jackson also failed to reveal several diplomatic appointments and thereby circumvented the Senate. Cf. chapter iii, p. 69, footnote 38.

[19]*Ibid.*, p. 313 (italics added).

President renominated Wise, only to have that unfortunate gentleman rejected for a third time, in the same day, by the emphatic vote of 29 to 2.[20] Even the President's few supporters in the Senate deserted him in his struggle with the Whig majority.

Actually the defeat was a double-barrelled one, since on March 2 the President had nominated Caleb Cushing, Webster's friend and Tyler's supporter in the House, to be Secretary of the Treasury in place of Forward, who had resigned under presidential pressure. When the Senate rejected Cushing on the first vote, the President sent a message of renomination which sarcastically took the Senate to task for rejecting his nominee on obviously partisan grounds. After noting Cushing's "consummate abilities" and "unquestioned patriotism," the President said:

> The respect which I have for the wisdom of the Senate has caused me again since his rejection to reconsider his merits and his qualifications. That review has satisfied me that I could not have a more able adviser in the administration of public affairs.[21]

Only the most vulgar sort of partisanship and churlish truculence could have led the Senate to reject again a man whose later successes marked him as one of the ablest public servants of his generation.

The President proved to be no less intractable when the 28th Congress met in December, 1843. Nor, for that matter, did the Senate yield anything on its part. Tyler had given recess appointments to James Porter of Pennsylvania and David Henshaw of Massachusetts to be Secretary of War and Secretary of the Navy, respectively. They, along with George H. Profitt of Indiana, nominated to be minister to Brazil, failed to receive senatorial confirmation on what were

[20] *Ibid.*, p. 314.

[21] *Ibid.* Tyler may not have been wholly sarcastic in repeating the nominations of Wise and Cushing. In 1832 he was personally doubtful of the desirability of consenting to Jackson's nomination of Van Buren to be minister to Great Britain. Nevertheless, he voted to confirm the appointment, saying to his son: "While I admitted that much of suspicion attached to him on account of recent occurrences, yet I did not think it wise or proper to rest on mere suspicion in rejecting him. He was qualified for the place, and I voted for him." Tyler, *op. cit.*, I, 427.

undoubtedly purely partisan grounds. Profitt had been a Tyler advocate in the House, while Porter and Henshaw were Democrats. The latter, in fact, had been Collector of the Port of Boston under Jackson and Van Buren. With respect to Porter and Henshaw the cry in the Senate had been that the President was trying to form a recess cabinet and circumvent the Senate. This was patently nonsense.[22] The result of this war with the Senate was to force the President to revise his cabinet further with the appointments of William Wilkins of Pennsylvania as Secretary of War and Thomas Gilmer of Virginia as Secretary of the Navy. The rejections, together with that of Cushing as Secretary of the Treasury, constitute the most remarkable violation in our constitutional history of the custom that the President's choice of cabinet members is not ordinarily to be fettered by senatorial rejection. About the most that can be said of the whole affair is that the Senate had its partisan day while the President moved forward to his prime objective, the annexation of Texas.

Tyler had particular difficulty in filling two vacancies which occurred in the Supreme Court during his administration. When Justice Thompson died in December, 1843, Tyler contacted Silas Wright to sound out Van Buren as a prospective nominee. Wright replied that such an action— one calculated to eliminate a prominent rival from the presidential race in 1844—would give the country a tremendous laugh. Thereupon Tyler nominated John C. Spencer, his Secretary of the Treasury;[23] when this nomination was

[22]Cf. *Niles Register*, LXV, 352; Benton, *op. cit.*, pp. 629-631; Hinsdale, *op. cit.*, pp. 119-120. Crittenden in the Senate predicted the rejections, just as he also predicted the nomination and confirmation of Wise in Profitt's place. Coleman, *op. cit.*, I, 216. A letter written by Webster in the *National Intelligencer*, Jan. 18, 1844, makes clear the party grounds on which the rejections were based. *Writings and Speeches of Daniel Webster*, XV, 189-191.

[23]In February, 1844, Crittenden wrote to Francis Granger: "Spencer's confirmation would have been a plain violation of all public and political morality, and would have been to make the Supreme Court an asylum for broken down, disgraced and guilty politicians." In March Thurlow Weed wrote Granger that "Spencer has terrible but just punishment. But it was hard killing him. He made a tremendous struggle for confirmation." Granger Papers.

promptly rejected, the President moved through intermediaries to secure either John Sergeant or Horace Binney,
both prominent Philadelphia lawyers. Both of these gentlemen declined on the grounds of advanced age and poor
health. In March, 1844, Tyler nominated Reuben H. Walworth, Chancellor of the State of New York. In the following month Justice Baldwin of the Supreme Court died,
leaving another vacancy for the President to fill. In June
the President became convinced that Walworth could not
be confirmed; so he again nominated Spencer, who had in
the interval resigned from the cabinet. For some reason the
President thought that:

> the circumstances under which the Senate heretofore de-
> clined to advise and consent to the nomination of John C.
> Spencer have so far changed as to justify me in my again
> submitting his name to their consideration.[24]

This move failed and the President again nominated Walworth, only to have the Senate adjourn with the nomination
on the table. To the vacancy caused by the death of Baldwin
in April Tyler nominated Judge Edward King of Philadelphia, but only after Buchanan had refused to accept the
nomination. The Senate failed also to act on King's nomination. In the regular session which met in December, 1844,
the President renominated both King and Walworth, only
to withdraw their names once again. He finally succeeded
in filling one of the vacancies with Judge Samuel Nelson of
the New York Supreme Court. The 28th Congress came to
an end with the name of Meredith Read, another Philadelphia lawyer, before it as a nominee to the other vacancy.[25]
Once again the Senate proved that even where it is not
empowered to act positively it may in fact paralyze the
constitutional functions of one or both of the other branches
of the government.

In March, 1842, the President had the opportunity to
spank the House verbally for a totally unwarranted inva-

---

[24]Richardson, *op. cit.*, p. 2181. Spencer, a New York Whig, had served Tyler in
the cabinet since 1841 and had thereby incensed the Clay Whigs.

[25]A full account of this story can be found in Warren, *op. cit.*, II, 107-120.

sion of the executive prerogative of making nominations to office. On March 21, on the motion of Representative Andrews, it was:

> *Resolved*, That the President . . . and the heads of the several departments be requested to communicate to the House . . . the names of such of the members (if any) of the 26th and 27th Congresses who have been applicants for office, and for what offices; distinguishing between those whose applications were made by friends, whether in person or in writing.[26]

The President's response to this invasion of executive privacy was prompt and vigorous. On March 23 he replied at length. It would have given him great pleasure to comply with this request for information, he said, were the call within the bounds of both law and sound public policy. On the contrary, however, this call was for two reasons a plain violation of executive right:

> All nominations to the Senate are official acts, which are matters of record, and are at the proper time made known to the House . . . and to the country. But the applications for office, or letters respecting appointments, or conversations held with individuals on such subjects, are not official proceedings, and cannot by any means be made to partake of the character of official proceedings, unless after the nomination of such person . . . the President shall think proper to lay such correspondence or conversations before the Senate.

There was, moreover, a higher duty which impelled him to refuse this demand:

> It becomes me, in defense of the Constitution and laws of the United States, to protect the Executive department from all encroachment on its powers, rights and duties. In my judgment, a compliance with the resolution . . . would be a surrender of duties and powers which the Constitution has conferred *exclusively* on the Executive . . . The appointing power, so far as it is bestowed on the President, is conferred without reserve or qualification . . . I cannot perceive anywhere in the Constitution any right conferred on the House . . . to hear the reasons which an

[26]*House Journal*, 27th Cong., 2nd Sess., p. 565.

applicant may urge for an appointment to office under the Executive department, or any duty resting upon the House ... by which it may become responsible for any such appointment.[27]

According to Tyler's view, the President's right of privacy in dealing with appointments to office was grounded in an executive autonomy which the Constitution conferred upon him. Tyler concluded by saying that this assumption of duty by the House of Representatives was "dangerous, impolitic, and unconstitutional."[28]

Although it is generally conceded that the President has a duty to make appointments to existing offices, it is also true that little can be done to force him to appoint to office, if he chooses not to do so.[29] In June, 1842, the Senate wanted to know when the superintendents of the armories at Springfield and Harper's Ferry had been removed, what successors, if any, had been appointed, and upon what authority any action was taken.[30] The Secretary of War replied that no successors had been appointed, since in the view of the President the duties of supervising the armories would be better performed under military, rather than civilian, direction. As a consequence, the Department of Ordnance had been directed to supervise the armories.[31] Its wits apparently dulled by a zeal for economy, the Senate took no further note of the President's action even though in this instance Tyler had, at his own discretion, virtually suspended offices created by Congress.

Appointment is ordinarily to an existing office, except for those appointments to diplomatic posts which the Senate was willing to confirm prior to 1855, and such private agents as the President might choose to employ in the conduct of foreign relations. In a strict sense, it has been suggested, the last-mentioned type of appointment is not to an office, since

[27]*Ibid.*, pp. 587-588 (italics added).
[28]*Ibid.*
[29]Corwin, *op. cit.*, pp. 89-90.
[30]*Senate Journal*, 27th Cong., 2nd Sess., p. 420.
[31]*Ibid.*, p. 433; cf. *Senate Document* No. 335, 27th Cong., 2nd Sess.

the standard of "tenure, duration, emolument, and duties"
does not apply.[32] Although Theodore Roosevelt is best known
among the Presidents for having employed numerous "vol-
unteer unpaid commissions,"[33] Tyler resorted to the use of a
commission to investigate alleged corruption in the New
York customs house in 1841-42 without express statutory
authority. The President carried on an extensive correspondence with the House over the question of his authority to
institute the commission which he had directed in May, 1841,
to undertake a thorough investigation of alleged malpractices. On February 7, 1842, the House "*Resolved*, That the
President . . . inform the House under what authority the
commission, consisting of George Poindexter and others, for
the investigation of the concerns of the New York custom-
house, was raised; what were the purposes and objects of
said commission . . ."[34] The President replied two days later:

I have to state that the authority for instituting the
commission mentioned in said resolution is the authority
vested in the President of the United States to 'take care
that the laws be faithfully executed, and to give to Congress from time to time information of the state of the
Union, and to recommend to their consideration such
measures as he shall judge necessary and expedient.'

The expediency, if not the necessity, of inquiries into
the transactions of our custom-houses, especially in cases
where abuses and malpractices are alleged, must be obvious to Congress, and that investigations of this kind were
expected to be made appears from the provision in the
twenty-first section of the act of 1799, which enjoins 'col-
lectors of the customs to submit their books, papers and
accounts to the inspection of such persons as shall be
appointed for that purpose.'[35]

He concluded his reply by saying that he would answer other
questions in the resolution at a proper future date. Clearly,
he rested his actions on his constitutional duty to supervise
the faithful execution of the laws and to secure information

[32]Corwin, *op. cit.*, p. 84.
[33]*Ibid.*, p. 85.
[34]*House Journal*, 27th Cong., 2nd Sess., p. 312.
[35]Richardson, *op. cit.*, pp. 1952-1953.

for legislative purposes. Moreover, the President had, by implication, statutory authority in the act of 1799.

The House waited until April 29 for the remainder of the President's views, but, having failed by then to receive them, it again directed the President to communicate the report of the commissioners.[36] The President answered the next day with a message in which he evidenced some pique and an unwillingness to act further in the matter:

Charges of malfeasance against some of those now in office will devolve upon the Executive a rigid investigation into their extent and character, and will in due season claim my attention. The readiness, however, with which the House proposes to enter upon the grave and difficult subjects which these papers suggest, having anticipated that consideration of them by the Executive which their importance demands, it only remains for me, in lieu of specific recommendations, which under other circumstances it would have been my duty to make, to urge upon Congress the importance and necessity of introducing the earliest reforms in existing laws and usages.[37]

This investigation, undertaken undoubtedly in good faith by the President, proved to be a two-edged sword. In so far as it revealed past malpractices, it embarrassed the Democrats, but in so far as it revealed then existing corruption, it hurt the Whigs. At best, it backfired politically in the President's face. Once the commission commenced upon its work of uncovering corruption and malpractices, it allegedly found that Curtis, the Collector, a staunch Webster wheelhorse in New York politics, was guilty, as his predecessors had been, of practicing frauds for the benefit of Massachusetts wool manufacturers. One of the commissioners, Poindexter, became convinced that the President, embarrassed by this revelation, was permitting Curtis's friends to poison his mind against Poindexter. The latter, therefore, wrote to the President on February 7, 1842, unburdening himself of his suspicions. The President, replying to Poindexter the next day, stated that the latter's suspicions of Tyler's lack

[36]*House Journal*, 17th Cong., 2nd Sess., p. 758.
[37]Richardson, *op. cit.*, pp. 2005-2006.

of faith in him were groundless, and that the information which he had sought to obtain from the commission was confidential in nature and intended for presidential eyes only, to be disposed of at presidential discretion. Poindexter, an anti-protective tariff man, had noised about among members of the House his charges that Curtis was engaged in fraudulent practices. Whereupon, anti-tariff members of the House succeeded in having Poindexter's personal views laid before the House.[38] Whigs like John Quincy Adams, who saw in the alleged findings of the commission an attempt to discredit the protective tariff, raised the cry that the whole affair was one more executive pretension to non-existent power. Profitt, however, reminded the members of the House that they had wholly approved of the President's actions during the special session of 1841, at which time the investigation was officially known to have started. The entire matter was conveniently dropped when Representative Underwood of Kentucky, a Clay handyman in the House, moved a resolution so phrased as to indicate the disapproval of the House respecting the President's action in initiating the commission. In approving the report of the Committee on Public Expenditures, the House announced the startling doctrine that it was "the opinion of the House that the President has no rightful authority to appoint and commission officers to investigate abuses, *or to procure information for the President to act upon, and to compensate such officers at public expense,* without authority expressly given by law." This resolution passed by the narrow vote of 86 to 83, after which, on the motion of John Quincy Adams, the whole matter was ordered to lie on the table.[39] The upshot of the affair was that Congress, in enacting H. R. 539, an appropriation bill, inserted a proviso forbidding the payment of agents or commissioners appointed by the President to conduct investigations until Congress had specifically appropriated the funds for such payments. The object of the legislation was, as the Attorney

[38]*House Journal,* 27th Cong., 2nd Sess., pp. 748, 768, 840. Cf. *Cong. Globe,* 27th Cong., 2nd Sess., pp. 475-477.

[39]*House Journal,* 27th Cong., 2nd Sess., pp. 748, 930, 932 (italics added).

General told the Secretary of War, to enable the legislative branch to "paralyze a function which it is not competent to destroy."[40]

The investigation of the customs house amply illustrates the interplay of executive and legislative power in our constitutional system. Despite the fact, however, that Congress acted to limit further investigations, even the Whigs did not assert that the President could not employ either an unpaid commission, a presidential agent, or one already provided an office by law. In other words, there was no attempt made to forbid *wholly* the use of executive investigations. Whatever may be the occasion for such inquiry, the question of the propriety of publicizing the results often arises. A particular advantage of executive inquiry, when compared with legislative investigation, is that the former can be conducted with a degree of secrecy which may be essential until all of the relevant facts have been gathered. Moreover, the personal reputations of persons connected with the investigation may well be better protected when the work is done quietly. At the same time it is important that any presidential claim of the right to keep executive secrets should not be debased by being used merely to cover up corruption and incompetence. It is evident that the President was denied the opportunity to maintain some degree of secrecy in the case of the New York customs house. An investigation of certain Indian affairs in 1841-42, however, had somewhat happier results in this respect.

In the spring of 1842 rumor had it that frauds had been perpetrated in the conduct of the affairs of the Cherokee Indian nation. As a consequence, on May 18, 1842, the House approved a resolution to the effect that "the Secretary of War be *required* to communicate to this House the several reports lately made to the Department by Lieutenant Colonel Hitchcock, relative to the affairs of the Cherokee Indians, together with all information communicated by him concern-

[40] *Opinions of the Attorneys General* 238. This view was expressed by Attorney General Nelson in discussing an investigation proposed by the Secretary of War, Sept. 21, 1843. Cf. Act of Aug. 26, 1842, 5 *Statutes at Large* 523 (524, 526).

ing the frauds which he was charged to investigate; also, all facts in the possession of the Department, *from any source,* relating to the subject."[41] On June 3 the Secretary of War replied to this call, saying that it was not consistent with the public interest to disclose the information demanded, since it was generally *ex parte* in nature and saying further that disclosure at this time would constitute an injustice to all concerned.[42] This refusal of an executive officer to give information to the House precipitated a debate which raged for six days in August, 1842, culminating in the passage of a series of three resolutions on the thirteenth of that month. One of these resolutions asserted that the House "has the right to demand from the Executive . . . such information as may be in their possession relating to subjects of the deliberations of the House, and within the sphere of its legitimate powers."[43] It was further claimed that the subject matter involved in the call of May 18 was within the legitimate sphere of the powers of an inquisitive House, and the demand was again made, *this time of the President,* that all information, "from any source," be supplied to the House.[44]

The President, carefully biding his time until the following January, administered a stinging rebuke to this brash invasion of executive discretion. In his message he pointed out that at the time of the call for information in May he had directed the Secretary of War, for the reasons stated in the Secretary's reply of June 3, not to disclose the information then available. He indicated further that the investigation had terminated without reaching a conclusion and that it might yet again be instituted. The President saw fit, however, to transmit all the information then in the possession of the investigating officer, with the exception of certain proposals made in the course of the investigation and certain views respecting personal character. Tyler, standing as the shield and defender of the Constitution, then launched into

[41]*House Journal,* 27th Cong., 2nd Sess., pp. 831-832 (italics added).
[42]*Ibid.,* p. 915.
[43]*Ibid.,* p. 1290.
[44]*Ibid.,* p. 1291.

an extended lecture on the obligation of the Executive to yield to the demands of the House for information in the possession of the former:

> If by the assertion of this claim of right to call upon the Executive for all the information in its possession relating to any subject of the deliberation of the House, and within the sphere of its legitimate powers, it is intended to assert also that the Executive is bound to comply with such call without the authority to exercise any discretion on its part in reference to the nature of the information required, or to the interests of the country, or of individuals to be affected by such compliance, then *I do feel bound, in the discharge of the high duty imposed upon me,* 'to protect, and defend the Constitution of the United States,' to declare in the most respectful manner my entire dissent from such a proposition.

Again asserting the doctrine of executive independence, based on his oath of office, Tyler claimed that his constitutional obligation to supervise the faithful execution of the laws conferred upon him an equal authority to inquire into the performance of duty by public agents. He added the sound observation that such inquiries must often be made in confidence lest "impertinence or malignity may seek to make the Executive Departments the means of incalculable and irremediable injury to innocent parties by throwing into them libels most foul and atrocious."[45] For him to yield to the inquisition of the House would be to deny to the President a discretion necessary for the proper performance of his duty and would render him wholly dependent upon that body for the performance of "a duty purely executive."[46] Must the President in such a case "become the instrument of such malevolence?" he asked. Although in this case the President claimed the right to be silent in order to protect the reputations of public servants under investigation, he reminded the House that when he had refused to comply

[45]Richardson, *op. cit.*, pp. 2073-2075 (italics added).
[46]*Ibid.* The President cited three instances in which his predecessors had declined to give information to Congress. Washington, in 1796, had refused such a call, as had Monroe in 1825. Jackson, too, in 1832 had denied the right of the House to obtain information in connection with the public lands.

with its demand to know what members of the 26th or 27th
Congresses had sought appointment to office, "no further
notice was taken in any form of this refusal."[47] He concluded
that by fair inference the silence of the House admitted that
the President has a discretionary authority to divulge or to
withhold information from the legislative branch. Adding
that he was apprehensive lest silence be mistaken for acqui-
escence, Tyler squeezed out the last drops of denunciation
against the action of Congress which forbade the payment
of charges incurred by investigations unless authorized by
special appropriation. "Of the policy of that provision of law
it does not become me to speak, except to say that the institution of inquiries . . . however urgent the necessity . . . is
thereby virtually denied to the Executive." He could not,
he added, assume any "portion of the responsibility," no
matter what might be the magnitude of the resulting evil.[48]
Thus is the inner structure of our constitutional system so
contrived that the constituent parts possess the means of
keeping each other in their "proper places"![49] Although the
President may claim an area in which he possesses an independent executive power, Congress is not necessarily powerless to check him, or even to thwart his plans.

While Tyler may have been emboldened in his defiance of
the House in this instance because its members were lame
ducks, the fact is that his sensitivities were easily stung by
any congressional actions that violated the constitutional
niceties. Especially was he alert to note what he thought
were invasions of executive right. When the Senate called
upon the Secretary of the Treasury for certain information
in 1844, Tyler launched into a lecture on protocol denying
the right of the Senate in executive session to address such
a request to a Secretary. In such a case the Senate "can only
properly hold correspondence with the President."[50] In his
"anxious desire" to lay the information before the Senate,
however, he complied with the request.

[47]*Ibid.*
[48]*Ibid.*, p. 2077.
[49]*The Federalist*, No. 51.
[50]Richardson, *op. cit.*, pp. 2173-2174.

The problems involving the appointing and removal powers, the scope of the President's power to "take care that the laws be faithfully executed," the extent of executive immunity to legislative inquiry, and the amount of authority accruing to the President by virtue of his oath were all matters of constitutional interpretation bearing little direct relation to statutes. But with the outbreak of unrest in Rhode Island in 1842, Tyler faced an issue which brought into question the President's constitutional military powers and their relation to statutory authority in cases of domestic violence or insurrection in a state.

Dorr's Rebellion afforded a test both of Tyler's judgment and of the President's military powers. It called into play the provision of the Constitution which guarantees to each state protection against domestic violence.[51] In addition, because of the facts in the case, it raised collaterally the question of what constitutes a republican form of government. From the standpoint of the Presidency, however, the sole question was whether or not Tyler had acted within the limits prescribed by law. When his policies in connection with the rebellion were questioned, the President maintained that he had acted solely in compliance with statutory law providing the means of suppressing domestic violence within a state, and totally without regard for the closely allied question of the "right" of revolution against an existing state government.

In 1841 throughout Rhode Island there occurred a number of meetings at which delegates were elected to a new constitutional convention. This revolt was under the leadership of Thomas Dorr, who had long been agitating for a more liberal suffrage. The delegates so "elected" formed a new constitution which was submitted to the "people," and

[51] *Const. of U.S.*, Art. IV, Sec. 4. Although there had been one state request for federal assistance prior to 1842 (Van Buren had been asked to intervene in the "Buckshot War" of Pennsylvania in 1838 and had refused to do so), the incident involved domestic violence but not insurrection against an established state government. Tyler, then, faced a unique situation. See Bennett M. Rich, *The Presidents and Civil Disorder*, pp. 51-54. Rich discusses Dorr's Rebellion on pp. 54-56 *passim*.

declared to be ratified. None of this was done with the legal sanction of the previously existing government—one based essentially on the charter originally granted by Charles II. Dorr's agitations grew so menacing that the charter government declared martial law.

On April 4, 1842, Sam King, Governor of Rhode Island under the charter government, wrote to President Tyler asking for the protection against domestic violence guaranteed to the states by the Constitution. At this time there was certainly no armed rebellion under way in Rhode Island; it existed only in the minds of the members of the charter government. Tyler carefully weighed the circumstances and examined the statutory basis for any action he might take before replying to Governor King that the President was empowered not to *anticipate* insurrection or violence, but merely to act when he was apprised of its existence. The President was thoroughly aware of the critical nature of the duty he had been called upon to perform. No man as sensitive to the rights of the states as Tyler was could face without serious misgivings the task of interposing Federal armed force in a struggle within a state. At the same time, there is reason to believe that there always lurked in the minds of most Southern politicians the fear that at some time they might have need to call upon the national government for just such help. It is undoubtedly for these reasons, at least, that Tyler determined to act in compliance with his legal duty, but to do so only when the need for his action had become clearly established. Portions of Tyler's letter to Governor King on April 11, 1842, are revealing:

I shall not adventure the expression of an opinion upon those questions of domestic policy which seem to have given rise to the unfortunate controversies between a portion of the citizens and the existing government of the State. They are questions of municipal regulation, with which this government can have nothing to do.

Thus, having disclaimed any intention of judging the moral merits of the claims of either side, Tyler admitted that it would be his painful duty to use armed force, should an

actual state of insurrection exist. By taking this action, however, he in effect recognized King as the lawful Governor of
Rhode Island:

There must be an actual insurrection, manifested by law-
less assemblages of the people or otherwise, to whom a
proclamation may be addressed and who may be required
to betake themselves to their respective abodes. I have
however, to assure your excellency that should the time
arrive . . . when an insurrection exists *against the government* of Rhode Island, and a requisition shall be made upon
the Executive . . . to furnish that protection which is guaranteed to each State by the Constitution and laws, I shall
not be found to shrink from the performance of a duty
which, while it would be the most painful, is at the same
time the most imperative.[52]

The statutory basis for any action which the President
might choose to take was to be found in the acts of February, 1795, and March, 1807. Together they provided that
the President could answer the call of the legislative branch
of a state, or, if the legislature could not be convened, of
the executive branch of a state, to supply troops from the
militia of any state or states, or a sufficient portion of the
regular armed forces of the United States, for the purpose
of suppressing insurrection.[53]

In May, 1842, the Dorrites sought to organize a new
government in Rhode Island by establishing the various
branches of government in Providence. This alarmed Governor King, who declared martial law and again applied to

[52]Richardson, *op. cit.*, pp. 2143-2144.

[53]Act of Feb. 28, 1795, 1 *Statutes at Large* 424: ". . . in case of an insurrection in
any state, against the government thereof, it shall be lawful for the President
. . . on application of the legislature of such state, or of the executive, (when the
legislature cannot be convened,) to call forth such number of the militia of any
other state or states, as may be applied for, as he may judge sufficient to suppress such insurrections."

Act of March 3, 1807, 2 *Statutes at Large* 442: ". . . in all cases of insurrection,
or obstruction to the laws, either of the United States, or of any individual state
or territory, where it is lawful for the President to call for the militia for the
purpose of suppressing such insurrection, or of causing the laws to be duly executed, it shall be lawful for him to employ, for the same purposes, such part of
the land or naval force of the United States, as shall be judged necessary . . ."

the President for armed intervention.[54] Again, however, the
President delayed any direct armed action. Instead, he took
steps to ascertain the true condition of affairs in the state
of Rhode Island by ordering Colonel Bankhead at Newport
to gain intelligence in the matter.[55] Meanwhile, he assured
Governor King of his belief that no real armed conflict would
be undertaken. The President demonstrated his desire to
avoid armed conflict in his letter to Governor King on May
9, 1842:

> I deprecate the use of force except in the last resort, and
> I am persuaded that measures of conciliation will at once
> operate to produce quiet. *I am well advised*, if the general
> assembly would authorize you to announce a general am-
> nesty and pardon for the past, without making any excep-
> tion . . . and follow it up by a call for a new convention
> upon somewhat more liberal principles, that all difficulty
> would at once cease . . . I have said that *I speak advisedly.*
> Try the experiment, and if it fail then your justification
> in using force becomes complete.[56]

In the President's mind the use of federally directed force
was a far greater evil than his modest proffer of advice, no
matter how reluctant he might be to interfere in a purely
state affair.

Despite assurances from the scene of action during the
early weeks of June that Dorr and his supporters would not
attempt a military coup, the situation became alarming at
the end of the month.[57] On the 23rd Governor King again
applied for military aid from the Federal government, but
in this case the President refused it on the nice ground that
the Rhode Island legislature was then sitting, and that,
therefore, the Governor's call to the President was on its
face illegal.[58] He assured the Rhode Island Governor, however, that a proper application for aid coming from the
charter legislature would "receive all the attention which

[54]Richardson, *op. cit.*, p. 2152.
[55]*Ibid.*, p. 2147.
[56]*Ibid.*
[57]*Ibid.*, pp. 2153-2154.
[58]*Ibid.*, p. 2156.

will be justly due to the high source from which such . . . shall emanate."[59] This step still left the back door open for the President, who was so reluctant to commit himself to the use of armed force. Within a week the President had deemed the situation sufficiently serious for him to instruct the Secretary of War to proceed immediately to the scene of action with broad discretionary power to call for armed intervention if a proper application were made to the President for this action. The Secretary was instructed to determine the true state of affairs, to issue a proclamation ordering the rebels to disperse, and to call on the Governors of both Massachusetts and Connecticut, if necessary, for militia "to prevent the effusion of blood."[60] In addition, the Secretary was directed to dispose the regular troops in the area in such a way as best to defend the city of Providence from assault.

When it became clear that Federal intervention was inevitable if the rebellion continued, the whole effort collapsed and a genuine crisis was averted. Of no little importance to Tyler personally was the fact that he had handled this affair according to the principle which he had enunciated in criticizing Jackson's policy in the nullification controversy of 1832; for then he said, "When he was called on for military force he should be disposed to inquire whether every other means had been exhausted before resort was had to the sword."[61] In the following year a new and more liberal constitution was adopted in Rhode Island under the auspices of the charter government.

There were three attempts made in the course of time to nullify the President's actions in this case. The first of these occurred in the Senate while the negotiations of April-June, 1842, were under way; the second occurred in the House in the spring of 1844; and the last occurred in the form of a

---

[59]*Ibid.*

[60]*Ibid.*, p. 2160. Cf. James Hart, *Introduction to Administrative Law*, 2nd ed. (New York: Appleton-Century-Crofts, 1950), pp. 228 ff. Spencer's action would have been the President's in contemplation of law.

[61]*Congressional Debates*, 22nd Cong., 2nd Sess., p. 21.

court case finally heard as *Luther* vs. *Borden* in the Supreme Court of the United States.[62] None of these efforts was successful.

To the Van Buren Democrats Dorr's Rebellion was grist for the political mill. As a consequence, on April 18, 1842, when the situation in Rhode Island was in a state of threatening flux, Senator Allen of Ohio introduced in the Senate a resolution which in substance demanded of the President all the information upon which he was acting in the Dorr case, as well as all the orders or instructions which he had issued to subordinates.[63] Despite Allen's repeated attempts to have the Senate consider this resolution, the most that he did was to introduce another resolution with a lengthy speech in which he said, in part, that:

> it was impossible for the Senate to close its eyes to the fact that there exists in that State a condition of affairs verging toward very serious consequences. It was impossible for the Senate to close its eyes to the fact that the President of the United States has, to some extent, interposed the Executive power between the two parties in that State. . . .[64]

Preston of South Carolina revealed the sentiment of conservatives by saying that he did not care to see a discussion of the matter at that time, and that he "would invoke the aid of every rule of the Senate that excludes debate."[65] Allen retorted that:

> the proposition is this: whether in the existing state of affairs (which the Senate knew to exist) that body would remain inert, inattentive, and careless, whilst the Executive . . . was pursuing a course which was calculated to make this government a party to a civil war. To say that Congress must wait until collision takes place, was to say that Congress must do nothing in the matter . . . Now he wished Congress to take action before the evil should arise . . . He made the motion that the sense of the Senate might

[62] 7 Howard 1 (1849).

[63] *Senate Journal*, 27th Cong., 2nd Sess., p. 299.

[64] *Cong. Globe*, 27th Cong., 2nd Sess., p. 446.

[65] *Ibid.*

be given . . . whether the Executive had the right to do that which was calculated to produce civil war.[66]

With the issue squarely before it, the Senate, by its inaction, refused to take the view that the President had no authority to act, or that in acting he was doing so unwisely.

The action of a Democratic House of Representatives in February, 1844, equally vindicated the President's judgment and actions respecting the whole matter. Although the House ordered a call for all the papers relating to his conduct in Dorr's Rebellion, it failed to censure Tyler in any way. The President's reply to this call so completely revealed his skillful handling of a delicate situation that even such debate as occurred in the House was aimed solely at the question of his authority to interfere in the affairs of a state "of his own mere notion" and without the consent of Congress.[67] The attempt was constantly made to cloud the issue of the President's duty to act under the Constitution and laws of the United States to suppress domestic violence with the moral question of the right of certain people in Rhode Island to revolt against an established government. To the Democrats the right of revolution was the paramount issue. In sending to the House the required papers the President met this issue unequivocally:

> I must be permitted to disclaim entirely and unqualifiedly the right on the part of the Executive to make any real or supposed defects existing in any State constitution or form of government the pretext for a failure to enforce the laws or those guarantees complied with because *the President* may believe that the right of suffrage or any other great popular right is either too restricted or too broadly enlarged. . . . For the Executive to assume such a power would be to assume a power of the most dangerous char-

---

[66] *Ibid.* The Senate later refused to receive a letter from Dorr, who claimed to be the "Governor" of Rhode Island. See *Senate Journal*, 27th Cong., 2nd Sess., p. 331.

[67] *Cong. Globe*, 28th Cong., 1st Sess., p. 407. This was the contention of Rep. McClernand of Ohio. Actually, as events demonstrated, it was an assertion which was wholly unsupported by the facts. The President had no intention, and no reason, to consult Congress.

acter. Under such assumptions the States . . . would have
no security for peace or tranquility. . . .[68]

The President was satisfied that the course he had followed
had produced a desirable change without violence and the
use of force.

The opinion of the court in the case of *Luther* vs. *Borden*
upheld, in effect, the right of Congress to vest in the President discretionary authority to act. The Court added that
by the acts of 1795 and 1807 Congress had vested in the
President the power to judge the existence of a specified contingency in which the government of the United States was
legally bound to act.

> He [the President] is to act . . . and consequently he
> must determine what body of men constitute the legis-
> lature, and who is the governor, before he can act . . . If
> there is an armed conflict . . . it is a case of domestic vio-
> lence, and one of the parties must be in insurrection against
> the lawful government. And the President must, of neces-
> sity, decide which is the government . . . before he can
> perform the duty imposed upon him by the act of Con-
> gress.[69]

The practical result of Tyler's actions was that the President
decided which of the contending groups was the government
of Rhode Island.

Tyler demonstrated in the case of Dorr's Rebellion a skilful capacity for blending his legal authority as the nation's
chief executive with the moral influence of the presidential
office.[70] He acted with restraint and firmness. He refused

[68]Richardson, *op. cit.*, p. 2137. In defending his refusal to use federal armed might
in the Dorr controversy Tyler must have recalled with satisfaction his opposition
to Jackson's threat to use force against South Carolina in the nullification im-
broglio in 1832. Tyler said then of Jackson's policy: "It is idle to talk of preserving a republic for any length of time with an uncontrolled power over the
military exercised by the President." Quoted in Chitwood, *op. cit.*, p. 113.

[69]7 Howard 43. The Court decided that it was bound by this decision of the political branches.

[70]Webster, who had been out of Tyler's administration for a year, congratulated
his former chief for his policy: "I write to signify to you how greatly I was pleased
with your message to the House . . . on the Rhode Island business. That paper
has given great satisfaction in this quarter to all sensible men of all parties.
Indeed, your conduct of that affair will appear hereafter, I am sure, worthy of

either to shy away from his plain duty or to act with pre-
cipitate haste. He refused to use his authority as a basis for
taking harsh measures when the spoken word would suffice.
In doing this he was able to adhere to his principle of not
extending unnecessarily the influence of the national government, while at the same time arriving at a solution based
upon conciliation and compromise. There is no higher mark
of a democratic statesman.

---

all praise, and one of the most fortunate incidents in your administration for your
own reputation. The case was new, and it was managed with equal discretion
and firmness." Tyler, *op. cit.*, II, 199.

Chapter V

THE CHIEF OF FOREIGN RELATIONS

IN 1799 John Marshall asserted in the House of Representatives that "the President is the sole organ of foreign relations."[1] This epigram raises a question as much as it answers
one. Does this say merely that the President is the *instrument of communication* between this and other states in the
world community, or does it also claim for the President the
authority to *formulate the policy* to be pursued in the conduct of this nation's foreign relations? Certain obvious answers to this query are evident with respect to particular
powers. While it is true that the framers were strongly influenced by the views of writers like Locke, Blackstone and
Montesquieu, who tended to view the power to conduct
foreign relations as one falling properly within the prerogatives of the Crown, it is equally true that they did not vest
control exclusively in the President. Hamilton was forced to
concede this in the Pacificus-Helvidius debate.[2] Congress
possesses, among others, the delegated powers to make war,
to raise and equip armies and navies, to define and punish
offenses against the law of nations, to regulate foreign commerce, to tax, to appropriate funds from the public treasury,
and, certainly, the power to make "all laws which shall be
necessary and proper" for carrying into effect not only its
own powers, but also those of the other branches of the
national government.[3] In contrast, the specific authority

[1]Quoted in Corwin, *op. cit.*, p. 216.
[2]See Edwin S. Corwin, *The President's Control of Foreign Relations*, pp. 11-12.
[3]*Const. of U.S.*, Art. I, Sec. 8.

107

which the Constitution grants to the President pales at first
sight alongside the congressional orbit of power. The President is Commander-in-Chief of the armed forces; he possesses the executive power; he shares with the Senate the
power to make treaties and appointments to office—notably
diplomatic office in this case; he receives ambassadors; and,
lastly, he is charged with the supervision of a faithful execution of the laws. Thus it is that Hamilton was forced to
assert, as Pacificus, the sweeping claim that "the general
doctrine of our Constitution is, that the *executive power* of
the nation is vested in the President; subject only to the
exceptions and *qualifications*, which are expressed in the instrument."[4]

The constitutional difficulty is that the President and
Congress, and the President linked especially with the Senate, have all been vested with some of the power necessary
to conduct foreign relations. Madison noted this in the Pacificus-Helvidius debate when he said that the two branches
of government could not, as Hamilton urged, possess *concurrent* powers over foreign relations. This, Madison said,
"would be as awkward in practice, as it is unnatural in
theory."[5] He urged that the powers possessed by each branch
were separate and distinct, with the lion's share of the important ones falling to Congress by express grant. It has
been suggested that the term *coordinate powers* is more accu-
rately descriptive of the powers vested in the legislative and
executive branches.[6] In those instances in which the framers,
intentionally or not, left gaps in the assignment of powers
to the two branches, it is the President who has generally
been able successfully to lay claim to inferred powers by
practical interpretation of the Constitution. For the truth
is that Hamilton's "general grant" theory has triumphed
over Madison's theory of legislative control. Moreover, this

[4]Quoted in Corwin, *President's Control of Foreign Relations*, pp. 11-12. The pertinent portions of the Pacificus-Helvidius debate are quoted extensively in chapter i.

[5]*Ibid.*, p. 22.

[6]Corwin, *President, Office and Powers*, p. 214.

tendency, now clearly evident, started with Washington.
Nonetheless, while the President may have secured the initiative in the formulation of foreign policy, Congress is not
of necessity left completely powerless to control him. A century and a half of constitutional development has amply
demonstrated that the President is legally "independent of
direction by Congress, though capable of being checked
by it."[7]

Despite the frequent displays of political bad blood between President Tyler and Congress over legislative policy,
especially during the life of the 27th Congress, Tyler's
achievements in the conduct of foreign policy are outstanding among those of the early Presidents. Although Tyler met
some congressional obstacles to success in the conduct of his
foreign policy, he was totally thwarted only once, and that
with respect to what must be considered a minor practical
matter.[8] Tyler assumed that the initiative was his, and he
never relinquished it to Congress. His view is particularly
notable since this relationship had not yet completely developed in the Presidency.[9] Congress, of course, did make some
attempts either to initiate policy or to nullify the results of
Tyler's initiative, but by and large, the policy which the
President proposed, or followed, was approved in the Senate
or the two houses. In fact, in the annexation of Texas, the
two houses were joined in sanctioning the President's measure in a unique manner. A state of cooperation between the
President and Congress, which alone can assure success in
the conduct of foreign relations, existed to a remarkable
degree in Tyler's administration despite his discord with the
Whigs on the prime domestic issues.

[7]*Ibid.*, p. 220.

[8]The Senate rejected the treaty with the German Customs Union. I do not count
the rejection of the Texas annexation treaty by the Senate as a mark of complete
failure in the light of subsequent events.

[9]*Ibid.*, p. 225. Corwin says: "Actually while now cooperation, now subservience,
has characterized the relations of Congress to the President at different times, yet
down to the Mexican War the former was the prevailing pattern, while since then
—and owing in part to that fateful precedent—it is the President who has more
and more called the tunes."

Either house of Congress may act within the scope of its powers to aid or to hamstring the President. Each house may do this in its own peculiar way, but one means open to both is to serve as a public forum in which debate on foreign policy may be a means of controlling the President. How successful this technique is depends wholly upon the circumstances in which it is used, and upon the personalities involved. A call for information from the executive branch can, of course, be embarrassing, but it may also be fruitless. A resolution used to express congressional opinion respecting foreign policy is likely to cause the President some bad moments if it does not support him.

In point of time, one of the first and most pressing of the problems of diplomacy facing Tyler when he became President was the settlement of the McLeod case. McLeod, a British subject, had been arrested by the authorities of the State of New York for his alleged participation in the burning of the ship *Caroline*, one of the incidents of the Canadian border warfare which had taken place in the latter part of the 1830s. After a lengthy interchange of correspondence between the American Secretary of State and the British Foreign Office, Britain assumed the position that McLeod had been acting as an agent of public force and was not, therefore, subject to the municipal law of the State of New York, but only to the law of nations. He could not, then, be held and tried for the crime of murder by that State.[10] Popular emotions were considerably fired by the incident at a time when other subjects of potential or actual negotiation between this country and Great Britain were also pressing for attention.[11]

In his message to the special session of the 27th Congress in May, 1841, the President recognized the strained nature of our relations with Britain but entertained at the same time the hope that a peaceful settlement could be reached

[10]For a discussion of the McLeod case see J. S. Reeves, *American Diplomacy under Tyler and Polk*, pp. 22-27.

[11]Among these were questions respecting the Maine and Oregon boundaries, suppression of the slave trade, the right of search, and our relations with Texas and Mexico.

in all matters.[12] He vigorously denied that Britain had any grounds for complaint respecting the course which this government had taken in the McLeod case. The national executive in this country could not intervene through legal processes in the proceedings of the state courts without an order from a proper tribunal. "The precise state of the proceedings at which such an order may be made is a matter of municipal regulation exclusively, and not to be complained of by any other government."[13]

Tyler accompanied this message with documents which explained the course of action already taken. The Secretary of State had instructed the Attorney General, at the direction of the President, to proceed to the scene of McLeod's trial at Lockport, New York, after showing to the Governor of the State of New York his instructions and authentic evidence that the British government recognized McLeod's act as one done by national authority. Webster also informed Crittenden, the Attorney General, that the President would direct a *nolle prosequi*, were this indictment pending in a court of the United States. Webster further informed Crittenden that the President wanted McLeod's counsel to seek a change of venue to get the trial away from the most excited areas of the state. The Attorney General was not to act as counsel, but he was to secure a skilful advocate for the defendant. In case the defense was overruled, he was to see that immediate steps were taken to remove the case to the United States Supreme Court on a writ of error.[14]

In pursuance of these instructions the United States District Attorney for the Northern District of New York appeared as counsel on behalf of McLeod.[15] This brought from Governor Seward and the President's critics in Congress the cry of federal interference in the affairs of a state. The President justified his action in a letter to Seward telling him

[12]Richardson, *op. cit.*, p. 1927.

[13]*Ibid.*, p. 1928.

[14]*Executive Documents and Reports of Committees*, 27th Cong., 1st Sess., Doc. No. 1, p. 25.

[15]Tyler, *op. cit.*, II, 208.

that the national government did not desire to interfere with the trial but that it had a necessary and legitimate interest in protecting itself in the conduct of its foreign relations so "that no just ground of complaint be furnished to other nations."[16]

Representative Floyd of New York, ever eager to protect the interests of his locality no matter what the national interest, introduced a resolution calling for information from the President in regard to McLeod's case. After incorporating the customary language requesting this information, if the President deemed its disclosure to be in the public interest, the House then proposed to require a detailed accounting of presidential actions: what civil or military officers had been directed to New York in connection with the trial of McLeod and whether by correspondence or by other means the President had given the government of Britain to understand that McLeod would be released or surrendered and, if so, "to communicate to this House copies of the instructions to, and the report of such officer."[17] For twelve days during the following three months the House debated this resolution—one which on its face was intended to embarrass the President, since he had already informed the House of both his actions and his intentions.[18] Representative A. V. Brown of Tennessee frankly admitted this motive in a speech on July 9 in which he shouted defiance at the President: "It is time, high time, for us to speak out boldly and without reserve. . . . Shall an American Congress be *afraid* to speak—afraid to call even for necessary information, lest, peradventure, it should embarrass our future negotiations? Sir, I am free to declare, that I desire to embarrass all such negotiations as have been lately going on."[19] On September 4, after John Quincy Adams had characterized the resolution as "a rank party measure," the House

---

[16]*Ibid.*, p. 210.

[17]*House Journal,* 27th Cong., 1st Sess., p. 189.

[18]See the speeches of Floyd and Gordon of New York, *Cong. Globe,* 27th Cong., 1st Sess., pp. 115, 123, 173, 174.

[19]*Cong. Globe,* 27th Cong., 1st Sess., p. 173.

ordered that the motion lie on the table.[20] A similar resolution moved by Allen of Ohio in the Senate in February,
1842, was permitted to die on the table without a word of
debate.[21]

The suppression of the African slave trade on the high
seas became a greatly agitated subject in the Tyler Administration. On June 13, 1842, the House agreed to J. Q. Adams'
resolution requesting that the President communicate to the
House, "so far as may be compatible with the public interest, a copy of the Quintuple Treaty between the five principal Powers of Europe, for the suppression of the African
slave trade."[22] It further requested a copy of the remonstrance of our Minister to France, Lewis Cass,[23] to the French
government against the ratification of the treaty, as well as
all correspondence between Cass and the government in
Washington. One week later the President declined to answer this call for information, saying that he lacked an
authentic copy of the treaty and that the communication of
the other requested papers "would not be compatible with
the public interest" at this time.[24] This reply was received
without a murmur of dissent in the House. The subject was
at this very time a matter of discussion between the Secretary of State, Webster, and the British envoy, Ashburton.[25]

Senator Thomas Hart Benton was not thoroughly satisfied with the manner in which the slave trade articles of the
Webster-Ashburton treaty were negotiated. He complained
"at the absence of all the customary lights upon the origin
and progress of treaty stipulations."[26] He was suspicious that
the origins of the articles were to be found in British proposals. Benton, despite his opposition to the treaty, was
powerless to prevent its approval by the Senate. In Decem-

[20]*Ibid.*, p. 428. The vote was 109 to 70.
[21]*Senate Journal*, 27th Cong., 2nd Sess., pp. 183, 186.
[22]*House Journal*, 27th Cong., 2nd Sess., p. 949.
[23]Cf. Tyler, *op. cit.*, II, 233.
[24]Richardson, *op. cit.*, p. 2011.
[25]See Tyler's message accompanying the Treaty of Washington, 1842; *ibid.*, p. 2011.
[26]Benton, *op. cit.*, p. 449. The negotiators, by agreement, kept no minutes. Cf.
Reeves, *op. cit.*, p. 44.

ber, 1842, however, he sought to chastize the President for
negotiating the ninth and tenth articles of the treaty, establishing the African squadron of the Navy for the suppression of the slave trade. On December 27, the Senate agreed
to a lengthy resolution moved by Benton requesting the
President to provide certain information, if this were compatible with the public interest. Among other things it requested the President to reveal how he knew, when he told
Congress so, that the course which the American government took toward the Quintuple Treaty "has excited no
small degree of attention and discussion in Europe." It further asked the President to indicate whether or not the
treaty had been communicated to this government, and, if
so, by whom and for what purpose. And, lastly, it requested
of the President "all information upon the negotiation of
the African squadron articles as will show the origin of such
articles and the history and progress of their formation."[27]
Archer of Virginia, Chairman of the Committee on Foreign
Relations, thought "that the Senate ought not on its own
account to send such a message to the head of any department of the Government."[28] The President thoroughly agreed
with him, for he said in reply that "agents of this government abroad obtained unofficially copies of it and sent it to
this government as political intelligence of some importance."[29] Moreover, the President added, with none too
gentle sarcasm, that it was no remarkable feat of intelligence
to deduce the fact of European interest in the attitude of
the United States toward the Quintuple Treaty. In an age
in which the public is informed of the actions and interests
of governments he could not see how the President could
fail to know the situation or why he should have to wait
for private information to be communicated to him. He
thought that it would not become him to debate this issue
with the Senate and he had nothing further to say in response to this question. As to the origins of the articles of

[27]*Senate Journal*, 27th Cong., 3rd Sess., p. 88.
[28]*Cong. Globe*, 27th Cong., 3rd Sess., p. 85.
[29]*Senate Journal*, 27th Cong., 3rd Sess., p. 88.

the Webster-Ashburton Treaty dealing with the slave trade, he answered with an air of injured surprise to Benton's questioning. These articles, he said, were proposed to the British at his personal direction and they were ratified by both governments. Saying that he thought his motives in negotiating these articles had been thoroughly understood by the Senate, he revealed his annoyance with novel inquiries into the conduct of the negotiations whereby the treaty was brought before the Senate. "I have," he said, "out of a profound respect for the Senate, been induced to make this communication in answer to inquiries, some of which, at least, are believed to be without precedent in the history of the relations between that body and the executive department."[30] The Senate accepted this scolding without comment.

Tyler refused three other calls by the House for information in the course of his administration.[31] Among those not refused, however, the resolution of February 2, 1843, is of some interest. Commodore T. A. C. Jones was made commander of the Pacific Squadron in 1841. In October, 1842, acting under the misapprehension that war with Mexico had commenced, he seized Monterey, the capital of the Mexican province of California, holding the city for only one day. The House demanded of the President copies of Jones' instructions at the time of his appointment as commander of the squadron as well as copies of all communications received from him relating to his "expedition for the occupation of the Californias."[32] The House ignored the courtesy of respecting the President's right to refuse those papers which he considered it necessary to withhold in the public interest. In his reply to the query of the House Tyler noted that the request had not been confined to such information as might safely be disclosed. In view of this fact, he lectured the

[30]*Ibid.*, pp. 92-93. The implication is clear in this passage that Tyler felt no legal obligation to reveal this information. Of course, this situation is different from that in which a treaty is still pending in the Senate. But there, too, the President has an undoubted power of selection over information of the sort Tyler utilized in connection with the Texas treaty.

[31]Cf. Richardson, *op. cit.*, pp. 1954, 2127-2128, 2173.

[32]*Ibid.*, p. 2080. Cf. Reeves, *op. cit.*, pp. 103-105.

House briefly on its right to obtain information from the executive:

> It may well be supposed that cases may arise even in time of peace in which it would be highly injurious to the country to make public at a particular moment the instructions under which a commander may be acting on a distant and foreign service. In such a case, should it arise, and in all similar cases, the discretion of the Executive cannot be controlled by the request of either House of Congress for the communication of papers.[33]

In this case, however, he could see no injury to the public interest in giving the House the information requested along with some which the House did not previously know about. This position served as ground for the President's refusal in May, 1844, to comply with a House request of January 3, 1844, for copies of the orders given to the commander of the squadron to suppress the slave trade.[34]

The relationship between the President and Congress in the formulation of our policy toward the Oregon territory is illustrative of the interplay of presidential and congressional control. As early as May, 1841, the President indicated his interest in the accelerated colonization of the Oregon territory.[35] In the following December he called to the attention of Congress, in his first Annual Message, a recommendation by the Secretary of War for the establishment of a chain of forts stretching from Council Bluffs, Iowa, to the Pacific Ocean.[36] By July, 1842, negotiations were nearly completed to settle the Maine boundary question, but not the Northwestern boundary question.[37] In view of this fact the President requested the Senate to consider his communication of the report of Lieutenant Wilkes' explorations in Oregon as confidential in nature.[38] The Senate did so. In his second

[33]Richardson, *op. cit.*, pp. 2080-2081.

[34]*Ibid.*, p. 2173. Tyler also refused to divulge the state of the negotiations over the Maine boundary in February, 1842; *ibid.*, p. 1954.

[35]*Ibid.*, pp. 1894-1895.

[36]*Ibid.*, pp. 1940-1941.

[37]See Reeves, *op. cit.*, p. 243. Cf. Tyler's second Annual Message in Richardson, *op. cit.*, p. 2049.

[38]Richardson, *op. cit.*, p. 2013.

Annual Message Tyler indicated that he had adopted Gallatin and Calhoun's plan of seeking an eventual adjustment of the boundary question only after the inevitable tide of emigration into the area should compel a practical settlement which recognized this fact.[39] At the same time, he expressed mild regret that the treaty of 1842 did not solve that problem successfully.[40] A year later the President said that our minister at London was under instructions to open the question again. He further reminded Congress of his previous recommendation that a chain of forts be built into the territory to protect the growing stream of emigrants into the Northwest.[41] Before the termination of his administration, the President allowed himself to hope that he might arrive at a satisfactory solution to the problem with the British. He told Congress that negotiations were pending in Washington and that, should they prove fruitful during the current session of Congress, he would communicate the result promptly.[42] The hope was, however, a vain one, and the matter was left for final adjustment in the Polk Administration.[43]

The sentiment in favor of the immediate adjustment of the Oregon boundary question on the basis of our claims, irrespective of British aspirations to the area, was strongly marked in Congress. Certain leaders of the Democratic party, notably Senators Benton and Linn of Missouri and Allen of Ohio, sparked a serious attempt to force the President's hand in the negotiations with Britain.[44] The first of several abortive efforts to do this came in August, 1841. On August 2 Senator Linn moved a resolution requesting the

[39]Cf. Reeves, *op. cit.*, pp. 241-242, 244.

[40]Richardson, *op. cit.*, p. 2049.

[41]*Ibid.*, pp. 2110-2111. Cf. Reeves, *op. cit.*, p. 245.

[42]Richardson, *op. cit.*, p. 2190. Cf. Tyler, *op. cit.*, II, 447-448. In his fourth Annual Message the President again recommended that Congress establish a chain of forts west to the Pacific.

[43]Cf. Reeves, *op. cit.*, pp. 249 ff.

[44]It should be remembered that this display of congressional impatience was probably not without some popular support. The question had been agitated for many years, particularly since the treaty of 1818. Cf. Reeves, *op. cit.*, pp. 224-242.

President to give notice to the British government that the
United States desired to end the agreement for the joint
occupation of Oregon.[45] Linn acknowledged that he had
heard some objections to his resolution based on the ground
that the phraseology of the measure might be offensive to the
President. Since this was so, he would agree, he said, to an
amendment which would refer the motion to the Committee
on Foreign Relations. This was agreed to, and the committee
promptly buried the resolution for the remainder of the
session.[46] The matter rested there until the treaty of 1842
revealed that the northwestern boundary question had not
been settled. With the meeting of the final session of the 27th
Congress, Linn and his supporters became more active in
their attempt to embarrass the President's actions (or inaction, as they suspected). The President's statement in the
second Annual Message that it had seemed neither possible
nor wise to attempt adjustment of the dispute in the course
of the Webster-Ashburton negotiations stirred Linn to
another of his resolutions. On December 22, 1842, he resolved
that the President be requested to inform the Senate why
agreement could not be had in the course of the adjustment
of the Maine boundary question, and further, what were the
nature and extent of the exploratory talks on the subject.[47]
Archer, in seeking to block the move, said that the propo-
nents of the resolution erroneously supposed that negotiations were at an end, but that this was not so. However, he
would agree to the resolution if there were added the usual
reservation that disclosure of the information was to be made
only if it were in the public interest. Benton, with his usual
bluster, answered King's observation that the resolution
sought to embarrass the negotiations by saying that "there
could be no reason for withholding the nature of the conference on these particulars. There is no necessity for state

45 *Senate Journal*, 27th Cong., 1st Sess., p. 131.
46 *Cong. Globe*, 27th Cong., 1st Sess., p. 325. *Senate Journal*, 27th Cong., 1st Sess.,
p. 203. A similar fate befell Linn's identical resolution of Jan. 4, 1842; *ibid.*, 2nd
Sess., pp. 66, 81.
47 *Cong. Globe*, 27th Cong., 3rd Sess., p. 74.

secrets in this country."[48]

The resolution, with Archer's amendment added, was passed, and the President replied to it the next day: "Measures have already been taken ... and under these circumstances I do not deem it consistent with the public interest to make any communication on the subject."[49]

On December 19, 1842, Linn had already introduced in the Senate a bill which was designed to place a much more serious obstacle in the path of the President's negotiations with Britain than could be done with a mere call for information. The bill provided for the granting of lands to settlers in the Oregon territory; it also included the President's oft-requested provision for the establishment of a chain of forts to the Pacific. But even more important, the bill commenced with a preamble which, if it were included in a bill enacted into law, was certain to arouse British anger. It was phrased as follows: "Whereas the title of the United States to the territory of Oregon is certain, and will not be abandoned; therefore ..."[50] The President's supporters attacked the preamble at once. When Senator Tappan moved that it be stricken out, Linn defended it frankly by saying that the select committee reporting the bill specifically included the preamble in view of the doubt existing in the public mind respecting the course of action which the administration intended to take. The intent was, he said, to reassure Americans that their right to emigrate to Oregon would be maintained. It was, he said, "absolutely necessary to quiet the public distrust of the course which the Government should take."[51] After determined efforts by Archer and Calhoun the preamble was stricken from the bill.[52] This success, however, did not remove all the difficulties from the measure. Since the bill proposed to grant to settlers certain

[48]*Ibid.*

[49]Richardson, *op. cit.*, p. 2064.

[50]*Cong. Globe*, 27th Cong., 3rd Sess., pp. 61-62, 99.

[51]*Ibid.*, p. 100. Linn and his followers suspected that the President did not intend to press our claim to 54 degrees, 40 minutes north, but would settle on the 49th parallel.

[52]*Ibid.*, pp. 105, 112.

pre-emption rights, the assumption was that the United
States had a clear and indisputable claim to the entire territory despite the treaty of 1818 providing for the joint
occupation of the area by the two countries. The United
States could scarcely give to settlers that which it did not
certainly possess, Calhoun said.[53] Senator Berrien of Georgia
stated the view which had the President's support. He
thought that the tide of emigration would fill up Oregon and
make future negotiation mere recognition of an accomplished
fact. Moreover, negotiation was an action conferred on the
executive by the Constitution, and Congress ought not to
interfere, especially since the President said that "a negotiation is actually pending."[54] Despite the President's objection, the bill passed by the close vote of 24 to 22.[55] Fortunately for the President, it was reported unfavorably by
Adams for the Committee on Foreign Affairs in the House.[56]
Thus, an action which amounted to a congressional vote of
no confidence in the President's conduct of the Oregon negotiations was thwarted, and he remained in control of the
situation, despite further efforts of this sort in the Senate.

In January, 1844, Senator Semple of Illinois moved a resolution requesting the President to give notice to the British
that the United States was abrogating the provision for the
joint occupation of Oregon.[57] In debate he offered what might
be called the "constitutionist" theory of the Senate's role in
the treaty process.

> I wish to indicate now to the President that we cannot
> agree to any treaty which shall provide for a joint occu-
> pation . . . Are we to sit here with our arms folded, and
> wait until a treaty is made, and then reject it? Have we

[53]*Ibid.*, p. 134. See the remarks of Choate and McDuffie supporting Calhoun; *ibid.*,
pp. 171, 198-201.

[54]*Ibid.*, p. 212. Cf. Reeves, *op. cit.*, p. 246.

[55]*Cong. Globe*, 27th Cong., 3rd Sess., pp. 240, 252.

[56]*Ibid.*, p. 297. There was no debate on this action in the House.

[57]*Ibid.*, 28th Cong., 1st Sess., p. 116. The House later passed an Oregon occupation bill which was defeated in the Senate when that body postponed consideration throughout the second session of the 28th Congress until March 3, 1845,
when, after a debate, it was again postponed (in effect, lost). Opponents again
claimed that it would embarrass negotiations. *Ibid.*, 2nd Sess., p. 387.

no power, no right, to *advise* the President what course in our opinion should be pursued? . . . The President himself should ask the advice of the Senate *before* a treaty is concluded. The Senate should *advise* first, and after it is signed, then consent to the treaty. . . . In this case, I am not sure that our advice is, or will be, obligatory on the President. He may or may not give the notice, even should this resolution pass; but it will be a strong indication and will scarcely be entirely neglected by the President. We have the right, however, to act on the subject, whether our action is regarded or disregarded.[58]

Although this theory was discredited in Washington's administration before it could become established usage, it was temporarily revived by Polk to deal with the Oregon boundary problem. It was also true that although the President's legal obligation to execute the resolution might be in doubt, he could not, in practice, totally disregard it without courting senatorial displeasure and possible non-cooperation at some future date.

Senator Miller of New Jersey challenged Semple in a somewhat oblique way by objecting to any attempt at a premature settlement by the legislative branch and not in the manner provided in the Constitution. He asked senators to reflect on the awkwardness of their position, if they should act now only to find themselves restricted by their vote in considering any treaty which might be placed before them in the future. Archer of Virginia claimed that the resolution would embarrass the President's negotiations already under way. A cautious James Buchanan said he "scarcely thought that any President . . . could be authorized to give that notice without the sanction of Congress." Sevier added that the real intent of the resolution was to clothe the President with the power to abrogate the treaty, "since he has no power *per se* to abrogate the existing convention."[59] The Senate rejected Semple's resolution by the margin of 28 to 18.

---

[58]*Ibid.*, p. 186.

[59]*Ibid.*, pp. 190, 353, 370, 417. While the matter was not a settled issue in 1844, the accepted practice today is that either the President or Congress possesses this power. See Corwin, *President's Control of Foreign Relations*, p. 112; and his

It is obvious that in the power of the purse Congress possesses authority which gives to that branch a potential, if not always controlling, voice in the conduct of foreign relations. Long-standing practice may accord to the President the power to propose, but is is within the province of the legislative authority to oppose policy by withholding grants of money. Since the power of appropriation is one in which the House has a customary initiative, it serves as one of the prime means by which that branch of Congress may seek to control the President in the formulation of foreign policy. It is equally evident that the division of authority under the Constitution requires the cooperation of the President and Congress. The relationship between the power to appropriate money and the appointing power is of some significance with respect to the conduct of foreign relations. While the President may appoint to regular diplomatic offices with the advice and consent of the Senate, and while he may employ private agents without the assent of that body, the fact is that there is little that such officers or agents can do without funds.[60] Thus Congress may, if it chooses, exercise a genuine control over foreign policy by withholding appropriations for diplomatic missions. It is equally evident that Congress is legally capable of withholding appropriations for the armed forces to curb presidential plans. Prior to 1855 Congress was not generally disposed to withhold funds for diplomatic missions and thus limit the President in his exercise of the power to employ regular diplomatic agents. The power of the purse

---

President, *Office and Powers*, pp. 238, 473-474. In 1841 an attempt was made in the *House* to secure the passage of a resolution requesting that the President enter into negotiations with the British in regard to U. S. citizens detained in Van Dieman's Land, but the move failed when Adams claimed that it would embarrass pending negotiations. The House members evidenced no sense of impropriety in debating the resolution even though such a resolution would appear to have no legal effect. *House Journal*, 27th Cong., 1st Sess., pp. 168, 173, 260, 468, 513. *Cong. Globe*, 27th Cong., 1st Sess., pp. 439-440. Tyler refused three other calls for information on the Oregon question. See Richardson, *op. cit.*, pp. 2127-2128, 2180, 2214-2215.

[60]The only test to distinguish a "regular" diplomatic officer from a "private" agent is the fund from which he is compensated and the presence or absence of senatorial confirmation. See Corwin, *President's Control of Foreign Relations*, p. 65.

was not, however, overlooked by some of Tyler's opponents in Congress.

At Tyler's request a bill to appropriate funds for diplomatic agents was reported by the House Committee on Ways and Means on July 29, 1841.[61] When the bill was read in the House, Ingersoll of Pennsylvania moved to strike out the provision for funds for the chargés at Sardinia and Naples, not out of personal or party malice, he said, but because these missions had originated in the House itself and no President had ever requested them. Moreover, there were not any duties to occupy a minister at either place. Millard Fillmore, chairman of the Committee of Ways and Means, said that it was enough for him to know that the President had officially asked for the appropriations. He thought Ingersoll's argument strange indeed. But Ingersoll continued by saying that he had been given to understand that the missions had been initiated by the House, "which was an abuse that was in danger of becoming inveterate . . . Nothing in the message of the present Executive, or in the communication of the Department of State . . . recommended them as necessary for the public service. These missions were supposed in this House to be useful."[62] It was not strange that he should attempt to strike out these provisions, he said, since it was the executive who was charged with the management of our foreign relations. Therefore, no mission ought to originate in the House.

In opposition to Ingersoll's move Caleb Cushing said:
There was on the table an Executive communication calling upon Congress to make the usual appropriations for the missions to the Courts of Naples and Sardinia; and, according to the ordinary course of legislation in reference to diplomatic appointments—as the foreign relations of the country were confided, by the Constitution, exclusively to the President, with the concurrent advice of the Senate, save so far as the House . . . had an ultimate control by the power to grant or to withhold the necessary supplies—the usual courtesy between the co-ordinate

[61]*House Journal,* 27th Cong., 1st Sess., pp. 284, 288.
[62]*Cong. Globe,* 27th Cong., 1st Sess., p. 393.

branches of Government led to an appropriation as a
matter of course, unless very strong reasons existed to
the contrary. Such instances were a very rare occurrence.[63]

John Quincy Adams then entered the debate in support
of Fillmore and Cushing, adding his great knowledge of the
entire subject. He said whether the mission had originated
with the House or as a result of an application of the President's powers was of no moment. The Constitution vested
in the President the authority to conduct foreign relations.
With the consent of the Senate he could appoint a minister
to any point on the earth and the House had nothing to do
with the matter, since the office of minister was created not
by the Constitution, but by the law of nations. The sole
authority given Congress over such presidential appointments lay in the power of the Senate to reject nominations
and in the power of the House to vote supplies. He could
recall no previous case in which the House had refused such
a grant despite a senatorial confirmation of nomination. This
was not the time, he thought, to set such a precedent.[64]

In the House the opposition to Ingersoll's move prevailed,
but the Senate, possibly in a fit of partisan anger, deleted the
provision for the two missions.[65] When the bill was returned
to the House, the provision for the mission was again included by disagreement with the Senate's amendment, and
in this form the bill passed as originally proposed.[66]

During the consideration of the appropriation bill for the
civil and diplomatic expenses of the government for the year

[63]*Ibid.*

[64]*Ibid.*, p. 394. Adams' theory of the origin of diplomatic offices was discarded by
the Act of 1855 describing both the posts and the salaries of diplomatic offices
but not of "special" presidential agents. Cf. Corwin, *President, Office and Powers*,
p. 157.

[65]*Cong. Globe*, 27th Cong., 1st Sess., p. 395. *Senate Journal*, 27th Cong., 1st Sess.,
p. 241. This action took place on Sept. 7, 1841, when partisan feeling over the
veto of the second bank bill had reached a fever pitch.

[66]*Cong. Globe*, 27th Cong., 1st Sess., p. 447. Strangely enough, J. Q. Adams raised
the cry for economy to support resolutions on Aug. 27, 1841, and March 15, 1842,
instructing the Committee on Foreign Affairs to "inquire into the expediency of
reducing the expenditures in the diplomatic department of the government, by
diminishing the number of ministers and other diplomatic agents abroad." *House
Journal*, 27th Cong., 1st Sess., p. 423; *ibid.*, 2nd Sess., p. 543.

1842, Senator Woodbury of New Hampshire moved the following amendment:

And provided further, That no part of this appropriation be applied, after the first day of July next, to the payment of special diplomatic agents abroad, appointed without the consent of the Senate, or any act of Congress authorizing it, nor for compensation to separate agents, appointed in either of these modes, for receiving and transmitting despatches.[67]

Woodbury defended his resolution by saying that "he wished to stop any establishment of new and permanent officers, like despatch agents, and on fixed salaries, without the sanction of Congress.... He thought, also, that a permanent diplomatic agent abroad, like one to Central America ... appointed since the 4th of March, 1841, and not nominated to the Senate yet, should not be sanctioned."[68] Buchanan objected to the amendment which would deprive the President of the power to appoint special diplomatic agents by denying him the necessary funds. He agreed that the salaries and duties of officers ought to be fixed by law but "our foreign intercourse is not of that nature at all."[69] Buchanan's view and long-standing practice were sustained as the Senate rejected Woodbury's amendment by a vote of 25 to 15.[70]

Tyler's request for a special appropriation to support an anticipated mission to China in 1843 resulted in a somewhat unusual action of the part of Congress. The circumstances

[67]*Senate Journal*, 27th Cong., 2nd Sess., p. 327.

[68]*Cong. Globe*, 27th Cong., 2nd Sess., p. 469.

[69]*Ibid.*, p. 473.

[70]*Senate Journal*, 27th Cong., 2nd Sess., p. 327. The vote was not along party lines. Both Buchanan and Woodbury were Democrats. It is uncertain whether Tyler had intentionally failed to make this nomination or not. When Jackson gave recess appointments to three commissioners to negotiate a treaty of commerce with Turkey in 1829 and let a whole session of Congress go by without nominating these individuals to the Senate, Tyler became incensed. In 1831 Tyler offered an amendment to an appropriation bill, authorizing remuneration to the commissioners but denying that such action was to be construed as senatorial approval of Jackson's action which deprived the Senate of its power to accept or reject diplomatic appointments. Tyler, *op. cit.*, I, 419-421. Tyler's regard for senatorial guardianship of the President's diplomatic agents seems to have cooled when he became President. See this chapter, p. 128.

of the case were such, however, as to preclude its becoming a precedent, although it foreshadowed the act of 1855 in which Congress set the grades and salaries of diplomatic officers.[71] On January 24, 1843, near the end of the life of the 27th Congress, Adams introduced in the House two bills on the recommendation of the President to provide for the future relations between this country and China and the Sandwich (Hawaiian) Islands, respectively. One bill provided that the sum of forty thousand dollars be appropriated and placed at the disposal of the President "to enable him to establish the future commercial relations between the United States and the Chinese Empire . . . the said sum to be accounted for by the President under the restrictions and in the manner prescribed by the act of first of July, one thousand seven hundred and ninety. . . ."[72] Adams moved to strike out the phrase "under the restrictions and . . ." saying that in talking with the Secretary of State he had learned that a failure to do this might "embarrass the negotiations." This amendment was passed, 96 to 59.[73]

The bill was not debated in the Senate until late on the last night of the session, March 3, 1843. Archer defended it by saying that the mission, a new one, would probably last for two years and that a large sum of money must, therefore, be appropriated.[74] Benton objected, saying that the bill was fraudulent on three points: "in the appointment of the agent —in the amount of his salary—and in the accountability of his expenditures. By the Constitution, all ministers are to be appointed by the Senate; but this minister to China is to be

7

[1]Cf. Corwin, *President, Office and Powers*, p. 250. Tyler made the recommendation in a special message, Dec. 30, 1842; Richardson, *op. cit.*, pp. 2066-2067.

[72]*Cong. Globe*, 27th Cong., 3rd Sess., pp. 195, 323. 1 *Statutes at Large* 128. This act, to be in force for two years, limited the President in making a payment for salary to any "minister plenipotentiary" to nine thousand dollars per annum. It also required an accounting of the monies used for the payment of such salaries and outfits if, in the President's judgment, they should be made public. If the President did not deem it advisable to specify the purposes for which the monies were used, he was required to indicate to Congress the amounts so spent. The accounting to Congress was to be an annual one.

[73]*Cong. Globe*, 27th Cong., 3rd Sess., p. 323.

[74]*Ibid.*, p. 391.

called an agent, and sent out by the President without the consent of the Senate; and thus, by imposing a false name upon the Minister, defraud the Senate out of their control over the appointment." He thought, moreover, that the whole mission was a plot to provide "for favorites . . . feeding out of the public crib."[75] Since the hour was near midnight, Woodbury of New Hampshire moved an amendment forbidding that more than nine thousand dollars be paid as salary to any one person in the mission. Archer agreed to this and it was adopted. Benton was still not satisfied with the plan and indicated, by his usual long-winded speech making, that he would fight the matter further.[76] To circumvent this ferocious opposition, Conrad moved a further amendment of some interest which was "to the effect that no *agent* be appointed without the consent of the Senate."[77] The bill was then enacted into law. Tyler apparently accepted this departure from practice in his haste to establish the China mission.

This act, in its final form, was a curious hybrid; it did not require the President to account for the use of the funds appropriated (as was the case with the contingent fund), but it did, in effect, set the grade and salary of the special minister to China. In debate Benton made much of the question of the title to be employed by this special agent. Obviously he could make a good case for requiring senatorial confirmation of this officer if it were established that he was an "ambassador, other public minister or consul."[78] Since the only test of what constitutes a special agent is the method of appointment and the source of the funds from which he is paid, it is really difficult to say precisely what position the special minister to China occupied.

[75]*Ibid.*, pp. 391-392. Apparently the salary maximum set by the act of 1790 was not again enacted, until the present case, but it did serve as a customary limit on such salaries.

[76]See Benton, *op. cit.*, pp. 512-513.

[77]*Cong. Globe*, 27th Cong., 3rd Sess. (italics added). The vote was 31 to 9 in favor of adopting this amendment.

[78]*Const. of U.S.*, Art. II, Sec. 2, Cl. 2; cf. Corwin, *President's Control of Foreign Relations*, p. 65.

On the night that the bill passed, the President nominated Everett, then Minister to London, for the post. Everett, although confirmed by the Senate at once, declined to leave England, and Cushing was appointed to the China mission by the President on May 8, 1843, the day on which Webster resigned from the cabinet.[79] Benton was particularly enraged at this action by the President. This recess appointment eliminated the possibility of Cushing's rejection by the Senate, were he nominated to that body by Tyler.[80]

After the details of the negotiation of the treaty to annex Texas had been made known to Congress by the President, some efforts were made in the Senate to criticize the President for his employment of Duff Green as a special agent. On June 10, 1844, Tyler replied to a resolution, apparently passed in executive session of the Senate, inquiring into the President's use of Green as such an agent.[81] On the seventeenth of the month Tyler replied to a further resolution of the Senate which requested the President to disclose the names of persons employed by him and paid out of the contingent fund. The President answered it with considerable reluctance and made a virtue of necessity. The contingent fund had always been at the disposal of the President, he said, to effectuate the objects contemplated in the appropriations. It was not required, nor was it intended, that the President should disclose either the names or the duties of

[79]Fuess, *op. cit.*, pp. 409, 412-413. For a detailed account see pp. 397-413. Cf. Benton, *op. cit.*, pp. 510-514. Originally Everett was to take the China mission, leaving London for Webster's graceful retirement from the cabinet. There was also a projected plan to create a special mission to Britain for Webster in case Everett did not wish to leave, but Adams indicated that this could not be put through Congress. The Cushing mission resulted in a treaty with China, approved by the Senate. *Senate Journal*, 28th Cong., 2nd Sess., p. 289.

[80]In this instance Tyler was merely following a precedent set by Washington. The latter concluded that if an appointee confirmed by the Senate declined his office after an adjournment of the Senate, his action created a vacancy which happened during a recess of the Senate. The President was empowered, therefore, by virtue of Art. II, Sec. 2, Cl. 3, to make a recess appointment in such a case. Cf. James Hart, *The American Presidency in Action, 1789*, pp. 125-126.

[81]Richardson, *op. cit.*, p. 2180. The details of the reply are unknown, since there is no record of this proceeding in the *Senate Journal*, the *Congressional Globe*, or Senate documents.

the persons employed by him in diplomatic intercourse, lest such revelations embarrass unnecessarily these activities. Nevertheless, the President felt he had no reason to hide the fact that he had paid Duff Green $1,000 "in undertaking negotiations then contemplated, but afterwards abandoned, upon an important subject." [82]

Tyler enjoyed some notable success in the use of the treaty power, even though he failed to secure ratification of the treaty to annex Texas. His failures can be explained principally in terms of partisan politics. During his administration Tyler submitted a total of fifteen treaties to the Senate. Of these only two were rejected outright; two more were so emasculated by senatorial amendments that they were rendered unacceptable to the other parties to them; a third was apparently buried and forgotten in the Senate.[83] Of those which were accepted, the most important in its day was the Webster-Ashburton Treaty of 1842. Of those which failed to receive senatorial approval, the most important, in one sense or another, were the treaty for the annexation of Texas and one with the German Customs Union.[84]

The negotiation of the Webster-Ashburton Treaty particularly demonstrated Tyler's strong personal interest in achieving the settlement of a dispute of sixty years' standing which, along with other problems, threatened to disrupt the peaceful relations between the United States and Britain. It also evidenced the extent to which the President may personally exercise the power to negotiate treaties. When the negotiations between Webster and Ashburton had reached a point of apparent breakdown in June, 1842, Webster re-

[82]*Ibid.*, p. 2181. The Senate again, on Feb. 4, 1845, inquired as to the President's use of Duff Green as a diplomatic agent in Texas, asking what salary was paid to Green and how he was appointed. The President replied that Green was not an agent to the government of Texas but, rather, was consul at Galveston. Further, Tyler indicated, Green was paid no salary and was acting under no special instructions. *Ibid.*, p. 2213. Cf. *Senate Document* No. 83, 28th Cong., 2nd Sess.

[83]For a detailed account see W. S. Holt, *Treaties Defeated by the Senate*, pp. 61, 63-83.

[84]These two are most important in the sense that they are both illustrative of the problem of presidential control of foreign relations. The failure of the Texas treaty is, of course, of some general historical interest.

ported, the President personally intervened in the matter:
The President has desired a personal interview with him
[Lord Ashburton], which has been had, and the President
has pressed upon him in the strongest manner the necessity of staying till every effort to effect the great object
of his mission shall have been exhausted. The President
feels, what all must feel, that if the mission should return,
rebus infectis, the relations of the two countries will be
more than ever embarrassed.[85]

Many years after the transpiration of these events the President told his son that "the negotiation with Lord A. was
conducted without protocol or letter. The letters were written after agreement, and each submitted to me and received
my correction. It may be too early to mention this fact publicly."[86] A year after the treaty had been ratified Webster
publicly acknowledged the President's personal role in this
highly successful enterprise.[87]

The treaty was sent to the Senate, accompanied by a
lengthy explanatory message from the President, on August
11, 1842.[88] On the twentieth of the same month the Senate
"advised and consented" to the treaty by a vote of 39 to 9.
Of the opposition, eight were Democrats and one a Whig.[89]
Fortunately, the party animosities which marked the discussion of the treaty for the annexation of Texas were miss-
ing in this instance. Nevertheless, it was remarkable that
this treaty was not made the object of partisan acrimony,
since at this time the relations between the President and
the Whig majority in Congress had reached the depths
of disunion.[90]

[85]Curtis, *op. cit.*, II, 105.

[86]Tyler, *op. cit.*, II, 242.

[87]*Ibid.*, II, 190. Cf. *ibid.*, p. 226. The President made several personal decisions of
significance respecting the treaty; *ibid.*, p. 225.

[88]Richardson, *op. cit.*, pp. 2015-2022.

[89]*Senate Journal*, 27th Cong., 2nd Sess., p. 699. Cf. Reeves, *op. cit.*, p. 56.

[90]By this time the President had vetoed the second tariff bill of 1842, and the
House, under the guidance of J. Q. Adams, was preparing its indictment of the
President for his use of the veto power. See chapter ii, *supra*. Holt concludes
that the political parentage of the treaty was doubtful and that this fact removed
any partisan opposition to its ratification. L. G. Tyler quotes Clay (without cita-

Senator Benton of Missouri was discontented with the manner in which the negotiations had been conducted. More than that, however, he complained of the fact that individual Senators had been carefully canvassed during the negotiations in order to secure their support for the treaty. He said that it was a well-known fact that certain Senators were consulted, not publicly but privately, "visiting the negotiators upon request for that purpose, agreeing to it in these conferences, and thus forestalling" the official action of the Senate. He abhorred the

> irregular manner in which the ratification of this treaty had been sought . . . and then sent here for the forms of ratification . . . I know I was not consulted myself; and I know many others who were not. All that I intend to say is, that I have reason to think that this treaty has been ratified out of doors! and that this is a great irregularity, and bespeaks an undue solicitude for it on the part of its authors, arising from a consciousness of its indefensible character.[91]

The skill with which Webster gained senatorial support for the treaty tends to emphasize the need for cooperation between the "coordinate" branches of the government in the conduct of foreign relations. Executive leadership is indispensable. Tyler was justifiably proud of this accomplishment.[92]

The treaty with the German Customs Union (Zollverein) is of particular interest as a rejected treaty because of the reasons assigned by the Senate for its refusal to advise and consent to the instrument. The treaty itself was undoubtedly popular with many agricultural interests in the country, and whatever may have been the constitutional reasons given

---

tion) as having said that Tyler was a "President without a party" who, in this instance, placed "himself upon the broad and patriotic foundation of the whole nation." Tyler, *op. cit.*, II, 225.

[91] Benton, *op. cit.*, p. 424.

[92] "So far the administration has been conducted amid earthquake and tornado, and yet if it had nothing else to point to but the English treaty as the result of the last eighteen months, I think it would be entitled to some small share of praise." Tyler to Tazewell (Oct. 24, 1842), Tyler Papers, Vol. II, No. 6433.

for its rejection, it must be counted a victim of partisan politics.[93] On April 29, 1844, Tyler sent the treaty to the Senate with a message in which he pointed to the advantages to be gained by various interests in this country by the ratification of the treaty. In particular, he said, favorable treatment was to be given to tobacco, rice, lard and cotton—in fact, the latter was to be admitted into the Customs Union free of duty. He added that the few concessions to manufactured items could not injure the manufacturing interests of the United States. Moreover, he conceded that since some of its provisions conflicted with existing tariff laws, it would be desirable for him to send a copy to the House for necessary legislative action should the Senate give its consent to the treaty.[94]

This portion of the President's message is notable in view of the constitutional ground on which the Senate purported to reject the treaty. The treaty itself was reported by the Committee on Foreign Relations without amendment on June 14, 1844, with an unfavorable report which opposed the treaty not on the ground of its substance but on the ground that it represented a novel and unwarranted departure from the established method of levying tariff duties. The committee complained that Congress would be bound for a period of three years to observe the restrictions imposed by a treaty obligation created by the President and the Senate. The power to make commercial regulations, the committee asserted, was conferred by the Constitution upon the legislative branch alone, the extent of the treaty power notwithstanding. Only the representatives of the people, Congress, sitting with "open doors, under the eye of the country," could properly gather the necessary information and understand the interests of the people. The committee concluded its condemnation of the treaty with the Whiggish

[93]This was Calhoun's view and it represents the conclusion of Holt. See Holt, *op. cit.*, p. 81. The first indication of the desire for this treaty was in the form of a House resolution, passed in 1837, requesting the President to negotiate reductions in foreign tariffs, particularly on tobacco. *Ibid.*, p. 78. Cf. Tyler's message reminding Congress of this fact; Richardson, *op. cit.*, p. 2192.

[94]Richardson, *op. cit.*, p. 2167.

view that:

To follow, not to lead, to fulfill, not to ordain, the law; to carry into effect, by negotiation and compact with foreign Governments, the legislative will, when it has been announced, upon the great subjects of trade and revenue, not to interpose with controlling influence, not to go forward with too ambitious enterprises—these seem to the committee to be the appropriate functions of the Executive.[95]

The reasons given by the committee, and accepted implicitly by the Senate, represented an extreme Whig view of the proper role of the President in the treaty-making process, since the Jay Treaty was a prior example of one which modified existing tariff laws.[96] Moreover, Tyler had indicated in a conciliatory manner his awareness of the problem in his message communicating the treaty to the Senate. In addition, there was no reason for the committee to be so sensitive to a situation in which the Senate and the President, through the exercise of the treaty-making power, had morally obligated Congress to enact enabling legislation. The committee's snide reference to the secrecy of the negotiations probably was prompted by partisan malevolence springing as much from Whig anger at the negotiation of the treaty for the annexation of Texas as from devotion to principle.[97] While the committee viewed with alarm the sanctioning of presidential initiative in tariff-making via the treaty route, it did at least limit itself to circumscribing only this boundary around executive initiative. The doctrine enunciated, however, is not wholly startling in view of the fact that Con-

---

[95]*Senate Journal*, 28th Cong., 1st Sess., pp. 445-456. This treaty contained a most-favored-nation clause. See Henry Weaton to Tyler (March 27, 1844), Tyler Papers, Vol. II, Nos. 6461-6464.

[96]The vote to lay on the table passed 26 to 18. Holt, *op. cit.*, p. 81. Cf. *Senate Journal*, 28th Cong., 1st Sess., p. 456.

[97]The Zollverein Treaty was submitted to the Senate precisely one week after the Texas annexation treaty. One of the Whig cries against the Texas treaty was the fact that the secrecy of the negotiations permitted the President to surprise the nation and the Senate with the issue. What pained them most was the fact that the issue was injected into the presidential campaign of 1844, thereby overshadowing all other issues. See further, this chapter.

gress to this day has continued to be unwilling to sanction enthusiastically this use of the treaty-making power.[98]

Since the treaty had not been rejected outright by a negative vote but had been merely laid on the table, the President again recommended its passage in his Annual Message to Congress in December, 1844. He indicated his belief that only a lack of time had prevented the Senate from acting favorably. For this reason, he said, he had instructed our Minister to Berlin to renegotiate the treaty. This negotiation was necessary since there was a limit of four months placed upon the time within which ratification must be had. This effort at renegotiation had, however, initially failed, he said. Nevertheless, in a few days Tyler was able to communicate to the Senate two confidential letters in which it was indicated that the Zollverein would waive the time requirement, if the Senate would act.[99] This the Senate did not do.

Few events in American political history have been more thoroughly examined than those connected with the annexation of Texas. There are, however, several aspects of the President's power to conduct foreign relations which warrant further attention.

Like the Maine and Oregon boundary questions, the annexation of Texas was not an issue which sprang forth, full grown, from the brow of the administration, as the Whigs would have led the public to believe in the campaign of 1844. Certainly some effort had been made in Jackson's adminis-

---

[98]The executive agreement based upon prior legislative authorization provides the principal means for present-day presidential tariff-making. However, three reciprocity treaties were consented to within the next sixty years: those with Canada in 1854, Hawaii in 1875, and Cuba in 1902. Thirteen others were rejected in this period. See B. H. Williams, *Economic Foreign Policy of the United States* (New York: McGraw-Hill, 1929), pp. 280-285.

[99]Richardson, *op. cit.*, pp. 2192-2206. Tyler could not resist reminding Congress that he had initiated the treaty "in strict conformity with the wishes of Congress as made known through several measures which it had adopted, all directed to the accomplishment of this important result." Jackson wrote Polk in September, 1844, that the votes of the Senators against this treaty ought to have the widest publicity; they should be "fully exposed to the people. . . . There never was such treachery to the laborer of the South and West, as the rejection of this treaty. I have been greatly astonished that the Democratic papers have said so little about it." Tyler, *op. cit.*, III, 149.

tration to annex Texas, although the matter had been allowed to cool during Van Buren's term.[100] As early as October, 1841, Tyler revealed to Webster his interest in annexing Texas to the United States.

I gave you a hint as to the *probability* of acquiring Texas by treaty. I verily believe it could be done. Could the North be reconciled to it, could anything throw so bright a lustre around us? It seems to me that the great interests of the North would be incalculably advanced by such an acquisition. How deeply interested is the shipping interest. *Slavery*—I know that is the objection, and it would be well founded, if it did not already exist among us, but my belief is that a rigid enforcement of the laws against the slave trade would in time make as many free States South as the acquisition of Texas would add of slave States, and then the *future* (distant it might be) would present wonderful results.[101]

In his first Annual Message to Congress Tyler said of Texas: "The United States cannot but take a deep interest in whatever relates to this young but growing Republic."[102] In his second Annual Message he reminded all concerned that the Monroe Doctrine applied to Texas and Mexico.[103]

Whatever may have been the President's intense interest in the subject, he deferred action until Webster had left the

---

[100]Cf. Reeves, *op. cit.*, pp. 70-89.

[101]Tyler, *op. cit.*, II, 126.

[102]Richardson, *op. cit.*, p. 1932.

[103]*Ibid.*, p. 2050. In this message, Tyler also extended the Monroe Doctrine (in effect) to include the Hawaiian Islands. He said: "It can not be but in conformity with the interest and wishes of the people of the United States that this community thus existing in the midst of a vast expanse of ocean, should be respected and all its rights strictly and conscientiously regarded; and this must also be the true interest of all other commercial states. Far remote from the dominions of European powers, its growth and prosperity as an independent state may yet be in a high degree useful to all whose trade is extended to those regions; while its near approach to this continent and the intercourse which American vessels have with it . . . could not but create dissatisfaction on the part of the United States at any attempt by another power, should such attempt be threatened or feared, to take possession of the islands, colonize them, and subvert the native government . . . the circumstances of the very large intercourse of their citizens with the islands would justify this Government . . . in making a decided remonstrance against the adoption of an opposite policy by any other power." *Ibid.*, pp. 2064-2065.

cabinet.[104] Webster's departure was a signal that annexation
was to be Tyler's remaining major objective—especially so
since he shifted his Secretary of the Navy, Upshur—fellow
Virginian and friend of Calhoun—to the post of Secretary of
State. With the choice of means made, Tyler set Upshur to
work on the negotiations almost at once. The President said
of this negotiation at a much later date: "I advised with no
one, consulted with no one, save Upshur, in taking the
initiative."[105]

A prerequisite to success, as the ratification of the Webster-Ashburton Treaty had clearly demonstrated, was assurance of the assent of two-thirds of the Senate. Although at
the very outset of the negotiations Upshur could not guarantee the success of the treaty to the Texans, he did in time
give them this very necessary assurance.[106] The President,
too, appeared to be sanguine, for in his third Annual Message in December, 1843, Tyler openly sent to Congress despatches received from the American minister to Mexico indicating that Mexico was threatening to fight if the United
States persisted in the pending annexation negotiations. He
seemed especially offended by the knowledge that Mexico
had made this threat on the basis of news reports in this
country of the coming discussion of a treaty of annexation
in the Senate. Bristling, Tyler expressed his indignation at
the notion that Congress, or the Senate, "the representatives
of a brave and patriotic people," should be frightened by
such empty mouthings. Should Mexico, however, be so fool-
ish as to wage war, Tyler asserted that the executive would
"with confidence throw itself upon the patriotism of the people to sustain the Government in its course of action."[107]
This open statement of intention left little ground for surprise when the annexation treaty was finally submitted to

[104]This may well have resulted from at least a regard for Webster's peculiar party
position. Cf. Reeves, *op. cit.*, pp. 92-111; Tyler, *op. cit.*, III, 130.

[105]Tyler, *op. cit.*, III, 396. Calhoun saw the significance of this shift; see "Correspondence of John C. Calhoun," p. 526.

[106]See Reeves, *op. cit.*, p. 134; and Upshur to Murphy (Jan. 16, 1844), Tyler, *op.
cit.*, II, 284.

[107]Richardson, *op. cit.*, pp. 2113-2115.

the Senate the following April. It also foreshadowed a prece-
dent-making step which the President took early in the following January. With the Texans apprehensive lest Mexico
should again commence active hostilities against them in the
event that annexation was achieved, they asked the American chargé, Murphy, to guarantee military assistance should
that eventuality materialize.[108] This guarantee Murphy gave
the Texans at once, saying that "as far . . . as my power and
authority may go, I will take care that my Government is
speedily apprized of your views and wishes, and that a sufficient naval force shall be placed in the Gulf of Mexico . . .
also, that measures shall be taken, *as required by you*, to
repel any invasion by land of a like character."[109] This sweeping promise, however, Murphy made at his own discretion.[110]
Van Zandt, the Texas agent in Washington, made a more
limited request of Upshur, asking the armed protection of
the United States for Texas "after the signing of the treaty,
and before it shall be ratified and receive the final action of
the other branches of both Governments, in case Texas
should desire it, or with her consent."[111] While the papers
transmitted to the House by the President disclose no reply
to this particular request, Nelson, Secretary of State *ad
interim* scolded Murphy for the pledge he had given the
Texans. Nelson said:

. . . the President . . . regrets to perceive, in the pledges
given by you . . . that you have suffered your zeal to carry
you beyond the line of your instructions, and to commit
the President to measures for which he has no constitutional authority to stipulate. . . .

The employment of the army or navy against a foreign
power with which the United States are at peace is not
within the competency of the President; and whilst he is
not indisposed, as a measure of prudent precaution, and
as preliminary to the proposed negotiation, to concentrate
in the Gulf of Mexico, and on the southern borders of the

[108]*House Executive Document* No. 271, 28th Cong., 1st Sess., p. 89.
[109]*Ibid.*, p. 90 (Feb. 14, 1844) (italics added).
[110]*Ibid.*, p. 92.
[111]*Ibid.*, p. 89 (Jan. 17, 1844).

United States, a naval and military force to be directed in the defence of the inhabitants and territory of Texas *at a proper time*, he cannot permit the authorities of that Government or yourself to labor under the misapprehension that he has power to employ them *at the period indicated by your stipulations.*[112]

After Calhoun succeeded Upshur as Secretary of State, Van Zandt's limited request for armed aid was reconsidered and acceded to by Tyler, who ordered the disposition of a naval force on the Gulf and land forces on the southwestern frontier. This was to occur "during the pendency of the treaty."[113] Since the action was ordered on April 11 and the treaty was signed the next day, the ambiguity in the President's position, as stated by Nelson in his message to Murphy, became a matter of academic interest. Tyler was *clearly* willing to take this action only "during the pendency of the treaty," as Calhoun said. Presumably the treaty was "pending" once it was signed by both parties. What was meant in Nelson's letter by the phrase "as preliminary to the *proposed negotiation*" is not really clear. Surely, Tyler stated a much more limited view than this *implied* in his public reply to the Senate resolution of May 13, 1844, calling for information on this matter. He said that in view of the Mexican threat to consider "the definitive ratification of a treaty" for the annexation of Texas by the United States a cause for war, he had sent the fleet to the Gulf of Mexico and troops to Fort Jessup at the Texas border to "apprise the Executive of any indication of a hostile design upon Texas . . . pending the deliberations of the Senate upon the treaty. . . ." He added:

> . . . it is due to myself that I should declare it as my opinion that the United States having *by the treaty* of annexation *acquired* a *title* to Texas which *requires only the action of the Senate to perfect it*, no other power could be permitted to invade and by force of arms to possess itself of any portion of the territory of Texas pending your deliberations

[112]*Ibid.*, p. 95 (italics added). This appears to have meant that our military action was to be confined to a demonstration of force during the negotiations.

[113]*Ibid.*, p. 96 (Calhoun to Van Zandt, April 11, 1844).

upon the treaty without placing itself in an hostile attitude
to the United States . . . justifying the employment of any
military means at *our* disposal to drive back the invasion.[114]

The absence of a successful challenge to this view in the
Senate allowed this construction of presidential authority to
stand. Of course, it was the President, not the Senate or
Congress, who had determined the existence of an interest
which this country would protect with its armed might
against invasion by another country.

After the treaty of annexation had failed to receive senatorial confirmation, the problem of the renewal of Mexican
hostilities became a matter of serious concern in Texas. Once
again, therefore, the question of the extent, if any, to which
the United States would intervene with armed force on the
behalf of Texas was raised. The situation was complicated,
of course, by the fact that, although the treaty had been lost
in the Senate, the issue was still pending before both the
House and the nation—the latter as the burning issue of the
presidential campaign of 1844. Calhoun informed the American chargé at Texas that the guarantee of protection continued to stand while the issue was still unsettled in this
country:

> As far as it relates to the executive department . . . [the
> President] is prepared to use all [his] powers for that pur-
> pose. But the government of Texas is fully aware that they
> are circumscribed by the Constitution within narrow limits,
> which it would not be possible for the President to tran-
> scend. *All that he can do is to make suitable representations*
> to the Mexican government against the renewal of war
> pending the question of annexation . . . *and to recommend*
> *to Congress to adopt measures to repel any attack* which may
> be made.[115]

Despite the equivocation contained in this startling reversal of opinion by the President, three days later Calhoun
informed the Texas agent in Washington that the orders of

---

[114]Richardson, *op. cit.*, pp. 2170-2171 (italics added). See Tyler's message of May
31, 1844, on the same subject, p. 2174.

[115]*House Executive Document* No. 2, 28th Cong., 2nd Sess., p. 50 (Sept. 10, 1844)
(italics added).

the previous April to the Army and to the Navy were still to be considered in force. In fact, they never had been canceled. These orders, the members of the cabinet felt, had stood the test of congressional examination successfully in May. Therefore, there was no reason for the President's doubts and equivocation.[116]

All of this clearly adds up to the conclusion that Tyler, while stating a rather bold position publicly, was extremely anxious to avoid making a precise commitment to the Texans —a commitment which was likely to embroil us in war with Mexico. Exactly on what ground he would have acted during negotiation, or even after the signing of the treaty, one can only speculate. After rejection of the treaty in the Senate, his first inclination was to deny his own authority to act. Why he so construed his powers it is difficult to say, since this country retained its "interest" in Texas no matter what means were employed to complete the act of annexation. Nevertheless, on second thought, backed by the urgings of his cabinet, he grew bold again.

While the treaty of annexation, submitted to the Senate on April 22, 1844, was rejected by that body in a vote that made it a party measure with the Whigs, it is of some interest to note that Tyler made serious and determined efforts to influence opinion in both the Senate and in the nation with a series of messages on the subject. This had apparently become a matter of necessity in view of Calhoun's letter of April 18 to Pakenham, the British Minister, placing the whole case in favor of annexation on the ground that it was necessary for the preservation of slavery.[117] The appeal of annexation, Tyler said in the message transmitting the treaty to the Senate, "appears to the Executive to be of an imposing, if not of a resistless, character [and] is made in the interests of every portion of the country."[118] On May 16,

---

[116]*Ibid.* Cf. Reeves, *op. cit.*, pp. 170-171.

[117]Detailed treatment of this correspondence can be found in Reeves, *op. cit.*, pp. 150-154. Cf. J. H. Smith, *The Annexation of Texas*, esp. pp. 200-219 *passim*.

[118]Richardson, *op. cit.*, p. 2161. Tyler did, however, allude to what he considered to be the danger of abolition in Texas if that country remained independent.

with the treaty still before the Senate, Tyler sent another message in which he sought to whip up the fear that if annexation were not now had, it was forever lost. Since last communicating to them, he said, he had decided that if there were any single argument against annexation it was that it should take place not now, but later. So alarming, however, was the tone of the papers he had to send to the Senate that it "is alike due to the Senate and the country that I should furnish any papers in my possession which may be calculated *to impress the Senate* with the correctness . . ." of his opinions.[119]

Tyler's action in now withholding, now revealing, information in his possession dealing with the Texas annexation was a further illustration of the President's unfettered discretion to give or to deny information to the houses of Congress. In either case he is free to pipe his tune to attract both public and congressional opinion alike. Even though this and other similar messages did not have the desired effect of securing senatorial consent to the treaty, it did sound a note in the public mind by playing upon one of the strongest of existing American prejudices—dislike of Britain.

On May 15, 1844, before voting to accept or reject the Texas treaty, the Senate removed the injunction of secrecy from most of the papers relating to the pending treaty. In taking this odd step the Senate said that its action should not be construed as a precedent. It merely claimed that secrecy was no longer necessary in regard to this "subject of great importance on which the will of the people of this Union ought to be consulted."[120]

Here was conclusive evidence that the Senate would not act on the treaty before its next session but wished to make annexation an issue in the presidential campaign of 1844. The Senate then rejected the treaty by an overwhelming

[119] *Ibid.*, p. 2171 (italics added). This correspondence reiterated charges of serious British attempts to forestall annexation. Cf. Smith, *op. cit.*, pp. 230-231.

[120] *Senate Journal*, 28th Cong., 1st Sess., p. 431. The documents may be found in *Senate Document* No. 341, 28th Cong., 1st Sess. On May 20 the injunction of secrecy on the speeches concerning the subject was removed. *Ibid.*, p. 435.

vote that appeared fatal to Tyler's hopes.[121]

On June 10, 1844, two days after the rejection of the treaty, Tyler took a determined and unprecedented step to secure his objective. He laid before the House of Representatives the Texas treaty along with all the documents which he had communicated to the Senate in executive session. He said to the House:

> The papers communicated embrace not only the series already made public by order of the Senate, but others from which the veil of secrecy has not been removed by that body, *but which I deem it essential to a just appreciation of the entire question.* While the treaty was pending before the Senate, I did not consider it compatible with the just rights of that body or consistent with the respect entertained for it to bring this important subject before you. The power of Congress is, however, fully competent *in some other form of proceeding to accomplish everything* that a formal ratification of the treaty could have accomplished, and I therefore feel that *I should but imperfectly discharge my duty to yourselves or the country,* if I failed to lay before you everything in the possession of the Executive which would enable you to act with full light on the subject, if you should deem it proper to take any action upon it.[122]

Tyler continued the message by repeating the reasons he had given previously for proposing annexation at that time—it was of benefit to the whole nation, and the British were conniving to strengthen an independent Texas. He ended the

[121]The vote, on June 8, 1844, was 35 to 16 against ratification. Of the affirmative votes cast, all but one were by Democrats. Seven Democrats and twenty-eight Whigs opposed it. Only one Southern Whig, Henderson of Mississippi, voted in favor of the treaty. There is nothing about this vote to sustain the charge that the plot to annex Texas was perpetrated by the "slaveocracy." See Smith, *op. cit.,* p. 273. By the time the Senate had voted on the treaty, the presidential nominating conventions had met; the Democrats overtly favored annexation, while the Whigs again remained silent (as in 1840) on a vital campaign issue. See Edward Stanwood, *A History of the Presidency from 1788 to 1897,* pp. 215-216, 220-221.

[122]Richardson, *op. cit.,* p. 2176. In removing the cloak of secrecy from the documents in its possession the Senate proved that it, too, could play the game of influencing public opinion. Tyler's counter-stroke demonstrated, however, the President's advantageous position.

message with this charge to the House: "The great question is not as to the manner in which it shall be done, but whether it shall be accomplished or not. The responsibility of deciding this question is now devolved upon you."[123]

Despite Henry Clay's objection to introducing the question into the presidential campaign of 1844, Tyler was persistent. He was vehemently criticized for this, and yet it is difficult to see what better occasion there could be for dramatically posing a single and overwhelming issue before the electorate. Moreover, Tyler did not shrink from continuing the fight for annexation even after all the hopes he might have had of being the Democratic nominee had vanished. This is a striking demonstration of the manner in which the President may focus public attention on an issue of great importance and force the matter to a final decision.[124]

With the victory of Polk in the campaign for the Presidency on a platform calling for the annexation of Texas, there was strong evidence that annexation was acceptable to the public. In his Annual Message to Congress in December, 1844, Tyler again urged the step, saying that it had passed—the "ordeal of public opinion." He noted that although the Senate had objected to annexation before the issue had been determined at the polls, its action was not due to lack of authority on the part of the President and the Senate. Brushing aside all memories of his bitter battles with Congress in 1841 and 1842, he modestly reminded Congress that he had urged it to act on annexation "as the best expounder of popular sentiment."[125]

It is but to state a truism to say that no matter how much personalities, local contests, and other factors may influence any presidential election, there is no method better known to determine what the public wants. Despite this fact, Tyler was pilloried by both the Democrats and the Whigs for introducing the Texas issue on the threshold of the campaign.

[123]*Ibid.*, p. 2180.

[124]For a detailed account of the Texas question in the campaign of 1844 see Smith, *op. cit.*, pp. 238-257, 297-321 *passim*.

[125]Richardson, *op. cit.*, p. 2196. Shades of the Protest Message!

Once the issue was joined, however, Tyler was on sound ground in construing Polk's victory to be one for annexation.[126] Two weeks later he sent another message to Congress urging annexation as a policy which served the national interest and not merely sectional ambitions. He said that he would have been blind to his highest obligations as President had he urged annexation in the interest of any one section of the country. He added that it was his pleasure to note that demonstrations of support for annexation "have proceeded from all portions of the Union."[127] All this effort might not have been necessary had Tyler prevented Calhoun from injecting the slavery question into the annexation issue.[128]

Placing the subject before the House for action "in some other form" was the master stroke.[129] The form chosen in the House was a joint resolution, which passed on January 25, 1845, by a vote of 120 to 98.[130] This resolution was silent respecting the role to be played by the President in the process of permitting Texas to become a state. It stipulated merely that Congress, by the passage of the resolution, consented to the erection of Texas as a state "with a republican form of government ..." It remained for the Senate to amend

[126]Holt concluded that the election of 1844 was the last one in the nineteenth century in which an issue of foreign policy was predominant. Holt, *op. cit.*, p. 59. Cf. Smith, *op. cit.*, pp. 234-257. It should be noted, however, that Tyler claimed (and there is no reason to doubt his claim) that he did not *originally* intend for annexation to become a controversial issue. Tyler, *op. cit.*, II, 321, 396. On the other hand, see Poage, *op. cit.*, p. 192; Smith, *loc. cit.*

[127]Richardson, *op. cit.*, p. 2209. In later years Tyler insisted in private letters that this was his true aim. Cf. Tyler, *op. cit.*, II, 425.

[128]Why Tyler permitted this is hard to say. It has been suggested that he was either the perpetrator or the unsuspecting victim of a plot to split both the Whig and Democratic parties along sectional lines. See chapter vi on this point. Cf. Reeves, *op. cit.*, pp. 150, 157.

[129]The idea of the joint resolution was not Tyler's. However, insistence on reaching his cherished goal was his even in the face of Calhoun's indifference to further action. See Tyler, *op. cit.*, II, 331. See also Henderson's resolution of June 8, 1844, calling for annexation "properly achieved by an Act of Congress admitting the people of Texas ... as a new State. ..." *Senate Journal*, 28th Cong., 1st Sess., p. 437.

[130]*House Journal*, 28th Cong., 2nd Sess., p. 265. For the text of the resolution see pp. 259-260.

the House's resolution by further providing "that, if the President of the United States shall, *in his judgment and discretion*, deem it most advisable, instead of proceeding to submit the foregoing resolution to the Republic of Texas as an *overture* . . . for admission, to negotiate [a treaty] with that Republic, then, *Be it resolved*, That a State . . . be formed out of the present Republic of Texas."[131]

Armed with this statutory authority, Tyler hesitated only long enough to consider the propriety of acting on either of the alternatives before him, since his term would end in but four days. With this in view, he called a meeting of the cabinet, and it was decided that the House-sponsored proposition to make an "overture" to Texas was to be preferred to the Walker amendment added by the Senate. Tyler decided further to send Calhoun to consult with Polk to determine the latter's sentiments respecting the choice of means open to the President. This was done, but Polk declined to commit himself. The next morning, March 3, 1845, instructions to act were sent to Donelson, our agent in Texas.[132] Thus, all but the final steps of annexation were taken under Tyler's guiding presidential hand.

For the last year of his administration Tyler was involved in accomplishing the second and last of his great objectives of foreign policy, the annexation of Texas. Despite his rebuff in the Senate, he achieved that goal. The initiative was his every step of the way, and, despite his errors of judgment respecting the temper of the Senate, without faltering he remained in control of the formulation and execution of this policy. It was a remarkable display of tenacity and single-mindedness, and a striking example of presidential leadership in the conduct of foreign relations at a time when this

---

[131]*Senate Journal*, 28th Cong., 2nd Sess., p. 215 (italics added). The Walker amendment passed by a vote of 27 to 25 in the Senate on Feb. 27, 1845. Cf. *House Journal*, 28th Cong., 2nd Sess., p. 527.

[132]Three years after these events transpired, Tyler wrote to his former cabinet members and asked them to confirm this account of the actions of the last few days of his administration. Tyler apparently did so because he was rather incensed at Calhoun's public boasts that he had been the directing force in annexing Texas. Tyler, *op. cit.*, II, 364-365.

characteristic of the office, now a commonplace, was not so thoroughly established as a feature of our constitutional system. In the words of one of John Tyler's most caustic critics, John Quincy Adams: "It is John Tyler's last card for a popular whirlwind to carry him through; and he has played it with equal intrepidity and address. He has compelled Clay and Van Buren to stake their last chance upon opposition to the measure *now*, and has forced himself upon the whole Democracy [the Democratic party] as their exclusive candidate for the Presidency next December."[133]

[133]Adams, *op. cit.*, XII, 22 (May 4, 1844).

Chapter VI

A PRESIDENT IN SEARCH OF A PARTY

DESPITE the acknowledged shortcomings of the American party system, there is no single instrument which serves as a more durable means by which the spheres of legislative and executive authority, so carefully separated and balanced against each other in the Constitution, are made to act in unison to form public policy. "The unplanned institution of organized partisanship" has been the principal means of bridging the theory of the separation of powers.[1]

Leadership is the mainspring of effective action. The institutionalization of leadership is a difficult undertaking at best, given the variable qualities of different human beings, but some of the framers thought that they had provided for it in the Presidency. According to their plan, the President was expected to lead by dealing directly with individual congressmen to gain support for his policies from among the various factions represented in the legislative branch. Obviously, support for the President would be given by congressmen on the merits of his measures, regardless of individual factional affiliations.[2]

This is what might be termed the ideal or constitutional theory of the President's working relationship with Congress. It is indispensable to the practical success of this theory that the President stand forth as the representative of the entire nation, even though congressmen may represent only sec-

[1]A. N. Holcombe, *op. cit.*, pp. 78-109, 238. Cf. E. P. Herring, *Presidential Leadership*, p. 8.
[2]Holcombe, *op. cit.*, pp. 239-240.

147

tions or localities. Accordingly, it is the President who represents the public interest; and it is the business of congressmen to sublimate their local interests and differences in the
national interest. Both John Adams and his son, John Quincy
Adams, studiously attempted to apply this theory in their
practice of the Presidency, and each was a notable failure in
so far as he was not re-elected.[3] According to the modern folk-
lore of the Presidency, "the President is commonly thought
of as representing the general welfare; Congress is the tool
of 'special interests.' In fact Presidential policy, however
'pure' in motivation, must mean the promotion of certain
interests at the expense of others."[4]

With the growth of political parties as instruments of partisanship, the President assumed at least the nominal position of party leader. Each President has in practice, however, been forced to rely upon his own talents and his own
conception of the public interest to sustain him in this position for any length of time. This is no mean task, since the
President lacks the "sanction of institutional controls or the
stimulus of party creed." He is thrown "back upon the politics of persuasion and manipulation."[5] These are the two
stumbling blocks of presidential party leadership: the lack
of party machinery so organized that the President can en-
force his views of public policy, and the lack of a profession
of fixed party faith—the principles upon which Burke thought
men united to advance the public interest. The means available to the President enabling him to play the role of leader
are few in number: he may use the patronage to strengthen
his hold on shaky congressional support; he may appeal to
the nation over the heads of Congress; he may, in fact must,
resort to the use of personal influence and manipulation.

It has been suggested that there are three basic elements
underlying the task of building parties; and perhaps they
also underlie the task of maintaining parties. First, the build-
ers of parties must find a working combination of interests

[3]*Ibid.*, pp. 241-243.
[4]Herring, *op. cit.*, p. 9.
[5]*Ibid.*, p. 24.

which will submerge their differences long enough to secure control of the Presidency and Congress as a prize. Second, they must be capable of making a non-rational appeal to the subconscious desires of human beings. This task involves exploiting "to the full the latent power of personality." It consists in making a hero for public consumption. Third, party makers must understand the "technique of sublimat‐ ing the specific economic interests of different political fac‐ tions by merging them in more general interests, which can be identified with the public interest of the whole body of the people."[6]

In the campaign of 1840, the Whigs succeeded remarkably in welding together an opposition party consisting of diverse and incongruous elements. The creation of the Whig party was an act of political miscegenation which wedded high tariff, pro-bank Northern National Republicans to Southern low tariff, anti-bank Jeffersonian Republicans, witnessed by a bridal party of Nullifiers, Anti-Masons, Virginia States' Righters and conservatives in general.[7] They chose as their presidential candidate not the acknowledged leader of the party, Henry Clay, but a military hero, an alleged plain man of the people, General William Henry Harrison. They totally ignored issues by declining to formulate a campaign plat‐ form.[8] It was a case where "an ounce of lead" was "worth more than a pound of sense."[9] As a reward to Southerners who resented Jackson's nationalist inclinations in the nulli‐ fication controversy, Tyler was nominated for the Vice-Presi‐ dency, an office which he had tried in vain to reach in the election of 1836.[10] So armed, the Whigs went forth in tri‐ umphant humbuggery to defeat the Democrats, whom they

[6]Holcombe, *op. cit.*, p. 92.

[7]There are two good histories of the party: E. M. Carroll, *Origins of the Whig Party*, esp. pp. 189-206; and A. C. Cole, *The Whig Party in the South*, esp. pp. 57-63. Cf. Herbert Agar, *The Price of Union*, pp. 285-292.

[8]Stanwood, *op. cit.*, pp. 190-191.

[9]Tyler used this caustic epigram to describe the rise of Richard M. Johnson to the Vice-Presidency under Van Buren. Tyler, *op. cit.*, I, 439.

[10]See Carroll, *op. cit.*, p. 164. Tyler was a Southern Whig candidate for the Vice-Presidency in this election on a ticket with Judge Hugh Lawson White of Ten-

considered to be the masters of demagoguery. In Virginia the Democrats complained that the Whigs "have raised in this state seventeen log cabins ornamented by two stuffed bear skins, one living bear, together with coon skins, brooms, gourds, and cider barrels innumerable. . . ."[11] The specific interests of each of the component groups in the Whig coalition were submerged in order to emphasize the ambiguous appeal of a candidate who was running as the common man *par excellence*. Relying upon the log cabin and hard cider campaign, the Whigs were careful to avoid making any appeal on the basis of Clay's "American System." To do so would have frightened away indispensable Southern votes.

The Democrats, in contrast to the Whigs, issued a nine-point platform in which they advocated a strict construction of the powers of the national government, the practice of rigid economy in government, and the separation of the monies of the national government from banking institutions. They opposed a protective tariff, the chartering of a national bank (an institution they considered subversive of "the liberties of the people"), the fostering of internal improvements by the national government, and the assumption of states' debts incurred for internal improvements. They denied the power of Congress to interfere with slavery in the states and adopted the "liberal principles embodied by Jefferson in the Declaration of Independence . . . which makes ours the land of liberty and the asylum of the oppressed of every nation . . . and every attempt to abridge the present privilege of becoming citizens and the owners of soil among us ought to be resisted . . ."[12] The planks of the Democratic platform are of particular interest when they are compared

nessee. While Tyler carried the states of Maryland, South Carolina, Tennessee and Georgia, Judge White carried only Georgia and Tennessee. In all, there were five presidential and four vice-presidential candidates in this campaign. Van Buren and Richard M. Johnson were the Democratic candidates for President and Vice-President. Van Buren was, of course, elected President outright, but Johnson was chosen Vice-President by the Senate. See Stanwood, *op. cit.*, p. 188.

[11]*Proceedings of the Democratic State Convention*, Charlottesville, Virginia, Sept. 9-10, 1840, Library of Congress.

[12]Stanwood, *op. cit.*, pp. 199-201.

with the legislative program which Tyler advocated during his administration.

Although Van Buren was their overwhelming choice for the Presidency, the Democrats had some difficulty in nominating a candidate for Vice-President. They finally solved the problem by naming no one at their Baltimore convention and allowing various candidates to be advanced in several areas.[13] Among these candidates, Tyler's friend Tazewell received the eleven electoral votes of South Carolina; William King of Alabama received no votes but was later appointed Minister to France by Tyler; and Polk, who received a single vote, succeeded Tyler in the Presidency.[14] The Whig coalition, united only in opposition to Jacksonian "executive usurpation," and animated by a conservative social bias, triumphed by a wide margin in the electoral vote but by a slim popular majority.[15]

In the selection of presidential candidates availability had triumphed over capacity. The plan of the framers to institutionalize leadership centering in the Presidency had apparently failed again (as it had under the rule of "King Caucus"). In the words of an able observer: "We see that political power shifts from the executive to the legislative branch and back again. Our system thus provides alternative institutional outlets, thereby facilitating the expression of changes in the political pattern of social forces in the country."[16] Leadership can be institutionalized immutably in neither Congress nor the President; with changing personalities and circumstances the focal point of control shifts.

While party is usually the tie that binds the President and

[13]When this fact is coupled with the knowledge that the Whigs had such a difficult time in selecting candidates in 1836, it becomes clear that party alignments were at this time highly unstable. The Democratic vice-presidential candidates were King of Alabama, Polk of Tennessee, Littleton Tazewell of Virginia, and Richard M. Johnson of Kentucky, the incumbent. Of these, Johnson received forty-eight electoral votes, Tazewell eleven, Polk one, and King none. *Ibid.*, pp. 198-199.

[14]Moreover, Tyler offered Polk the post of Secretary of the Navy in 1844, but he refused the nomination.

[15]The popular votes cast resulted in a close vote of 1,200,000 to 1,100,000. The electoral vote was 234 to 60. Cf. *ibid.*, pp. 203-204.

[16]Herring, *op. cit.*, pp. 7-8.

Congress in a general way, it does not prevent an impasse
between them. This was certainly the case in Tyler's administration. As Vice-President, he could do no more than thwart
temporarily the Whig program by casting a tie-breaking vote
against a measure which offended Southern Whig scruples.
This sort of action could be overcome through the exercise
of strict party discipline even in the rather closely balanced
Senate. When Harrison died, however, and Tyler succeeded
to the Presidency, the party without principles which had
elected him to a position of presumed impotence paid dearly
for the success it had bought at the polls.

John Tyler was a Democrat or Jeffersonian Republican
during all his early political career. In 1827, and again in
1832, he favored Jackson as the least offensive in the choice
of evils before the country. "To . . . Gen'l Jackson I have
entertained the strongest objections; there are even *now*
many, many others whom I would prefer, but every day that
passes inspires me with the strong hope that his administration will be characterized by simplicity—I mean Republican
simplicity."[17] His faith in Jackson was strengthened when the
latter vetoed the Maysville Road Bill. Tyler told Tazewell,
"this is good as a first step, and greatly raises my hopes and
confidence. The banner of Mr. Clay and the corruptionists
will now be unfurled, and *parties will be more distinctly
marked.*"[18] Tyler was enthusiastic when Jackson vetoed the
bill to extend the charter of the national bank, and he voted
to sustain him.[19]

Tyler's break with Jackson came slowly and reluctantly.
Even while he enthusiastically supported Jackson's actions
in opposing the bank and the Maysville Road Bill because
these moves were in accord with Tyler's anti-nationalist sentiments, he was forced by his conscience and constitutional
principles to resist Jackson's use of the prerogative. He opposed Jackson's recess appointments which circumvented
senatorial confirmation (or rejection); he opposed Jackson's

[17]Tyler, *op. cit.*, I, 379.
[18]*Ibid.*, p. 412 (italics added).
[19]Chitwood, *op. cit.*, p. 125.

appointment of newspaper editors to public offices as a violation of the principle of free press; he denounced Jackson's
removal of federal deposits from the Bank of the United
States as an unconstitutional violation of the statutes, and
he supported the resolution censuring Jackson for his acts.
South Carolina's Ordinance of Nullification and Jackson's
vigorous nationalism in responding to the Force Bill were
enough to shake Tyler deeply, for he opposed both. He did
not entirely refuse his support to Jackson thereafter, but the
conviction grew on him that re-election in 1832 had turned
Jackson from his States' Rights faith and had made him a
nationalist. "Livingston," Tyler said, "is to be the man to
rule the roost, for sooth; and if his counsel prevails, the Constitution may be construed . . . to mean everything and anything."[20] By 1834 he gloated with his friend Tazewell:

I look back with increased satisfaction to the position we
assumed while were here [in the Senate] together, and
bring myself readily to believe that but for the resistance
we from time to time urged, even in the hey-day of Jack-
sonism, against executive usurpation, the present condition of things could never have been brought about. It
requires numerous strokes of the axe to bring down the
oak, and the exposure of every encroachment committed
by a popular administration on constitutional rights is
absolutely necessary for preserving free government.[21]

When the power of Jackson's popularity reached into the
Virginia General Assembly in 1836 and secured the passage
of a resolution requiring the Old Dominion's senators to vote
to expunge from the Senate Journal the resolution censuring
Jackson, John Tyler resigned, claiming that any mutilation
of the Journal was an unconstitutional act. He could well
afford the luxury of his principles, for he was already the
vice-presidential candidate for States' Rights Whigs in Maryland, North Carolina, Georgia and Virginia.[22] Not until four
years later, however, was he to taste victory in pursuit of
this office. He did so then on votes cast for William Henry

[20]Tyler, *op. cit.*, I, 423, 489.
[21]*Ibid.*, p. 496.
[22]*Ibid.*, pp. 520, 534, 536.

Harrison, nominated by the nationalist wing of the Whig party.

Despite the professed enthusiasm of the party faithful for their new chief when Tyler became President, the leaders of the Whigs were not quite so certain of their own unreserved support for him. John Quincy Adams predicted that "the policy of Mr. Tyler will look exclusively to his own election for the next four years, and that of Webster will be to secure it for him; that Mr. Clay will be left to fight his own battles with the Land Bill, without aid or support from the administration, and . . . between Tyler and Webster there will be a concert for mutual concession between North and South. Clay will soon be in unequivocal opposition."[23] Clay, too, saw no good in the accession of Tyler to the Presidency. He wrote Judge Beverly Tucker in April, 1841, saying, "I can hardly suppose that V. P. Tyler will interpose any obstacle to the adoption of the measures on which the Whigs are generally united. Still, his administration will be in the nature of a regency, and regencies are very apt to engender faction, intrigue, etc."[24] Shortly after the opening of the special session of the 27th Congress, Clay wrote to E. M. Letcher, a Kentucky friend, and acknowledged that the Whigs had been ensnared in their own trap. "There is reason to fear that Tyler will throw himself upon Calhoun, Duff Green, etc., and detach himself from the great body of the Whig party," Clay said. "A few days will disclose. If he should take that course, it will be on the bank."[25] Clay already knew that Tyler would rather not propose any specific bank plan and that he would veto any such plan as might offend his strict constitutional scruples.[26]

Outside of the Clay Whig camp, the men close to the President had their own suspicions. Tyler's intimate, Wise, indicated the course which he thought Clay would follow:

Clay is wholly impracticable; he is beyond conference or

[23]Adams, *op. cit.*, X, 405 (April 20, 1841).
[24]Tyler, *op. cit.*, II, 30.
[25]Coleman, *op. cit.*, I, 156-157.
[26]See chapter i, p. 20 *supra*.

advice, and you and I had better not approach him. Tyler will veto his full-grown central monster . . . a national bank, and he is madly jealous enough of T.'s running for a second term to make it a point now to drive him to a veto if he can. Let him do it. The veto kills Clay; and Webster and his personal friends take shelter under T., and the united opposition forces him back in a war with centralism—Clay for the focus.

This presents the whole campaign to you. Clay is the same man he was in 1828. He is a national, out and out . . . and wages war of extermination to all republican strict construction. He has . . . ability to stand alone; Webster has not, and flies before him. We humble the latter to us, and must combat the former. Regard Clay as the opposition to Tyler's administration ultimately.[27]

The bank became the issue on which a President was to be made or unmade.

The observations of Adams, Wise and Clay are particularly notable, since they predicted the courses which Tyler was eventually to follow. However, since they were to some degree mutually contradictory, Tyler pursued first one course and then the other. As events demonstrated, Tyler's first course was to attempt to conciliate those elements of the Whig party which opposed Henry Clay and which could be formed into an alliance of North and South. This was to be accomplished with the aid of Webster and other Whigs who were willing to go along with the administration. When this plan failed, Tyler was forced by his position on issues to seek the outright support of the Democratic party. When it appeared to Tyler that his second political tack was probably a failure, he allowed himself to become an independent third party candidate who might or might not have a strong appeal in the South and in certain key states of the North.

The move to re-charter a bank of the United States was, of course, the prime issue of the summer of 1841 in the special session of the 27th Congress. Moreover, the principal actors in this political drama were quite aware of the disruptive potential of this issue. As we have seen, Tyler fur-

[27]Tyler, *op. cit.*, II, 38.

nished a bank plan only when called upon by Congress to do so, and this plan was not followed strictly in formulating the first bank bill. When Tyler vetoed this bill, Clay raised the cry that one of Tyler's objects in doing so was to disrupt the Whig party and force a realignment of parties.[28] Calhoun, for his own selfish reasons, feared that Clay's bank bill would fail to pass Congress but that the plan recommended by the President would pass and be signed. "This," he said, "I fear, and it is the only thing I do. I should much rather Clay's bill should pass and be vetoed."[29] For his part, Tyler thought that he saw President-making in the whole controversy. As a consequence, when he was faced with the second bank bill, which, like the first one, offended his constitutional scruples, he proposed to include in his veto message an announcement of his intention to limit his ambitions to a single term in office, his current term. He said that he refrained from doing so, however, only after consultation with his cabinet, who advised against it. Moreover, previously he had deleted from his Inaugural Address a similar statement only when pressed by personal friends to do so. His aim, in both cases, was to remove the bank question from the partisan struggle over the Presidency in 1844, so that the matter could be settled on its merits.[30] Sorely beset by this tumultuous contest for control of the Whig party, Tyler wrote his friend Tucker in confidence, saying, "every day the more convinces me how little real patriotism was mixed up in the late contest. The great mass is always true to the country, and governed by correct motives, but the noisy demagogue has his eye for the

---

[28]*Cong. Globe*, 27th Cong., 1st Sess., Appendix, pp. 364-365. Representative Stuart of Virginia made much of the fact that when he went to see the President at the White House in the hope of framing a satisfactory second bank bill, he found Tyler "engaged with a distinguished *Democratic* Senator." Tyler, *op. cit.*, II, 77.

[29]"Correspondence of John C. Calhoun," p. 481.

[30]This statement was corroborated by Duff Green and Webster in letters published Dec. 29, 1842, and June 9, 1843, respectively. Tyler, *op. cit.*, II, 27-28, 340. Tyler had no fixed opinion regarding the one-term issue. In 1830 he thought that the trouble with the President's succeeding himself was that his first term was devoted to electioneering for a second. At the time, however, he preferred the re-election of Jackson, who was, he thought, most likely to be opposed by Clay—as he was in the election of 1832. *Ibid.*, III, 62.

most part fixed on selfish ends. Are we destined ever again
to see the day when the good of the country is to be the
great consideration with political parties? I fear not."[31]

With Tyler's veto of the second bank bill, the split with
the Whigs was complete and final.[32] The issue had been
joined by irreconcilable forces. Clay had forcibly learned
Tyler's intentions and had, in turn, sought the fulfillment
of his own by holding sway over his congressional followers
with the despotism of an oriental potentate. "Old Hickory
himself never lorded it over his followers with authority more
undisputed or more supreme."[33] The session had been spent
in President-making, as Profitt charged in the House when
he said:

> from the first meeting of Congress up to this hour, there
> has been a determination of the part of some gentlemen
> to create an issue with the President. His constitutional
> scruples, well known and openly avowed, have been sneered
> at, and, under the pretext of avoiding them, the most ab-
> surd and evasive propositions have been presented to him,
> with a full knowledge that they could not receive his sanc-
> tion. In the expressive language of the gentleman (Botts
> of Virginia), there has been every means used to "head
> him"—to make him sign a bill which neither his conscience
> nor judgment approved ... [or] by refusing his assent, to
> become an object of abuse and misrepresentation for those
> who hate him, and look upon him as standing between
> them and the objects of their ambition.[34]

[31]*Ibid.*, II, 53 (July 28, 1841).

[32]Calhoun said on Aug. 1, 1841, *even before* the veto of the second bank bill, that
the split between Tyler and the Whigs was complete. "Correspondence of John
C. Calhoun," p. 484.

[33]The New York *Herald*, quoted in Chitwood, *op. cit.*, p. 217. Clay apparently
"lorded it" over the Kentucky legislature, too, for his resignation from the United
States Senate is recorded in the following interesting terms: Clay presented the
credentials of "John J. Crittenden, chosen a Senator by the Legislature of the
Commonwealth of Kentucky, 'to fill the vacancy occasioned by the resignation
of the honorable Henry Clay'; and having announced to the Senate the resignation of his seat, retired." This was the same Crittenden, of course, who had
resigned from Tyler's cabinet in the previous September. *Senate Journal*, 27th
Cong., 2nd Sess., p. 262.

[34]*Cong. Globe*, 27th Cong., 1st Sess., p. 389. Cf. Bott's "coffee-house letter," Tyler,
op. cit., II, 112.

The manifesto of the Whigs of Congress, issued after a party caucus on September 13, 1841, marked the formal break between President Tyler and the Whig party. Declaring that the special session of Congress had been called to enact the Whig program which had been generally understood by the electorate in the campaign of 1840 (even though not announced in a platform), the Whigs found that their President had proved himself treacherous by thwarting those aims. Tyler had, they said, used the veto power not to sustain his conscientious scruples, but rather to alter the existing party alignments:

... Too many proofs have been forced upon our observation to leave us free from the apprehension that the President has permitted himself to be beguiled into an opinion that, by this exhibition of his prerogative, he might be able to divert the policy of his administration into a channel which should lead to new political combinations, and accomplish results which must overthrow the present divisions of party in the country ... The last persons in the government who would seem to have been intrusted with his confidence on those embarrassing topics were the constitutional advisers which the laws had provided for him. ... We are constrained to say that the President, by the course he has adopted in respect to the application of the veto power to two successive bank charters, each of which there was just reason to believe would meet his approbation; by his withdrawal of confidence from his real friends in Congress and from the members of his cabinet; by his bestowal of it upon others notwithstanding their notorious opposition to leading measures of his administration, has voluntarily separated himself from those by whose exertions and suffrages he was elevated to that office through which he reached his present exalted station.[35]

Caleb Cushing replied with a counter-manifesto in which he urged the Whigs of the country to ignore the "caucus dictatorship"[36] which had broken with the President. He

[35]*Niles Register*, LXI, 35-36.
[36]This was Cushing's term—a favorite with Tyler's supporters. The editor of the *National Intelligencer* claimed that caucus discipline had enabled the Whigs in Congress to stand together on the measures of the special session against the President. *National Intelligencer*, Oct. 2, 1841.

solicited their support for the present administration instead of hoping for "some contingent possibility" four years hence.[37]

Tyler's reaction to the calamitous party brawl was to set up himself and his few supporters as a non-party administration in the sense that he hoped to draw support from the moderates of both parties. He told Thomas Cooper, a friend: "The new cabinet is made up of the best material. Like myself they are all original Jackson men and mean to act upon Republican principles. We hope to sustain by no intrigue, but by the faithful discharge of our public duties— and if we go down, it will be no small degree of comfort to us that we have intended the public good and have worked faithfully to accomplish it."[38]

To Webster he expressed his fear that the administration would face a tremendous storm, and that it could look only to the country, not the politicians, for support: "My information from all parts of the country is encouraging, and although we are to have a furious fire during the coming winter, yet we shall, I doubt not, speedily recover from its effects. Our course is too plainly before us to be mistaken. We must look to the whole country and to the whole people."[39] Upshur, Tyler's new Secretary of the Navy, wrote to Tucker, saying:

He [Tyler] is now determined to take a middle course, avoiding ultraism on both sides, and aiming at the approbation of the temperate and sober minded of both parties . . . I verily believe that he is determined on this course. He speaks of his re-election without any sort of reserve, as a thing that may or may not be, and as a thing which he may or may not seek. . . . *The mere game of politics is one at least at which he will certainly be beaten. He has no chance but in placing himself on broad principles, and adhering to them with boldness and independence.*[40]

---

[37]Benton, *op. cit.*, pp. 359-360. Cf. Fuess, *op. cit.*, pp. 323-325.

[38]Tyler Papers, Vol. II, No. 6405 (Oct. 8, 1841).

[39]Tyler, *op. cit.*, II, 104 (Oct. 11, 1841).

[40]*Ibid.*, p. 247 (Dec. 12, 1841) (italics added). This is a significant appraisal of Tyler as a politician by one of his intimate associates of long acquaintance.

A few days later Upshur added to this information by telling
Tucker:

> If you will reflect on the condition in which we found the
> government you will estimate the difficulties with which
> we have to contend. We came in against all parties, and
> of course *without any support except what our measures
> would win for us*. We knew that the government must go
> on, and we knew that it could not go on without a party
> to sustain it. Of course, it became necessary that we should
> *create a party*. On this subject we have consulted together
> freely and without reserve. We have *all agreed*, without a
> single exception, that our only course was to administer
> the government for the best interests of the country, and
> to trust to the moderates of all parties to sustain us. . . .
> But you certainly do Tyler some injustice in supposing
> that he pays any more court to the *locos* than to the other
> party. His appointments show the reverse; they are made
> indiscriminately from both parties; but the greater part
> from the Whigs. He avoids alike Clay-men and Benton-
> men, for there is nothing to choose between them.[41]

Calhoun's keen analysis of the party situation, and his
statement of his own position, lend further clarity to the picture as it stood after the veto of the second bank bill and
the breakup of the original Harrison cabinet. On September 12, 1841, the day after Tyler's first cabinet resigned, he
wrote a lengthy letter to A. P. Calhoun in which he said:

> The effect of the double veto is to defeat the bank at least
> for the next three or four years. That is a great gain; but
> I fear it will in the end lose us as much if not more than
> we shall gain.
>
> From all I can see, Mr. Tyler will attempt a middle
> course, or rather stop where he is. In his last veto he speaks
> with approbation of all the measures of the Extra Session,
> with the single exception of the bank bill.
>
> If he should take the course I suppose, the consequence
> will be, that he will draw to him all that portion of our
> party who were opposed to a bank, but in favor of the

---

[41]*Ibid.*, p. 154 (italics added). This apparently refers to the situation when Upshur
joined the reformed cabinet in Sept., 1841. In short, Upshur thought that Tyler
was avoiding the nationalist wings of both parties.

other measures, or at least not opposed. At the head of these, I regard the Pennsylvania interest. That state is in debt, and is inclined to the Tariff . . . such also I fear is the feeling of her prominent men in Congress, particularly Mr. Buchanan. It is that interest, I am inclined to think, that has been consulted in the formation of the new Cabinet. Mr. Forward is a Pennsylvanian and a tariff man, and his appointment to the Department of the Treasury must have a controlling influence over that and all connected measures. . . .

If I am right in these impressions, our situation . . . will be one of great embarrassment. Tyler will certainly be opposed by the Whigs. If we join in that opposition we shall be confounded with them; but if we oppose them, and defend Tyler and his administration, we shall sink down to the level of their principles and policy, and lose all the fruits of our passed [*sic*] efforts . . . I see but one way to act, and that requiring great caution and prudence; to stand fast on our principles, propose but few measures, and to oppose or support the measures proposed by Whigs or administration, just as they accord with or oppose our principles and policy. Taking that course, the administration would be so weak, as to be compelled to take shelter under one or the other party, and would more probably under ours than with the Whigs.[42]

There is nothing which can be added to Calhoun's prediction of the course Tyler was to follow as a non-party leader only to learn how fruitless such a position is for a President. Given the platform of the Democratic party in 1840, and his own previous record, there was no other organized partisan group to which Tyler could turn with any genuine hope of gaining support for his policies or for his own re-election, should he aspire to it. Tyler apparently did not realize this fact in 1841. After the elections of 1842, however, he unblushingly awaited the advances of the Democratic party.

The composition of the cabinet which Tyler chose in September, 1841, to replace those members of the original Har-

[42]"Correspondence of John C. Calhoun," pp. 487-489.

rison cabinet who resigned strikingly illustrated Tyler's determination to take a middle position while maintaining his
nominal connection with the Whig party. Tyler considered
himself a moderate and a true Whig. Webster, who remained
as Secretary of State, was far and away the most notable
Whig politician aside from Henry Clay. Webster could hope
to draw to Tyler the support of New England Whigs, even
though J. Q. Adams personally despised Tyler.[43] John C.
Spencer of New York was a prominent Whig whose appointment to the cabinet came as a surprise, since he was thought
to oppose Tyler. His entry into the cabinet, however, tended
to balance to some extent the loss of Granger, the former
Postmaster General, who was close to Thurlow Weed and
was not warm in his regard for Clay. Forward, the new Secretary of the Treasury, was a Pennsylvanian, and, as Calhoun
observed, was apparently selected to please the interests of
that key state. The remainder of the new cabinet members
came from the South. Upshur, Secretary of the Navy, had
been appointed to the General Court of Virginia while Tyler
was Governor. He was a "Republican" strict constructionist
who apparently greatly admired Calhoun. Legaré, the new
Attorney General, was a South Carolinian strongly opposed
to Calhoun and classed by Vernon Parrington as a Southern
Federalist possessing one of the finest legal minds in the
ante-bellum South.[44] Wickliffe, the new Postmaster General
from Kentucky, was the fly in the political ointment. He
and his family were the bitterest of Clay's political enemies
within the Whig party in that state. Moreover, Wickliffe had
family ties with Calhoun. This appointment was a clear indication that the President had declared open war on Clay.[45]
There is no known record which reveals to what extent

[43]Calhoun concluded, however, that the Clay Whigs looked upon Webster as the
controlling personality in Tyler's administration. For this reason Clay had de-
tached nearly all the Whig party from the administration, leaving the Democrats
coldly suspicious of Tyler. *Ibid.*, pp. 508-509.

[44]V. L. Parrington, *Main Currents in American Thought* (New York, Harcourt
Brace, 1927), II, 114-124.

[45]See Poage, *op. cit.*, pp. 102-106; Chitwood, *op. cit.*, pp. 277-281. See chapter iii
supra for additional information about cabinet members.

Tyler used the patronage below the level of cabinet and diplomatic posts to build a following of faithful office holders. Immediately after his break with the Whig party Tyler did, however, direct the Postmaster General to forbid the appointment of newspaper editors to office as postmasters. This bit of proscription hit the opposition presses quite hard and provided loaves and fishes for the new faithful.[46] The Democrats complained that Tyler removed office holders merely for their opposition to him, but his official organ, The *Madisonian*, denied that this had been done on a wholesale basis.[47]

Without a doubt, however, appointments to office were made with an eye to securing support for the President.[48] Tyler's appointments to important offices indicated rather clearly, moreover, the extent to which he was wooing either party.[49] After the spring of 1843 it was quite clear that it was the Democrats whom he favored. Yet, whatever may have been the extent of Tyler's efforts to build a party following, the professional politicians thought his activities laughable. William A. Marcy of New York mocked the President's efforts in observing that "Captain Tyler, poor soul, thinks the people have discharged all their party leaders and are coming en masse to his relief. The office seekers tell him so because they know he wishes to believe it. He is a doomed man; deaf to the honest voice of warning—blind to the visible prognostics of the future."[50]

[46]James E. Pollard, *The Presidents and the Press*, p. 219.

[47]See Chitwood, *op. cit.*, p. 371. Horace Greeley complained to Cushing that too many "Loco Focos" were being left in office. He said: "I hold . . . that simple justice demands the confiding of at least half the valuable offices to that party which for twelve years has been denied any." Fuess, *op. cit.*, pp. 337-339.

[48]Cushing denied in the House that Tyler was "selling" offices to the supporters of his measures, but this denial was probably nonsense. See Fuess, *op. cit.*, pp. 378-379.

[49]Late in his administration Tyler was apparently engaged in making numerous removals and appointments for faithful service. Several letters indicate as much. See Tyler Papers, Vol. II, Nos. 6490, 6492, 6500 (Alexander Gardiner to Tyler). See further "Correspondence of John C. Calhoun," p. 602. On July 10, 1844, Calhoun said that Tyler was making appointments without regard to the wishes of his Secretaries. However, early in 1844 Tyler offered two Whigs, John Sargeant and Horace Binney, appointment to the Supreme Court. See chapter iv *supra*.

[50]Quoted in Oscar D. Lambert, *Presidential Politics in the United States, 1841-1844*.

The bitter party strife which marked the relations between the President and the Whigs in the regular session of the 27th Congress resulted in the longest session of Congress up to that date—one of 269 days. It was, in fact, popularly dubbed the "Long Parliament."[51] Although Clay resigned his seat in the Senate on March 31, 1842, he continued to maintain his hold over the Whig party. Tyler had failed, as Calhoun observed, "in conciliating his old friends, though they give him their support whenever they can consistently with their principles and policy."[52] The President, with his small following of loyal supporters, was faced with the nationalist opposition of the Clay Whigs and the Van Buren Democrats.[53] With the nation in the pit of a financial crisis, the President's "Exchequer Plan," a substitute for the Whigs' bank bills, did not get even a reasonable hearing in the House.[54] On the other hand, the President used the veto power to thwart the Whig majority in its plan to enact both a protective tariff and the continued distribution of the proceeds from the public land sales.

The incessant wrangling of the parties in this session, the action of the House in censuring the President for his use of the veto power from corrupt motives, and the Democrats' landslide victory in the congressional elections in the fall of

---

p. 87. Cf. Calhoun to Duff Green (April 2, 1842) and Calhoun to T. G. Clemson (April 3, 1842) in "Correspondence of John C. Calhoun," pp. 507-509. Calhoun said that the administration was very weak with "not one open advocate in the Senate; and not more than four or five in the House. It is unsteady, without fixed purpose of any kind, except to create a third party. . . . Webster is regarded as the controlling spirit, and he has become almost universally odious. . . . Clay has been able to detach almost the entire body of the whigs from the administration, while they have failed to make any impression on the Republican ranks."

[51]J. B. McMaster, *History of the People of the United States*, VII, 65. Writing to Robert McCandlish on July 10, 1842, about the state of our relations with Mexico, Tyler revealed his dissatisfaction with this Congress, with which he was yet to have the worst possible relations: "Is it not abominable that this miserable Congress should not even yet have passed the Army or Navy appropriation bill, thereby subjecting the country to be brow-beat by the captive of San Jacinto? More than seven months in session, and nothing done." Tyler, *op. cit.*, II, 173.

[52]"Correspondence of John C. Calhoun," p. 507.

[53]*Ibid.*, p. 499.

[54]Cf. Fuess, *op. cit.*, pp. 340-345.

1842—all convinced the President that the nation was with
him, even if the party managers were not. He revealed his
state of mind to Tazewell in October, 1842:

I am still destined, my dear Sir, to navigate the barque
of State amid all the convulsions and agitations of faction.
The *Ultras* of both the prevailing factions will not consent
to ground their arms, although the signal defeat which
one has encountered would teach wisdom to both. Is there
any other course for me to pursue than to look to the
public good irrespective of either faction? Or can I best
acquit myself of my important duties by yielding myself
into the hands of a party calling itself Republican, but
which I fear has a cohesion of party without a cohesion of
principle? My strong determination is to hold, as I have
heretofore done, the politicians of both parties and of all
parties at defiance, and to continue to act [illegible] on
patriotic motives and broad principles of public good. But
the difficulty in the way of administering the government
without a party is undoubtedly great. From portions of
the Democratic party I have received an apparently warm
support, *but while the Ultras control in the name of party,* I
fear that *no good would arise from either an amalgamation
with them or a too ready assent to their demands for office.* Do
I ask you too much when I desire that you place yourself.
in my situation and tell me what course you would pursue
under similar circumstances? You are the only person living of whom I would seek counsel upon such a question
and what you shall say to me will be confined to myself
and fully weighed.[55]

This confession to a man who must be considered Tyler's
most confidential adviser indicated clearly that Tyler, despite the urgings of extremists like Wise (and possibly Upshur), was still far from convinced that his experiment in
"constitutional administration" was a failure.[56] His doubts

[55]Tyler Papers, Vol. II, No. 6433 (Oct. 24, 1842).

[56]Cushing so described the administration in debate in the House when he said
that the issue was between a constitutional administration by the President and
a party administration led by a chief in Congress. Fuess, *op. cit.,* p. 378. Wise
in particular seems to have aimed at a coalition of Tyler's forces with those of
Calhoun early in the administration. This may well explain his bold action in
approaching Calhoun's friends with the offer of appointment as Secretary of
State in 1844 without Tyler's previous consent or suggestion. See p. 168 *infra.*

of its future effectiveness, however, had grown upon him. At least, Tyler had come to realize the extreme difficulty of the position of a President who attempted to place himself "above" parties in the hope that he could govern successfully through the appeal of non-partisanship.

As early as April, 1842, Alexander Hamilton, one of Tyler's personal friends who appears to have been a sort of presidential errand boy, wrote to the President urging that he change his cabinet. Significantly, he told the President "our cause is spreading among the people. . . . Your position is beautiful, but Webster and Spencer must leave your cabinet —no mistake."[57] By September of that year a move was on foot to get Forward out of the cabinet, but Tyler evidently refused to remove him outright. The plan was to make room for Caleb Cushing as the new Secretary of the Treasury.[58]

It will be recalled that the contemplated reorganization of the cabinet did not actually occur until the spring and summer of 1843. Forward resigned in March, 1843, Webster resigned in May, and Legaré died in June. Tyler's choice of replacements for these officers indicated without a doubt his future plans with respect to both policy and party. His choice of the Virginian, Upshur, as Secretary of State, and Nelson, a Maryland Democrat, as Attorney General evidenced his interest in pursuing intensively the annexation of Texas. His choices indicated, too, that Tyler hoped no longer to cling exclusively to his non-party position. Upshur, of course, was one of the original Virginia States' Rights men with whom Tyler surrounded himself. In addition to Nelson, Tyler chose two other Democrats to fill the recess vacancies in his cabinet. They were David Henshaw, a former Jackson party wheelhorse in Massachusetts,[59] and James Porter, brother of the Democratic Governor of Pennsylvania. It will be remembered that the latter two appointments caused a row between

5

[57]Tyler Papers, Vol. II, No. 6423 (April 23, 1842).

[58]Forward was apparently considered incompetent in office. See Tyler, *op. cit.*, II, 104; Tyler Papers, Vol. II, No. 6430, Sept. 15, 1842. Cushing was rejected by the Senate. See chapter iv, p. 85.

[59]He had been Collector of the Port of Boston under Jackson and Van Buren.

Tyler and the Senate when Congress met in December, 1843, resulting in the rejection of both Porter and Henshaw. These two gentlemen were then replaced by Thomas Gilmer, the ex-Governor of Virginia who was strongly interested in Calhoun's fortunes, and William Wilkins, a Pennsylvania Democrat.[60] Calhoun's analysis of the importance of the Pennsylvania interest to Tyler's political fortunes was totally correct.[61]

The appointment of a Dr. Martin as chief clerk in the Department of State tends further to confirm the move to attract a following of Democrats. Tyler found this appointment personally embarrassing after it was made because of the doctor's enmity to Webster. Tyler wrote to Legaré: "In regard to Dr. Martin, my embarrassment is even greater than your own. I considered his appointment not only due to his deservedly high standing, but to sound policy. It would have an effect equally substantial with the appointment of a Democrat to the Head of the Department, and was calculated to make all things smooth and easy."[62]

The following October Amos Kendall, a Jackson stalwart who had been Postmaster General under Old Hickory, wrote Tyler a letter in which he displayed his eagerness for the appointment as public printer. "The emoluments of this station would be an inexpressable relief to me under the existing circumstances," he said, "yet I do not seek or desire them at the expense of injury to the Democratic Party.... If, however, such shall be the concurrence of circumstances at the meeting of Congress, that the printing in question can be given to me *without injury to our common cause* . . . I shall

---

[60]A brief note from Calhoun to R. M. T. Hunter on Sept. 13, 1843, adds weight to this view. Calhoun said: "I am glad to hear that Gilmer is right. It is important that Wise should go with us . . . What is Rives doing?" "Correspondence of John C. Calhoun," p. 549.

[61]This conclusion is further borne out by Tyler's conversion to advocating and accepting the mildly protective tariff of 1842. Wilkins was the unsuccessful candidate of a coalition of Southern and Pennsylvania Democrats for Speaker in the 28th Congress. This plot was intended to discourage the candidacy of Van Buren in 1844. *Ibid.*, pp. 898-899.

[62]Dr. Martin had been removed from this office to make room for Fletcher Webster at the outset of Harrison's administration. Tyler, *op. cit.*, III, 112.

receive it with joy and gratitude. . . ."[63]

The deaths of Secretaries Upshur and Gilmer in mid-February, 1844, coupled with the resignation of Spencer in May of that year, gave Tyler additional opportunities to make cabinet appointments. Calhoun, who had recently withdrawn from the race for the Democratic presidential nomination, was selected to replace Upshur as Secretary of State. Henry A. Wise claimed the exclusive honor of effecting this move, and his claim has not been denied. By pointed intimation he offered the post to Calhoun through mutual friends and then told the President what he had done. Tyler was angered but did not feel that he could back down on the issue; so Calhoun received the appointment.[64] This was the most that Tyler's associates who were the secret admirers of Calhoun were able to do.[65] The effect of the appointment, however, was to

[63]Tyler Papers, Vol. II, No. 6442 (Oct. 20, 1843) (italics added). Kendall admitted another interest in receiving the appointment: "I shall receive it with joy and gratitude which will be shared by more hearts than one and more tongues than one will unite with that of a husband and father in overflowing thankfulness to the authors of so great a good."

[64]Wise, *op. cit.*, pp. 223-225. Wise's version of his actions in slipping Calhoun into the cabinet is repeated in Coit, *op. cit.*, pp. 361-362. Of the appointment Calhoun said: "The possible reason I can see for accepting the Department, should it be offered, as far as duty is concerned, is limited to the pending negotiations relating to Texas and Oregon. They are both, I admit, of vast importance; especially to the West and South. . . . Is there reasonable hope that a treaty for annexation . . . can be made with Texas, and that the Oregon question can be settled? If so, I do not see how I could withhold my services, if required by the President. . . ." "Correspondence of John C. Calhoun," p. 574. A week later he told his daughter: "I have been offered the State Department . . . and I am strongly appealed to through Mr. McDuffie [Senator from South Carolina] and others to accept. The appeal is to my patriotism . . . in behalf of the South. My repugnance to accepting is every way great." *Ibid.*, p. 576. Accepting the post meant, of course, that Calhoun became a part of the very administration which he had intended to aid only in so far as it contributed to his nomination for the Presidency by the Democrats in 1844.

[65]There is much evidence to support the conclusion that Wise, Upshur and Gilmer all worked to secure the nomination of Calhoun before his cause was lost with the Democrats. Calhoun was informed of the negotiations with Texas at a time when they were still supposedly highly secret. Thus, even Tyler's intimates were working against him. "Correspondence of John C. Calhoun," pp. 900-906. Tyler is said to have been keenly aware of the unfortunate political implications of Calhoun's appointment as far as the annexation of Texas was concerned. Tyler, *op. cit.*, II, 292, 295. Cf. Poage, *op. cit.*, pp. 130-132.

enmesh securely the question of the annexation of Texas in the partisan controversy over slavery.

In addition to Calhoun, John Y. Mason, a Virginia Democrat, was appointed Secretary of the Navy, but only after feelers to Polk had been rejected by that worthy. Mason, a States' Righter, remained in the cabinet when Polk succeeded Tyler.[66]

The President's final cabinet appointment was that of the rather obscure George M. Bibb of Kentucky to the office of Secretary of the Treasury. Aside from the fact that Bibb was another former Democratic Senator who, like Tyler, had broken with Jackson in 1834, his appointment had little known political significance. The most that probably can be said is that he was an "old school Republican" of Virginia birth who added sectional weight to a cabinet which, by May 1844, was composed almost exclusively of Southerners.

In courting the support of the Democrats Tyler did not overlook the opportunity to flatter two of their most prominent leaders. In December, 1842, in his second Annual Message to Congress, Tyler recommended that the fine imposed on Jackson at New Orleans be remitted by Congress, saying, "it is believed that the remission of this fine and whatever of gratification that remission might cause the eminent man who incurred it would be in accordance with the general feeling and wishes of the American people."[67] In 1843 Tyler sent an expedition to Oregon under the command of Lieutenant John C. Fremont, Senator Benton's son-in-law, only to receive rather dubious gratitude from the old man.[68]

As early as January of 1843 Tyler sounded out Thomas Ritchie of the Richmond *Enquirer* with respect to his prospects for the Democratic nomination. Ritchie replied that although Tyler had done much to aid the Democrats by the policies which he had pursued, the party managers were not inclined to accept as their candidate a man who had done so

[66]Tyler, *op. cit.*, III, 133-134.

[67]Richardson, *op. cit.*, p. 2062. Congress passed an act remitting the fine after a bitter debate. Benton, *op. cit.*, p. 509.

[68]Benton, *op. cit.*, pp. 579-581; Tyler, *op. cit.*, II, 292.

much to hurt them in the campaign of 1840.[69] In September, 1843, Tyler wrote a letter to George Roberts in which he earnestly sought the support of his friends for his re-election.[70] In the same month he addressed a confidential letter to an unknown correspondent, to whom he said:

I write you hastily . . . but I am anxious to make a suggestion relative to your course relative to the Syracuse convention. It has occurred to me for some time that the Calhoun press of the North, if there be one at all, looked altogether to our papers to carry on a war with Van Buren. Now whatever may be done in New York and elsewhere, I think your press should preserve a dignified reserve. Publish the proceedings and say nothing about them—or but very little as that 'you fear that they may have a disastrous bearing' or something of that sort. We have nothing to hope from either faction—so let them fight it out. Prudence, my dear Sir, prudence is the word. There will be no harmony in any convention nor do the parties desire it. They will all run upon their own hooks under the belief that a Whig cannot be elected or succeed before the H. of R. composed as it is of a large majority of Democrats . . . Hold off as much as possible and let your fire be directed at Clay. He broke up the Whig party for his own selfish ends. Use my name as little as possible in your paper.[71]

This letter contains the unmistakable suggestion that Tyler at this time considered the choice of the President by the House of Representatives in 1845 as being a distinct possibility. Conceivably he looked upon himself as a candidate for such a choice. This conjecture is reinforced by a report to Calhoun from Virgil Maxcy, who told of his conversations with Upshur in December, 1843. Upshur revealed then that the negotiations with Texas were nearly completed, and that Tyler was so determined to secure the annexation of Texas that should the Texan minister *fail to sign* the treaty, the

[69]*Niles Register*, LXIV, 394.

[70]*William and Mary Quarterly* (First Series), XIX, 216.

[71]Tyler Papers, Vol. II, No. 6441 (Sept. 13, 1843). The reference is to the selection of Van Buren for the Democratic candidacy in 1844 by the New York State Democratic convention. Tyler thought he saw growing discontent with Van Buren among the rank and file of the Democratic party.

President "will adopt some other mode of bringing the matter before Congress."[72] Upshur was convinced that the issue
would rally the South around a Southern candidate, split
Clay and Van Buren on the annexation question, and throw
the election to the House, where Southerners would not vote
for either Clay or Van Buren. Moreover, Maxcy reported
Upshur as saying that "the President has some hopes that
he may become that Southern candidate."[73]

Thus, possibly by the end of 1843 Tyler came to the conclusion that his experiment in presidential leadership had
failed to attract to him sufficient organized partisan support
to make him a major party contender for re-election in 1844.
After this time, all his party building efforts seemed to have
but one aim—to prevent the election of either Clay or Van
Buren in 1844.[74] He sought to remove Van Buren from the
race by offering him an appointment to the Supreme Court,
but intermediaries rejected this. He considered Clay damaged, but not beaten, by the Democratic victory in the congressional elections of 1842. He viewed his own prospects
with a mixture of doubt and hope.

We have Tyler's word that he remained an active aspirant
for re-election until August, 1844, only to achieve two objectives. He wished to force the Democrats to drop Van
Buren as their candidate and to advocate openly the annexation of Texas. In explaining his acceptance of a nomination
by the "Tyler Party" convention in Baltimore on May 27,
1844, the President said:

> At the time of my acceptance of the nomination, although
> a large and overwhelming majority of the [Democratic]
> party had been brought into power by the people, as if for
> the express purpose of sustaining me in what I had done,
> yet that very party had made no public movement indica-
> tive of a friendly feeling, and a portion of its members,

[72]"Correspondence of John C. Calhoun," p. 903.

[73]*Ibid.*

[74]Writing *two days before* he sent the Texas annexation treaty to the Senate, Tyler
said: "Parties are violently agitated. Clay will most probably come out against
Texas, and then Van will seek to come in on Texas and my vetoes. For that we
are ready to do battle." Tyler, *op. cit.*, II, 307.

who seemed to control the rest, exhibited the bitterest hostility and the most unrelenting spirit of opposition. Under the circumstances there was but one course left to me consistent with honor, which was to maintain my position, unmoved by threats and unintimidated by denunciations.[75] In view of Van Buren's presumed strength among the Democrats, Tyler had now relinquished any hope of being their nominee. His convention met in Baltimore on the same day as the regular Democratic convention. He accepted his own nomination to the laughter of the Whigs and the discomfort of the Democrats. A week after these events occurred, Tyler told his daughter that "the Democrats are terribly alarmed at their own doings and are now looking to me for help. Clay's election over Polk is nearly certain and they, or many of them, anxiously desire to run a Union ticket with me and Polk. They universally admit now that I would have beat Clay. I have no cause to regret what has transpired. . . . I can continue the contest or abandon it with honor."[76]

Tyler made it his policy to "make these men feel the great necessity" of his cooperation.[77] His fear was that, if he withdrew from the canvass, his followers would receive shabby treatment at the hands of the regular party managers. Accordingly, after the Democratic leadership held numerous worried consultations expressing their fear of the inroads of "Tylerism" on their chances of success, they contrived the plan of sending an emissary to the President to promise fair treatment to Tyler's loyal followers. This was arranged, and with the promise that the Tylerites would be welcomed as brothers in the Democratic camp, the President issued a public statement, withdrawing from the race on August 20, 1844.[78]

An examination of the principal measures favored by Tyler, as well as of those which he opposed through the

[75]*Ibid.*, p. 343. Tyler called the Democratic victory in 1842 the "greatest political victory within my recollection." *Ibid.*, p. 341.

[76]Tyler Papers, Vol. II, No. 6419 (June 4, 1844). This letter suggests that he had not yet made up his mind to withdraw from the presidential race.

[77]Tyler, *op. cit.*, II, 710.

[78]*Ibid.*, pp. 338-349; III, 139-149.

exercise of the veto power, will show immediately that Tyler was generally in accord on paramount issues with the professed aims of the Democratic party. Above all, he and the most of the Democrats agreed on the two leading constitutional questions of the day—the construction of the powers of Congress and the proper use of the veto power. Throughout his administration Tyler advocated the strict construction of the powers of Congress, and when he was called upon to apply this principle, he did so. He vetoed the bank bills as constituting invalid construction of congressional powers. Not all his actions pleased the Democrats, however. While he signed the Apportionment Act of 1842, he did so under great doubt that Congress could require the states to elect representatives from districts created for that purpose. This act was bitterly assailed by the Democrats as an illegal extension of national power. Nevertheless, he did advocate and approve an act of August 29, 1842, providing for the removal of certain cases from state to Federal courts.[79] Moreover, he further antagonized many Democrats when he intervened with the threat to use the armed forces to suppress Dorr's Rebellion. His advocacy and approval of the mildly protective tariff of 1842 was disapproved almost wholly by the Southern free-traders, but Northern Democrats, particularly in Pennsylvania, applauded it. His use of the veto power elicited cheers from the Democrats—so much so that their platform in 1844 said:

> We are decidedly opposed to taking from the President the qualified veto power by which he is enabled . . . to suspend the passage of a bill, whose merits cannot secure the approval of two thirds of the Senate and House of Representatives . . . and which has thrice saved the American people from the corrupt and tyrannical domination of the Bank of the United States.[80]

[79] 5 *Statutes at Large* 539. This act grew directly out of the McLeod case and dealt essentially with foreign affairs. It could probably be argued, therefore, that Tyler did not consider this an inconsistent view of the extent of national authority. After all, the school of strict construction in this country has been concerned *principally* with the narrow interpretation of the powers of Congress relating to domestic, not foreign, affairs.

[80] Quoted in Stanwood, *op. cit.*, p. 215. After the bank vetoes, Jackson wrote that

On other specific matters of policy Tyler and the Democrats were in general accord. They both opposed internal improvements of a local nature and congressional interference with slavery in the states; they worshipped rigid economy in the operations of the government. The second time around, in 1842, Tyler disapproved the distribution of the proceeds from the public land sales; he did this, however, on grounds of policy, not of constitutionality, as the Democrats did in their 1844 platform.[81] When the Democrats embraced the annexation of Texas in their platform in 1844, the general accord with Tyler's policies was strongly marked.[82]

At the same time, it should be noted that until September, 1841, Tyler had generally agreed with the Whigs on the measures which constituted their legislative program. He had signed the act repealing Van Buren's sub-treasury system, the Whigs' bankruptcy act (a measure bitterly opposed by the Democrats), the loan act, and the bill to distribute the proceeds from the public land sales. Tyler, then, actually approved Clay's program of 1841 except for the bank and the protective tariff. The latter, of course, became the major issue and a point of violent disagreement between the President and Congress in the next session of Congress in 1841-1842. Finally, Tyler's vigorous efforts to suppress the slave trade by negotiating the African Squadron articles of the Webster-Ashburton Treaty were calculated to secure the support of both the Upper South and the North, irrespective of party lines. These facts made the Whig charges of Tyler's treachery, raised in September, 1841, rather hollow. Henry Clay could not afford to let John Tyler stand as a good Whig.

"in the ability and determination of the President to maintain the government on principles purely republican" he had the utmost confidence. Tyler, *op. cit.*, II, 292.

[81]Tyler signed a distribution act in 1841 (undoubtedly to secure some Western support) only because it provided for suspension of distribution if the tariff rates exceeded those of the Compromise Act of 1833, or in the event of war.

[82]In fact, if not in campaign oratory, the Democrats agreed with his Oregon policy, since Polk settled for the 49th parallel as our Northern boundary. Tyler left this matter to Calhoun, who was opposed to any American claim beyond the 49th parallel. Cf. Reeves, *op. cit.*, pp. 248-249.

By the end of the third session of the 27th Congress in August, 1842, however, Tyler's disagreement with the Whig's financial measures—the heart of their program—made it clear that he had broken with them irrevocably. On these fundamental legislative issues Tyler had followed a course practically identical with that of Jackson.

On at least three major issues Tyler appealed to the people for support over the heads of Congress. He fought the bank bills by his use of the veto power and then frankly rested his case upon the foundation of popular approval. In this there is little doubt that he was sustained. Never again did the Whigs advocate the chartering of a national bank as an article of party creed. He battled the Whigs in the summer of 1842 on the issue of tariff and distribution, and here, again, he secured the policy which he thought the public good required. His "Protest Message" to the House was an open appeal for public support. It is difficult to object to Tyler's interpretation of the Democratic landslide in the autumn elections of 1842 as an overwhelming public endorsement of his course of action. The annexation of Texas was the last issue which he forced into the arena of popular discussion, and again no one could say that he did not find adequate support for this policy.

Nevertheless, the startling and significant fact to be gained from Tyler's record is that he failed utterly to build effective, organized partisan support for his administration. He neither created nor captured a party which was capable of giving him national support both on the hustings and in Congress. He had committed the unpardonable sin of offending the professional party managers by being a turncoat—a political apostate.

Tyler was undoubtedly hampered by the lack of an organized and powerful press—the prime medium of communication in his day. In fact, he did make an attempt to organize a partisan press, but these efforts were a miserable failure.[83]

---

[83]Cf. Pollard, *op. cit.*, pp. 211-225. He may even have had difficulty in holding the reins of the *Madisonian*. In January, 1844, he wrote J. B. Jones, the editor: "Your paper leans too much to Clay. Beware of those around you. You should preserve

Against him were arrayed the trumpets of both the Clay and the Van Buren presses which took their cues directly from the powerful *National Intelligencer* and the *Globe* in Washington. Under such circumstances the battle for the minds of men, the battle to control the formation of public opinion, was already half lost. Only the crisis issues, not the petty political intrigues of the Washington scene, could be known to the general public. Modern presidential leadership without access to the media of communication would be impossible; it was no less impossible in Tyler's administration.

In conclusion, it can be said that John Tyler was the victim of a basic misconception of the working of the American party system. He thought that he could build organized partisan support for his measures and for his re-election solely on the merits of his policies spiced here and there with the salt of patronage. Though they rarely appear to be, if the party allegiances of voters were the result of rational and conscious choice, Tyler's hope of building a party of moderates, or even of immoderate opponents to nationalism, was well founded. Tyler learned too late, however, that while a President may enjoy support for his policies from many quarters regardless of party bond, it is to existing organized partisan groups that he must turn to sustain himself in office. He thought that a party could be built from scratch on the basis of a creed—more yet, a consistent creed. He longed to see a division of the parties on the general issue of broad versus strict construction of the powers of Congress. Tyler counted himself a guardian of pure Jeffersonian principle, unpolluted by federalist nationalism. His scorn of party loyalty, his constant references to "factions" and factionalism stamp him a politician raised in the uni-party era of the Virginia dynasty. Throughout almost all his adult years be-

---

an exact balance. All opposition to Van Buren should rest on his unavailability. . . . Many things may yet occur to change the direction of public opinion. It is also fatal to connect my name with Mr. Webster's as in the commentary on the Columbus convention. Remember always that mine is an isolated position. There are several persons who want to control the Madisonian. Hold firmly the reins." Tyler Papers, Vol. II, No. 6449.

fore reaching the Presidency Tyler had drawn his sustenance from men who well remembered Washington's solemn warnings against the "baneful spirit of faction" and that natural impulse for revenge which it engenders. If Tyler treated the link of party lightly, he had seen others do the same. His friend Tazewell, a Whig for a few years, had been a Democratic candidate for Vice-President in opposition to him in 1840. Clay was once a Jeffersonian Republican like Tyler. Calhoun had been Vice-President under Jackson only to turn Whig and return Democrat in less than a decade. Both the Whigs and the Democrats had several candidates for Vice-President in 1836, just as the Democrats had in 1840. Party loyalties and the party system were in a state of ferment and remained so during Tyler's lifetime. In fact, there was no party system as we know it today. Instead there was a loose aglomeration of alliances grouped around personalities, except during Jackson's administration. Once he retired from office his own party commenced to disintegrate, so that Van Buren could not hold the members together. Clay, Webster, Calhoun, Van Buren, Tyler and others were some of the factional leaders who had followings of varying size. Every one of these leaders was feverish with hope as he gazed upon that brightest star of them all—the Presidency.[84] The confederations which were temporarily contrived to secure the nomination and election of candidates during this period of factionalism melted under the heat of partisanship in office. As Tyler said in 1844: "Did the federal portion of the Whigs indulge a dream that when we went into union with them to produce a change in the administration, that thereby we had covenanted to lay at their feet our principles, our judgments and all our thoughts and emotions?"[85] In the Presidency John Tyler remained what he had been as a vice-presidential candidate—a factional leader of the Democratic party.

---

[84]Carroll, *op. cit.*, pp. 173-174.
[85]Tyler to M. S. Sprigg (Aug. 20, 1844), Tyler Papers, Vol. II, No. 6480.

Chapter VII

A JACKSONIAN WHIG

WRITING in *The Federalist* Hamilton observed: "There is an idea, which is not without its advocates, that a vigorous executive leadership is inconsistent with the genius of republican government." Washington, Jefferson and Jackson, each in his own way, agreed with Hamilton in urging the contrary doctrine that "energy in the Executive is a leading character in the definition of good government."[1] Among these Presidents the credit must go to Jackson for not merely reviving the office but for remaking it.[2] In his hands the Presidency was claimed to be as truly representative of the people as Congress could be, and when it became necessary in his view of things Jackson lashed Congress with the veto and appealed to the people to sustain him. After a generation of congressional dominance, the Presidency was claimed to be on a plane with the other branches, with the imperious Jackson buttressing his policies with the new dogma of autonomous executive prerogative. Tyler and his fellow strict constructionists could applaud Jackson's vetoes, for they had worshipped a lifetime before the altar of strict construction in communion with the spirits of Jefferson and Madison. They could not, however, stomach either Jackson's use of the prerogative in derogation of the Senate or his nationalist convictions in the nullification controversy. The suspicion lingers, too, that the symbolic union of the presidential office

---

[1] *The Federalist*, No. 70, p. 454.
[2] Corwin, *op. cit.*, p. 22.

179

with the enfranchisement of the masses held a new terror for these Southern conservatives. Senator John Tyler beheld with incredulity a President who would "throw himself forward as the most prominent advocate of one of the aspirants to the succession, and then have the affrontery to *breathe* the name of Jefferson."[3]

John Tyler entered the White House thoroughly schooled in a constitutional theory upon which he had based his whole political career. He regarded the Union as a compact to which the sovereign states were parties in the creation of their agent, the government of the United States. In response to the Force Bill he said: "I have been reared . . . in the strongest devotion to the great and enduring principles of the report and resolutions of 1798-9 [the Virginia and Kentucky Resolutions] . . . When therefore the President requires of me to admit that this is *a unit gov't.*—a *social* and not a *conventional* system—that the people of all the Union acting as *one community*, and not the *States* acting as *separate* communities, adopted the constitution . . . whatever may be the consequences personally to myself I say nay to these doctrines. . . . If I stand alone in opposition to them, I am ready to abide my fate. . . ."[4] If Tyler believed that state legislatures should be the sentinels guarding the Constitution against a too liberal interpretation of congressional authority, he believed no less that the Senate of the United States was a proper guardian to prevent abuse of the executive powers. As Jackson's enlargement of executive power grew apace, Tyler could tell his daughter that "even here the President's powers are too great."[5] As Senator, then, Tyler was in the somewhat contradictory position of sustaining Jackson's vigorous use of the veto in opposition to legislation offending the States' Rights men, while condemning "King Andrew's" exercise of his appointing, removal and

---

[3]Tyler to W. F. Pendleton (Oct. 26, 1837), Tyler, *op. cit.*, III, 67.
[4]*Ibid.*, p. 64. At this time Tyler urged the submission to the states of a constitutional amendment to settle the power of Congress to incorporate a bank. *Ibid.*, I, 489.
[5]*Ibid.*, I, 549.

supervisory powers over his subordinates. Tyler was yet to learn once he was inside the White House that the Presidency assumes dimensions which sometimes appear to be awesome and frightening when viewed from the Senate chamber.

Standing almost alone, deserted by the party which had elected him and supported only by a "corporal's guard," with veto piled on veto, Tyler destroyed Clay's nationalist legislation so hated by the strict constructionists. Ironically, John Tyler, who had left the Senate rather than see that proud body prostrated by a dominating President, met the Whig fury over his own vetoes with the claim that the President is as much the representative of the people as Congress is. Although Tyler was no legislative leader in the sense in which we expect a President to be today, neither for that matter were most of his predecessors. His chief legislative success lay in a courageous use of the veto justified by a difference of view between the President and Congress. He rationalized the vetoes of the bank bills with the claim that Congress did not have the power to enact them. But this practice was soon dropped in favor of a frank admission that the President did not agree with Congress on policy and, therefore, would not sign an objectionable bill. Such was the case with Tyler's disapproval of the tariff and distribution bills in 1842. His use of the veto matched Jackson's in courage even if not in political effect, although the same interests were for the most part served in both cases. Tyler became the first President to cast off the cloak of constitutional argument and openly to base his veto on the ground that Congress' action was unwise. While it is true that his refusal to sign objectionable bills did not provide a positive legislative program of the sort we expect from our Presidents today, his influence was controlling over those domestic issues which were most important in his administration—the bank, the tariff, and the distribution of the revenue from the public lands.

On the other hand, Tyler refused to assume a position of positive legislative leadership. He declined to do more than to tell Congress in general terms what measures were desirable. He usually did not submit the drafts of bills except when called upon by Congress to do so. In this regard Tyler was a Jeffersonian who believed that the President's function in the legislative process was merely to inform Congress and to forbid the passage of bills by refusing his assent to them. To this extent, also, he deferred to Whig denunciations of active executive leadership of the law-making machinery. This practice was by far the weakest element in Tyler's otherwise vigorous conduct of the Presidency.

In his actions as Chief Executive Tyler emphatically rejected the notion that the President is subject to the guardianship of either Congress or his cabinet. When the Whigs asserted that the cabinet was a council by which the President must be guided in making policy, Tyler encouraged the resignation of every member of the group selected by Harrison and subservient to Clay. He did this in the face of what he thought was a plot to force his resignation from the Presidency for lack of administrative chiefs. Furthermore, he handled the potentially explosive Dorr's Rebellion with rare firmness, tact and skill. He was equally firm in claiming for the President the right to judge what information is to be yielded or withheld from Congress—especially when the public disclosure of information may injure both a public and a private interest. Finally, he added at least one precedent to the theory of the executive power in claiming for the President a right of investigation to be inferred from his oath and the injunction to take care that the laws be faithfully executed. Although he added nothing to the theory of the appointing power, he was careful to avoid what he thought was Jackson's abuse of the authority to make recess appointments. In resubmitting to the Senate the names of several of his most important nominees, Tyler learned at least that the Senate can be captious in the performance of its advisory function.

As Chief of Foreign Relations Tyler made a record which was to be equalled by few of his more immediate predecessors or successors, unless possibly by Polk. Threatening dis-

putes with Great Britain over the McLeod case, the right
of search on the high seas, and the Maine and Oregon boundaries were never permitted to erupt into conflict. By the
end of his administration he had failed only to adjust the
Oregon boundary question. In the annexation of Texas there
can be no question that from the moment Tyler decided to
act on this problem until he left the Presidency, he held the
initiative. When the Senate rejected the annexation treaty,
he took his case in a unique manner to the House and to the
country, where it can be said that the question was fairly
settled through the democratic process. He succeeded in this
endeavor, moreover, despite the severest partisan opposition
to his policy. In a similar manner he secured the ratification
of the Webster-Ashburton Treaty at a time (August, 1842)
when the Whig opposition to him had reached a point of
emotional frenzy. He never reflected the slightest doubt that
the Constitution gave the President the whip hand in the
conduct of foreign relations.

It is one of the paradoxes of the office that a President
must seek to balance his position as chief of his party with
an equal need for support of his policies from all quarters
of the nation regardless of partisan lines. He owes his office
to the efforts of the party which put him there and, yet,
once in power, his success as a leader rests in no little measure upon his securing a broad base of popular approval.
Tyler, in driving away the Whig irreconcilables under Clay
and appealing to the nation for support of his measures,
failed to achieve this delicate and very necessary equilibrium.
As a matter of fact, since Tyler seems to have premeditated
this break, the vituperation hurled at him made him something of a political ascetic who saw high duty in his trial
by slander.

At the same time his sacrifices were not intended to be
fruitless. His stand on the rechartering of the bank, the protective tariff, and the annexation of Texas should have
pleased the dominant planter-interests of the South as well
as many of Jackson's followers. Tyler's fundamentalist strict
construction of the powers of Congress as a necessary prin-

ciple of the federal union ought to have attracted many of the same groups. His efforts to settle the right of search on the high seas and to strengthen the Navy and seacoast defenses should have appealed to the New England shipping interests. His approval of the mildly protective tariff should have brought him closer to the manufacturing interests (as it apparently did in Pennsylvania) and should have done him little harm with those who had accepted the Compromise Tariff of 1833. As a cultured Virginia gentleman and slave owner, he should have symbolized to the Whigs the conservative bias which was the only tie common to all elements of that party. And yet, he failed completely to attract sufficient strength from existing parties to form a new party or to capture an existing one. But like a blind Sampson pulling the temple down upon his horrified tormentors, Tyler almost singlehandedly destroyed the presidential prospects of both the nationalists, Van Buren and Clay. Tyler's flirtation with the "Pennsylvania interest" presaged the new Democratic combination of Southerners and Northern "Doughfaces" who controlled the party until the break of 1860. His hope of realigning the parties was only partly successful, and once denied renomination he had to content himself with the knowledge that he had not compromised those convictions which he considered basic to the preservation of the Union.

If he had had a good press, Tyler might have achieved a considerable measure of support for himself. He might have displayed himself to the public and thereby carried the battle to his opponents, but he was schooled in the retiring and gentlemanly politics of Virginia, where, he claimed, the office sought the man. Only once did he travel through a part of the nation—to Boston for the dedication of the Bunker Hill Monument in June, 1843. His Whig opponents sneered at this gesture, and John Quincy Adams absolutely refused to appear on the same platform with Tyler. He claimed that the trip was a snare whereby Webster might "whistle back his Whig friends whom he had cast off" and a pageant to "bedaub with glory John Tyler, the slave-breeder, who is coming with all his court, in gaudy trappings of mock royalty, to receive the homage of hungry sycophants, under the color of doing homage to the principles of Bunker Hill martyrdom."[6]

It is easy to overlook the fact that Tyler entered upon the duties of the presidential office under circumstances unique in American history. It was symbolic of his independent conduct of the office that his first decision was to claim that he had succeeded to the Presidency and was not merely acting as President. He did so conscious of the political storm whose clouds had already gathered. In his Inaugural Address he told the nation so, and he told his friends so in the privacy of personal letters. It is a tribute to his steadfastness of purpose, no matter how harshly one may judge Tyler for his policies in office, that he repeatedly asserted the doctrine of executive independence even though he had succeeded to the office only upon the death of his predecessor. Today we accept this as a commonplace; Tyler had the courage and the foresight to set the precedent and to adhere to his independent position in the face of the vilest obloquy during his four years in office.

After he had left office, John Tyler wrote to his son Robert, saying:

if the tide of defamation and abuse shall turn, and my administration come to be praised, future Vice-Presidents who may succeed to the Presidency may feel some slight encouragement to pursue an independent course. In no other contingency will any one thus situated be anything more than a mere instrument in the hands of the ambitious and aspiring demagogues; the executive power will be completely in abeyance and the Congress will unite the legislative and executive functions.[7]

---

[6]Adams, *op. cit.*, p. 382. Adams expressed "disdain to be associated with the mouth worship of liberty from the lips of the slave-breeder." The next day his bile spilled over and he added: ". . . how could I have witnessed the sight of John Tyler's nose, with a shadow outstretching that of the monumental column—how could I have witnessed all this at once without an unbecoming burst of indignation or of laughter?" *Ibid.*, p. 383.

[7]Tyler, *op. cit.*, II, 107 (March 12, 1848).

There is little that the commentator can add to this statement. From the outset of his term, he was determined to act in what he conceived to be the public interest, no matter what the cost in terms of party strife. Since he occupied a unique position and stood opposed to the aims of a powerful party, it was necessary that he claim for himself not only the legal but also the moral authority of the Presidency in order to forestall attacks upon him. He was prepared to be a President without a party.

It is undoubtedly due to the bias of the Whig version of history that Tyler has been so long maligned as a vacillating, treacherous, obdurate and vain man who was one of the worst of our Presidents.[8] His record in office demonstrates that he was a man of courage, honesty and determination who chose to follow a course of policy which he thought served the public good better than the one proposed by Henry Clay. Had he decided to play the role of a manageable nonentity, he might well enjoy today the reputation of having been a patriotic although somewhat colorless President. He refused to do so and thereby precipitated a tremendous struggle for institutional dominance within our constitutional system.

The English historian W. E. H. Lecky introduced his account of William Pitt the younger with a masterful and perceptive analysis of the qualities of mind and character which produce political success in modern times. Such qualities as originality or profundity of thought, capacity to deal with principles, perception which grasps the finer shades of thought or emotion "can be of little or no service in practical politics . . . The politician deals very largely with the superficial and the commonplace; his art is in a great measure that of skilful compromise, and in the conditions of mod-

---

[8]This view is expressed by Chitwood, *op. cit.*, Binkley, *op. cit.*, p. 99, and Poage *op. cit.*, p. 99. For kind judgments see Turner, *op. cit.*, p. 490, and George P. Garrison, *Westward Extension, 1841-1850 (The American Nation: A History*, Vol. XVII), p. 65. The bitterest of Tyler's critics would include John Quincy Adams, whose *Memoirs* are replete with vitriolic denunciations of Tyler. See also H. E. von Holst, *The Constitutional and Political History of the United States*, James Shouler, *History of the United States of America*, Sargent, *op. cit.*, and others.

ern life the statesman is likely to succeed the best who possesses secondary qualities to an unusual degree, who is in the closest intellectual and moral sympathy with the average of the intelligent men of his time, and who pursues common ideals with more than common ability."[9] It is perhaps too much to say that Tyler was a man possessed of intellectual endowments which removed him from the mainstream of the common sentiments of his times, although something of that sort is true. He was a man of parts and polish. His state papers reflected a grasp of principle which was to be his political undoing and a fluency of expression which was a cut above the effulgence of the age of euphuism. In his manner we have the word of his worst enemies that he was a man of tact and culture, inclined to be conciliatory in conversation but unbending when his principles were challenged.[10] He had the courage and obstinacy necessary for beating back the attacks of his assailants. At the same time he simply lacked the vulpine craft which is the mark of a highly successful politician. Lacking the common earthiness of a Jackson or the eloquence of a Lincoln, his administration seemed never to be dedicated to the achievement of any of the great ideals for which leaders are honored.[11] Bitterly denounced by his enemies, who were many, he was extravagantly eulogized by his friends, who were few.

One cannot safely say that Tyler enhanced the prestige of the Presidency while he was in office. The vilification of his administration by his contemporaries was so intense and

[9]W. E. H. Lecky, *A History of England in the Nineteenth Century*, 9 vols. (New York: Appleton, 1903), V, 261.

[10]After attending a wedding party at the White House, J. Q. Adams observed that the polish of the President and his family matched that "of the most accomplished European courts." Adams, *op. cit.*, XI, 174.

[11]If anything, Tyler was something of a prophet of doom and the defender of a faith destined for destruction. In his fourth Annual Message he took the occasion to warn against the dire effects of political parties divided on the slavery question. Such "opinions, entirely abstract in the States in which they may prevail and in no degree affecting their domestic institutions, may be artfully but secretly encouraged with a view to undermine the Union . . . until at last the conflict of opinion . . . may involve in general destruction the happy institutions under which we live." Richardson, *op. cit.*, p. 2190.

pervasive as to make the business of exhuming opinions from the grave hazardous at best. In retrospect, however, surely Tyler must command admiration for his political courage, as well as respect for his honesty of conviction and personal dignity in office. If power is nourished with use, the Presidency did not languish in his hands. His vetoes were in defense of the Constitution as he understood it and his protest message was in the name of the people of the United States to protect the executive power. Under his guidance foreign relations were conducted with foresight and audacity. Courteous in his official dealings with Congress, he nevertheless successfully resisted every effort of the congressional opposition to violate the principle that neither branch should encroach upon the powers of the other or abdicate its proper functions within the constitutional scheme. In doing so he learned that his own views of the proper scope of the President's powers had to be molded to fit the circumstances in which they were exercised.

The question whether Tyler added some intangible measure of influence to the Presidency knows no quantitive answer. In the absence of qualities of leadership in Tyler one is forced to view his administration from the standpoint of his contribution to the theory of the Presidency and his actions in using the powers bequeathed him by his predecessors. At the very least, he determined for the future the tradition that a President by accident may use his official powers with a vigor and purpose undiminished by his peculiar position. Like Jackson alone before him, Tyler stood adamant in defending his office against the Whig dogma of legislative guardianship of the executive. The struggles of his administration were largely those fought by Jackson over the same issues, with the same weapons, amongst many of the same principal adversaries. The Whigs entered office in 1840 determined to restore the President and Congress to their proper relationship—with Congress calling the tunes. Tyler fell heir to the Presidency determined to preserve the Union as a compact of sovereign states as long as it was within the power of his office to do so. As the perspicacious

Madison noted, ours is a system in which ambition is made to counteract ambition; the interests of the man are connected with the rights of the place. The Whig counter-revolution foundered on the rocks of executive independence, for John Tyler proved to be a Jacksonian Whig.

SELECTED BIBLIOGRAPHY

Memoirs of John Quincy Adams, ed. CHARLES FRANCIS ADAMS. 12 vols. Philadelphia: Lippincott, 1876.

AGAR, HERBERT. *The Price of Union.* Boston: Houghton Mifflin, 1950.

BEARD, CHARLES A. *The American Party Battle.* New York: Macmillan, 1929.

————. *The Economic Origins of Jeffersonian Democracy.* New York: Macmillan, 1915.

BENTON, THOMAS H. *Thirty Years' View.* 2 vols. New York: Appleton, 1858.

BERDAHL, CHARLES A. *War Powers of the Executive in the United States.* Champaign: University of Illinois Press, 1920.

BINKLEY, WILFRED E. *President and Congress.* New York: Knopf, 1947.

BLACK, H. C. *The Relation of the Executive Power to Legislation.* Princeton: Princeton University Press, 1919.

BROWNLOW, LOUIS. *The President and the Presidency.* Chicago: Public Administration Service, 1949.

BURGESS, JOHN W. *The Middle Period, 1817-1858.* New York: Scribners, 1897.

"Correspondence of John C. Calhoun," ed. J. FRANKLIN JAMESON, *Annual Report of the American Historical Association,* 1899. Washington: Government Printing Office, 1900. Vol. II.

CARROLL, E. M. *Origins of the Whig Party.* Durham: Duke University Press, 1925.

CHITWOOD, OLIVER P. *John Tyler, Champion of the Old South.* New York: Appleton-Century, 1939.

The Works of Henry Clay, ed. CALVIN COLTON. 10 vols. New York: Putnam's, 1904.

191

COIT, MARGARET. *John C. Calhoun*. Boston: Houghton Mifflin, 1950.

COLE, A. C. *The Whig Party in the South*. Washington: American Historical Association, 1913.

COLEMAN, MRS. CHAPMAN (ed.). *The Life of John J. Crittenden*. 2 vols. Philadelphia: Lippincott, 1873.

CORWIN, EDWARD S. *The President, Office and Powers* (3rd ed.). New York: New York University Press, 1948.

————. *The President's Control of Foreign Relations*. Princeton: Princeton University Press, 1917.

CURTIS, GEORGE T. *Life of Daniel Webster*. 2 vols. New York: Appleton, 1872.

"Diary of Thomas Ewing, August and September, 1841," *American Historical Review*, XVIII (October, 1912).

FARRAND, MAX. *Records of the Federal Convention*. 3 vols. New Haven: Yale University Press, 1913.

The Federalist, ed. EDWARD MEAD EARLE. New York: Random House (Modern Library), 1937.

FISKE, JOHN. *Essays, Historical and Literary*. 2 vols. New York: Macmillan, 1902.

FORD, HENRY JONES. *The Rise and Growth of American Politics*. New York: Macmillan, 1898.

FRASER, HUGH R. *Democracy in the Making*. Indianapolis: Bobbs Merrill, 1938.

FROTHINGHAM, P. R. *Edward Everett, Orator and Statesman*. Boston: Houghton Mifflin, 1925.

FUESS, CLAUDE M. *The Life of Caleb Cushing*. 2 vols. New York: Harcourt Brace, 1923.

GARRISON, GEORGE P. *Westward Extension, 1841-1850*. (*The American Nation: A History*, ed. A. B. HART, Vol. XVII.) New York and London: Harpers, 1906.

Reminiscences of James A. Hamilton. New York: Scribners, 1869.

HART, JAMES. *The American Presidency in Action, 1789*. New York: Macmillan, 1948.

HERRING, E. PENDLETON. *Presidential Leadership*. New York: Farrar and Rinehart, 1940.

HINSDALE, MARY. *A History of the President's Cabinet*. Ann Arbor: University of Michigan Press, 1911.

HOCKETT, HOMER C. *The Constitutional History of the United States*. 2 vols. New York: Macmillan, 1939.

HOFSTADTER, RICHARD. *The American Political Tradition*. New York: Knopf, 1948.

HOLCOMBE, ARTHUR N. *Our More Perfect Union*. Cambridge: Harvard University Press, 1950.

————. *The Political Parties of Today*. New York: Harpers, 1924.

HOLT, W. S. *Treaties Defeated by the Senate*. Baltimore: Johns Hopkins Press, 1933.

HORWILL, HERBERT W. *The Usages of the American Constitution*. London: Oxford University Press, 1925.

LAMBERT, OSCAR D. *Presidential Politics in the United States, 1841-1842*. Durham: Duke University Press, 1936.

LASKI, HAROLD J. *The American Presidency*. London: George Allen and Unwin, 1940.

LEARNED, H. B. *The President's Cabinet*. New Haven: Yale University Press, 1912.

LEVIN, PETER R. *Seven by Chance: The Accidental Presidents*. New York: Farrar Straus, 1948.

McLAUGHLIN, ANDREW C. *A Constitutional History of the United States*. New York: Appleton-Century-Crofts, 1935.

McMASTER, JOHN B. *A History of the People of the United States*. 8 vols. New York: Appleton, 1910.

MILTON, GEORGE F. *The Use of Presidential Power, 1789-1943*. Boston: Little Brown, 1944.

Opinions of the Attorneys General, ed. BENJAMIN F. HALL. Washington: Robert Farnum, 1852. Vols. III and IV.

PARKS, JOHN H. *John Bell of Tennessee*. Baton Rouge: Louisiana State University Press, 1950.

PATTERSON, C. PERRY. *Presidential Government in the United States*. Chapel Hill: University of North Carolina Press, 1947.

POAGE, GEORGE R. *Henry Clay and the Whig Party*. Chapel Hill: University of North Carolina Press, 1936.

POLLARD, JAMES E. *The Presidents and the Press*. New York: Macmillan, 1947.

REEVES, J. S. *American Diplomacy under Tyler and Polk*. Baltimore: Johns Hopkins Press, 1907.

RICH, BENNETT M. *The Presidents and Civil Disorder*. Washington: Brookings Institution, 1941.

RICHARDSON, JAMES D. (ed.). *The Messages and Papers of the Presidents*. 20 vols. New York: Bureau of National Literature, 1914.

SARGENT, NATHAN. *Public Men and Events.* 2 vols. Philadelphia: Lippincott, 1875.

SCHLESINGER, ARTHUR M., JR. *The Age of Jackson.* Boston: Little Brown, 1945.

SCHURZ, CARL. *Life of Henry Clay.* 2 vols. New York: Houghton Mifflin, 1889.

SHOULER, JAMES. *History of the United States of America.* 6 vols. New York: Dodd Mead, 1889.

SILVA, RUTH C. *Presidential Succession.* Ann Arbor: University of Michigan Press, 1951.

SMITH, J. ALLEN. *The Spirit of American Government.* New York: Macmillan, 1911.

SMITH, J. H. *The Annexation of Texas* (revised ed.). New York: Barnes and Noble, 1941.

SMITH, W. H. *History of the Cabinet of the United States of America.* Baltimore: Industrial Printing Co., 1925.

STANWOOD, EDWARD. *A History of the Presidency from 1788 to 1897.* 2 vols. Boston: Houghton Mifflin, 1898.

SWISHER, CARL B. *Roger B. Taney.* New York: Macmillan, 1935.

TAFT, WILLIAM HOWARD. *Our Chief Magistrate and His Powers.* New York: Columbia University Press, 1925.

THACH, C. C. *The Creation of the Presidency.* ("The Johns Hopkins Studies in History and Political Science," Ser. 40, No. 4.) Baltimore: Johns Hopkins Press, 1922.

TURNER, FREDERICK J. *The United States, 1830-1850.* New York: Holt, 1935.

TYLER, LYON G. *The Letters and Times of the Tylers.* 3 vols. Richmond: Whittet and Shepperson, 1885.

VON HOLST, H. E. *The Constitutional and Political History of the United States.* 8 vols. Chicago: Callaghan, 1879.

WARREN, CHARLES. *The Supreme Court in United States History.* 2 vols. Boston: Little Brown, 1947.

The Letters of Daniel Webster, ed. C. H. VAN TYNE. New York: McClure Phillips, 1902.

The Private Correspondence of Daniel Webster, ed. FLETCHER WEBSTER. 2 vols. Boston: Little Brown, 1857.

The Writings and Speeches of Daniel Webster, National Edition. 18 vols. Boston: Little Brown, 1903.

WILSON, JAMES G. (ed.). *The Presidents of the United States.* 4 vols. London: Gay and Bird, 1895.

WILSON, WOODROW. *The President of the United States.* New York: Harpers, 1916.

WISE, HENRY A. *Seven Decades of the Union.* Philadelphia: Lippincott, 1881.

Congressional Globe, 27th Congress, 1st, 2nd, and 3rd Sessions; 28th Congress, 1st and 2nd Sessions.

John Floyd Papers (MS), Library of Congress.

Gideon and Francis Granger Papers (MS), Library of Congress.

Historical Statistics of the United States, 1789-1945. Washington: Government Printing Office, 1949.

Journal of the House of Representatives, 27th Congress, 1st, 2nd, and 3rd Sessions; 28th Congress, 1st and 2nd Sessions.

Journal of the Senate of the United States, 27th Congress, 1st, 2nd, and 3rd Sessions; 28th Congress, 1st and 2nd Sessions.

Niles National Register. Baltimore: 1841-45. Vols. LX-LXVII.

John Tyler Papers (MS), Library of Congress.

Tyler's Quarterly Historical and Geneological Magazine. Vols. I-XV.

William and Mary Quarterly, 1st and 2nd Series.

INDEX

A

Adams, John Quincy: opinion of Tyler, 11-12; recognizes Tyler as President, 17; protests executive dictation, 38 n38; opposes vetoes, 48; proposes amendment of veto power, 53; on nature of diplomatic offices, 124; appraises Tyler's Texas policy, 146; predicts Tyler's policies, 154; sneers at Tyler, 184; mentioned *passim*

Agent, diplomatic: Woodbury would limit use, 125; Senate refuses to cut funds for, 125, 127-128, 129 n82; Benton criticizes, 126-127

Allen, William, Sen.: on succession, 14; on Dorr's Rebellion, 102

Appointing power: Tyler criticizes Jackson's use of, 69 n38, 70; Tyler invites senatorial scrutiny, 83-85; Calhoun observes Tyler's practices, 83; Tyler denies House has power over, 89; *see also* Agent, Patronage and Senate

Appointments, recess: Tyler construes power, 70 n39; of Henshaw, 75; of Porter, 75; of Cushing, 128 and n80

Appropriations: Congress denies and paralyzes an executive function, 92; and foreign relations, 123-127

Archer, William S., Sen.: defends Tyler's "cabal," 65; and foreign relations, 118-119

B

Bank of the United States: in Tyler's Inaugural Address, 19-20; Tyler's plan, 28, 31-32; Tyler writes Clay about, 29; Tyler opposes, 30, 40-44, 152; role of cabinet respecting, 35, 37; as a party issue, 39-40, 45 n58, 154-158 *passim*, 173

Bell, John: quoted, 37

Benton, Thomas Hart, Sen.: opposes bank legislation, 42 n50; seeks information on foreign affairs, 114; on diplomatic agents, 126-127; criticizes Webster-Ashburton Treaty, 131

Bill-drafting: by executive, 27, 31-32, 34-35, 37

Botts, John Minor, Rep.: negotiates bank bill with Tyler, 36 n31; charges Tyler with perfidy, 45 n58; proposes impeachment of Tyler, 54

C

Cabinet: Tyler's use of, 35, 37, 71-72, 145; theory of tenure, 58; Tyler retains Harrison's, 58; Clay's influence, 60; Tyler's control of, 62-64, 69; Tyler ignores, 66-67; unofficial advisers, 66-67; revision of, 67-69, 74-75, 162, 166-167; number of appointments by Tyler, 73; partisan alignments, 75, 166-169; Senate rejects nominations, 85

Calhoun, John C.: appraises Tyler, 40, 160-161, 168; predicts cabinet revision, 67; enters cabinet, 75; comments on patronage, 83; fears bank legislation, 156; as Secretary of State, 144, 168; intrigue, 167 n60; mentioned *passim*

Checks and Balances: generally, ix-x; Madison quoted, 2; Tyler and Congress, 189

Clay, Henry: on presidential powers, 4; as legislative leader, 39; views on veto, 42-43; opposes "vote of no confidence," 54 n82; criticizes Tyler's "cabal," 65; proposes constitutional amendments to limit President, 71